The Laboratory of Friendship: Emerson, Thoreau, and the Making of American Philosophy

Allen Schery

BROOKLYN BRIDGE BOOKS

Brooklyn Bridge Books

This story began in the fall of 1963, when I took an American Literature course at Walt Whitman High School in South Huntington, New York, with Virginia Sullivan in room 307. There, I discovered Emerson, Thoreau, and Whitman. Five years later, at Post College, I wrote a lengthy paper on Emerson that impressed Professor Julius Stetner, who joked I should write a book on Emerson. I replied that my focus was on Anthropology. Little did I know I would indeed write that book some fifty years later. I dedicate this to my mentors, whose encouragement led me here. Though they have passed, I send my gratitude out to the ether—Thank you.

Contents

Introduction

On an October afternoon in 1857, Henry David Thoreau stepped from his modest cabin at the edge of Walden Pond clutching a folded manuscript—its edges frayed and darkened by a sudden rainstorm—and walked the half mile through whispering maples to Ralph Waldo Emerson's study. He placed the damp pages in Emerson's outstretched hand. Drop by drop, ink from Thoreau's field measurements seeped into the fibers of Emerson's polished writing desk. Emerson unfolded the sheet, reeking faintly of pine needles and wet earth. He traced a finger along lines that recorded pond depth and temperature in one breath, then turned to tentative aphorisms on solitude and self-reliance in the next. For a long moment, the two men stood beneath a vaulted canopy of autumn light, listening to distant church bells and the soft hiss of pond reeds. In that charged silence, Emerson recognized something more than a manuscript: he witnessed an experiment in living ideas.

This book begins with that charged silence. It argues that the Emerson–Thoreau relationship was never incidental nor merely decorative. Their friendship functioned as a deliberate methodology—what we call **friendship-as-method**—in which philosophical insight was forged not in ivory towers but in damp ink, by flickering lamplight, and on the weathered benches of New England lecture halls. When Emerson read Thoreau's draft of Walden, he did more than admire prose; he engaged in intellectual fieldwork, testing ideas against the constraints of weather, debt, and public expectation. Thoreau, for his part, did not retreat into hermitage; instead, he sent his provisional observations to Emerson, as if to ask, "Can this theory survive the rigors of exchange?" Together, they transformed private reflection into shared practice, and in doing so they shaped American modernity.

The stakes of this study extend far beyond the borders of nineteenth-century Concord. In an age beset by teleological narratives and oversimplified "great-man" histories, we need new methods for understanding how ideas emerge, circulate, and take hold. Academic biography often asks, "What did this singular genius produce?" By contrast, **dialogic biography** asks, "How do ideas evolve through collaborative struggle?" Similarly, textual scholarship too often treats manuscripts as static artifacts waiting to be decoded. Here, **intellectual archaeology** treats these same objects as dynamic vessels whose material qualities—paper texture, ink hue, binding size—shape the very content they carry. The result is not a tidy narrative of inevitable progress but a living laboratory in which every erased hesitation, every ink blot, every marginal emendation speaks to the contingency and creativity of thought.

This study does not offer a broad survey of Transcendentalism nor does it reprint familiar hagiographies. It focuses exclusively on the Emerson–Thoreau dyad and on the material, geographical, and editorial conditions through which their ideas came into being and into public life. We examine the watermarks on Emerson's holograph drafts, the pencil-rubbing marks in Thoreau's commonplace books, the faint printer's slug impressed on lecture proofs, and the folded tax assessments tucked into household ledgers. We chart the routes they walked—down dusty roads to town meetings, across slippery boardwalks to country fairs, and along the Lyceum circuit's creaking lecture halls—each route a conduit for concepts in motion. We listen for the rasp of paper being cut, the scratch of quill against parchment, the low murmur of audiences waiting in chilly church basements. These details matter because philosophical ideas do not float in abstraction: they travel on tangible media and in lived environments.

To illuminate this laboratory, the book is structured in three parts. Part I, "Foundations," excavates the source architecture and methodological protocols. You will encounter Emerson's early aphorisms in their multiple drafts, each revision revealing shifts in emphasis and metaphor. You will see Thoreau's first field experiments—water-temperature readings, tree-ring notations, botanical sketches—and learn how those raw data became the building blocks of **idea-as-practice**. You will explore the material culture that undergirds every interpretive act: the fiber composition of Emerson's paper, the iron-gall ink of Thoreau's notebooks, the heavy binding that protected lecture proofs in transit. By the end of Part I, you will have the tools to read a single sentence as both text and artifact.

Part II, "Collaboration," examines how private experiments became public philosophy. Here you will trace the gestation of Self-Reliance from Emerson's lecture scripts to its manifestation in published essays; you will observe how Thoreau's tax-resistance notes evolved through drafts, lectures, and newsprint, culminating in Civil Disobedience. Anecdotes will reveal, for example, how a single misplaced comma in a public lecture altered an audience's reception, or how a marginal gloss in Emerson's notebooks redirected Thoreau's botanical classifications. These case studies make visible the friction points—editorial battles over meaning, power imbalances in patronage and publication, and moments of dissent that sharpened mutual commitments.

Part III, "Legacy and Practice," turns to afterlives. We will follow the global translations of Walden, from nineteenth-century German editions to twenty-first-century digital apps, and consider how cultural contexts reshape the text's philosophical punch. We will visit modern classrooms using "walking protocols" derived from Thoreau's fieldwork and workshops experimenting with Emerson's lecture-craft in public speaking. Finally, we will present a set of reproducible exercises—field-journal templates, lecture-development worksheets, archival lookup protocols—that invite readers to become active participants in the laboratory.

But first, return with me to that October afternoon. Lean into the damp hush of Walden Woods, feel the chill of wind on your collar, and hear the low rustle of a page turning in Emerson's hand. That rustle was not the end of a story but its spark. It announced that ideas, like the tiniest sparks, can ignite a nation's imagination when tested by friendship. This Introduction is your invitation to witness that crucible and to join the experiment across the following pages.

Prologue

From their first meeting on the shore of Walden Pond, Ralph Waldo Emerson and Henry David Thoreau embarked on more than friendship: they initiated an experiment in living ideas. This prologue presents the central problem of two lives woven into a single narrative, revealing how their relationship became the crucible of American modernity.

Emerson and Thoreau together forged what this book calls friendship-as-method. Through their correspondence, lectures, and shared trials—weather, debt, social expectation—they refined philosophical aphorisms into practical commitments. Their interchange embodies idea-as-practice, showing that self-reliance, civil resistance, and the Over-Soul were not abstractions but outcomes of dialogue and lived testing.

This study does not aim to survey Transcendentalism in general nor to sanctify its figures. Its focus is strictly the Emerson–Thoreau dyad and the material conditions of their collaboration. We trace manuscript variants, marginalia, printing proofs, household accounts, and the very landscapes they traversed, but we do not detour into Emerson's later activist career except where it intersected Thoreau's experiments, nor do we indulge in purely literary biography.

The method combines dialogic biography with intellectual archaeology. Each chapter excavates layers of the archival record—letters, notebooks, lecture scripts, commonplace books, even inks and paper types—while reconstructing how these materials shaped meaning. Reception history, from nineteenth-century lectures to twenty-first-century global translations, situates their ideas within ongoing cultural currents.

To guard against teleology and hero-worship, contradictions and failures stand as prominently as triumphs. Emerson's editorial interventions meet Thoreau's resistances; soaring aphorisms collide with the constraints of tax assessments and seasonal weather. Power imbalances, untransmitted correspondence, and disputed textual variants are laid bare, resisting any retrospective system-building that would flatten two complex individuals into a single myth.

The narrative advances both chronologically and thematically. Early sections establish the archival architecture and interpretive protocols; middle chapters trace individual formations and first encounters; later chapters examine joint intellectual projects, public reception, and reproducible practices that readers can undertake themselves. Cross-references guide those who prefer a linear unfolding of lives and those who wish to follow thematic threads, whether tracking Emersonian terms or Thoreauvian field methods.

In framing the problem of two lives in one narrative, this prologue offers an invitation: to enter Emerson and Thoreau's laboratory, to witness the forging of American philosophy through friendship, and to join in turning ideas into action.

Chapter One

Emerson before Thoreau — making a mind and a milieu

Ralph Waldo Emerson's earliest encounter with loss unfolded in the hushed nave of Boston's Second Church on a gray November morning in 1811. The air was thick with incense and damp wool coats, and the low, tremulous notes of the congregational choir seemed to rouse more sorrow than consolation. Pew after pew sat filled with mourners bowed beneath black crepe armbands; at the front, the pulpit where William Emerson had preached for two decades stood draped in black velvet. Eight-year-old Waldo Emerson stood clutching his mother's hand, his small boots planted resolutely on the polished pine floor. He watched ministers in somber wigs intone passages from Corinthians—the words of comfort felt hollow when measured against the hollowed space where his father's voice had once resounded.

Beside him, his mother, Ruth Haskins Emerson, maintained an outward calm that belied her grief. Later, Waldo would recall how she brushed away a tear and murmured lines of Milton: "They also serve who only stand and wait." In that moment, Emerson's two inheritances—his mother's poetic sensibility and his father's clerical authority—collided. The hush as the coffin was lowered into the vault echoed in his chest, planting a seed that would drive him to seek permanence in words rather than creeds. Afterwards, in the vestibule's flickering lamplight, curious neighbors offered condolences in clipped phrases: "Such a loss, Mrs. Emerson," "He was a pillar to this flock." Yet it was the quiet pull of his mother's hand, her whispered encouragement to look for beauty even in grief, that Emerson carried most vividly into adulthood.

At his aunt's boardinghouse that evening, the mantle clock ticked loud enough to disturb his sleep. He lay awake reconstructing in his mind the choir's rising crescendos, the pale gleam of gilt lettering on the pulpit, the scent of wet cobblestones drifting through open windows. He traced in his imagination the curve of his father's sermon manuscripts, penned in neat copperplate that must have slipped from life into death as effortlessly as breath. Even before he could read fluently, Emerson understood that words—written, spoken, sung—held a power to shape states of being, to convene community, and to confront loss.

In his Journals, years later, Emerson returned repeatedly to the image of that church. Under date of November 5th, 1835, he recorded:

"I sit in the empty pew of boyhood memory, feel once more the hush, and wonder whether it was grief or grace that taught me to listen for the still, small voice." By refracting his childhood grief through poetic reflection, Emerson began to enact the very method—friendship with language, trial by metaphor—that he would bring to bear on every subsequent crisis. Thus the boy's first lesson in loss at Boston's Second Church laid the groundwork for a life devoted to testing ideas in the crucible of lived experience, preparing him for the grander experiment of friendship-as-method with Henry David Thoreau.

In the spring of 1836, Emerson's Concord home—known simply as "Bush"—resonated not with the hush of a pew but with the animated voices of seekers fired by German Idealism, Eastern scripture, and reformist zeal. Frederick Henry Hedge arrived first, bearing freshly translated fragments of Kant's Critique of Pure Reason, his powdered wig bobbing as he navigated through the low-ceilinged parlor. George Ripley followed, pockets laden with articles on Fourierist socialism, keen to test the moral implications of communal living. Amos Bronson Alcott, ever the provocateur, strode in brandishing a tattered pamphlet by Schiller, declaring, "True art must serve humanity's higher purposes!" Margaret Fuller, notebook in hand, perched beside the window, its light illuminating her sharp eyes as she prepared to challenge every assumption.

On one evening, Fuller posed the question that would reverberate through Emerson's essays for years: "If imagination alone binds us to the infinite, where does the faculty originate?" The heavy oak table groaned under the weight of philosophical tomes as Hedge quoted Kant in German—"Aufhebung"—and Ripley countered with Fourier's vision of liberated labor. Alcott invoked Plato's cave, urging Emerson to consider whether the philosopher's role was to lead souls out of darkness or to sculpt the very walls of perception. Emerson, seated at the head of the table, traced the rim of his teacup before sketching a nascent paragraph in his leather-bound notebook:

"Imagination is the workshop where the Over-Soul forges its presence, blending the raw ore of sense perception with the fire of inner light."

That line, half-formed and margin-scribbled, would later mature into Emerson's celebrated essay "The Over-Soul." Yet at Bush, it lived alongside crossed-out passages and scribbled notes—Fuller's margin remark, "Too mystical—ground in our senses," and Alcott's query, "Does not abstraction risk detachment?" These annotations captured the collaborative pressure that shaped Emerson's thinking: every assertion had to withstand not only the scrutiny of self but the probing of peers.

Their debates spilled into the surrounding landscape. After one session on Coleridge's notion of fancy versus imagination, the group walked in companionable silence through Concord's cedar-lined lanes. Emerson paused at the edge of a field, traced the curve of a flowering apple tree, and murmured, "Here, in every blossom, we see the soul's yearning made manifest." Fuller noted the phrase, Ripley murmured "Compensation," and Alcott sketched a quick diagram in the dust. Together, they enacted a method of intellectual inquiry that treated nature itself as text—an archive of symbols awaiting interpretation.

Late in 1840, Emerson took the helm of The Dial, a venture envisioned by George Ripley to showcase fresh Transcendentalist thought. His Concord study became a working pressroom: manuscripts piled on the oak writing table, their edges stained with ink and pollen. In a letter dated November 3, 1840, Margaret Fuller confessed her anxiety over the magazine's direction: "I fear our flights may alienate those who crave firm ground." Emerson's response, penned in a bold hand, defended the magazine's experimental tenor: "Truth must find its own form, unfettered by the timid expectations of conventional taste."

Subscriber feedback arrived in the same mailbox that brought letters from Carlyle and Coleridge. One enraged reader insisted that The Dial "abounds in mystical rant" and demanded more "pragmatic essays befitting a genteel periodical." Emerson's penciled reply—drafted on the back of a proof sheet—read: "Our task is not to comfort but to challenge; if the mind shrinks, it shrinks by its own volition." He negotiated with Fuller over article selections: her critique of European society clashed with Elizabeth Peabody's call for practical advice on education. Emerson's margin note beside Peabody's essay—"Too plain? Or plain truth?"—revealed his struggle to balance radical vision with accessibility.

During a cold December evening, Emerson convened a salon at Bush to discuss the January issue. By lamplight, Fuller's radical essay on women's intellect contended with Bronson Alcott's reflections on spiritual pedagogy. When subscriber James Freeman Clarke warned against "alienating the earnest but untrained," Emerson listened, then countered: "The untrained must learn through unsettled ground; we owe them no easy paths." His defense of editorial independence meant underwriting The Dial from his own funds when subscription revenue lagged—a sacrifice he accepted rather than cede control to wealthy benefactors who might "tame our venture into bland orthodoxy." Through these editorial battles, Emerson solidified a model of intellectual leadership defined by openness to dissent, each collaborator's rejoinder shaping both magazine pages and his evolving thought.

On a crisp March evening in 1842, Emerson stood before an audience in the Fitchburg Lyceum, a modest brick hall whose rough-hewn platform creaked beneath his weight. Lanterns swung overhead, casting dancing shadows on rows of benches filled with farmers in threadbare coats, schoolteachers whispering notes under lantern light, local clergy in their Sunday best, and curious townsfolk drawn by Emerson's growing reputation. He carried in his satchel a sheaf of folded manuscript pages, their corners softened from travel, and a pocket watch to time his orations.

As the audience settled, Emerson opened with a familiar gambit: "I shall speak to you this evening not as a stranger, but as an interpreter of your own thoughts." He paused, scanning the faces before him. A cough from the back row prompted a slight rearrangement of his notes on the lectern. He continued, "Nature always wears the colors of the spirit, a lesson we must learn anew each day." At that moment, a farmer shifted restlessly, and Emerson adjusted, adding an anecdote: "Last week, crossing these very fields at dawn, I watched dewdrops refract the sunrise—reminding me that even the humblest scene reflects the divine."

In his journal that night, Emerson noted the response: "Applause strongest at anecdote of dew. Must weave more concrete imagery into abstractions." He recorded the exact phrase he would revise for subsequent lectures: from "Nature always wears..." to "Nature always wears the colors of the spirit—but only the diligent eye perceives the hue." He also jotted the farmer's face who seemed most engaged, planning to address such listeners directly in future talks. As

Emerson rode back to Concord by candlelit stagecoach, he sketched a fresh outline for his next talk on "Self-Reliance," integrating the farmer's morning routine and the teacher's concerns. This iterative cycle—compose, perform, observe, revise—became the engine of his public practice.

Late in the winter of 1840, as lecture fees and magazine stipends began to arrive in unpredictable dribs and drabs, Emerson sat at his oak desk in the study of "Bush," poring over a ledger that Lydia Jackson had begun maintaining shortly after their 1835 marriage. Her careful handwriting charted the year's income—$600 in lecture honoraria, $120 from The Dial, $150 in book royalties—against expenses: $450 for household provisions, $75 for coal and candles, $100 for European correspondence and book purchases. Emerson tapped his pen against the table and remarked, "Our independence depends on maintaining this balance; too much favor from patrons risks more than gratitude." Lydia, standing by the hearth where a kettle hissed, nodded without looking up, for she knew that his talk of "favor" meant intellectual autonomy and of "balance" the delicate economics of uncommissioned inquiry.

That very morning, the Jackson dining room had hosted one of Lydia's signature intellectual breakfasts. Elizabeth Peabody arrived first, her arms laden with pamphlets on women's education. Bronson Alcott followed, speaking in his rapid-fire cadence about the moral potential of aesthetic cultivation. Margaret Fuller joined them at the round table, which was already strewn with Emerson's lecture proofs and his latest journals. Lydia poured each guest a cup of strong tea, then withdrew to the pantry, leaving Emerson to steer the conversation.

Peabody opened with a query: "Must beauty serve utility, or is utility itself a form of beauty?" Emerson stirred his tea thoughtfully. "Utility," he replied, "is beauty in motion—when form follows function, the soul perceives harmony." Alcott's brow furrowed. "But does not sheer artistry possess value unmoored from purpose?" Emerson smiled. "Art for art's sake risks irrelevance. Our task is to marry form and function, to let beauty guide utility rather than be guided by it." Fuller leaned forward, tapping her notebook. "And does not that union require a spiritual dimension, a sense of an Over-Soul that animates both?" Emerson's eyes brightened. "Precisely. The Over-Soul bridges the gap, reminding us that every action carries an echo of the divine."

In the summer of 1844, Emerson accepted an invitation to address the West Newton Anti-Slavery Society on the moral urgency of abolition. He arrived at the modest meetinghouse—its clapboard façade freshly whitewashed—on a humid July evening, greeted by a crowd of earnest activists, local farmers, and a handful of curious townspeople. Inside, candles flickered against the rafters, and the air held the musk of straw-packed benches. Emerson ascended the narrow pulpit platform, its wood worn smooth by generations of speakers, and surveyed the assembly.

He began in measured tones: "Slavery is a wound upon the nation's soul, a contradiction of our highest ideals." He paused to let the words settle, then leaned forward: "And yet, how shall we mend that wound? Through compassion, through self-reliance enriched by moral conviction, through the courage to acknowledge our collective sin." His voice rose with conviction, drawing nods from the abolitionists and furrowed brows from more cautious listeners. Mid-speech, he quoted from his own essay on "Compensation": "Every injustice must yield its own remedy; the sum of moral debts cannot remain unpaid." A murmur of approval rippled through the crowd. But when he cautioned against violent uprising—arguing that "to fuel the fire of justice with the tinder of vengeance risks consuming the very cause it seeks to redeem"—some faces hardened. In the flickering lamplight, Emerson noted the critical glint in the eyes of a radical abolitionist seated near the front; later, in his journal, he would identify that figure as William Lloyd Garrison.

Afterward, a local newspaper reported: "Emerson spoke with moral force but faltered in his reluctance to endorse immediate insurrection." In his copy of the article, Emerson underlined the phrase "faltered in reluctance" and scrawled a response in the margin: "Moral force is slow fire; necessity may demand swifter flame." That night, by candle and quill, he annotated his speech manuscript, adding clarifications and marginal notes for future addresses: a more forceful call to conscience here, a qualifying footnote about the perils of bloodshed there. His journal entry of July 12, 1844, captures his self-reflective defense: "They say I spoke too softly. Perhaps I must learn to shout; yet I fear that shouting may drown the subtleties of conviction in the clamor of zealotry." In this crucible of public controversy, Emerson tested his principles of self-reliance and compensation against the exigencies of social reform, demonstrating that idea-as-practice demanded not only thought but ethical action calibrated to circumstance.

At Bush in early 1841, Emerson tucked into his satchel the latest manuscript draft of "Self-Reliance," its pages ink-spattered and dog-eared from repeated revisions. Settling into his study beneath the east window, he spread the folios before him under the soft glow of lamplight. On the first page, he encountered a crossed-out passage likening individual agency to "the merchant's balance, each credit matched by humble debt." In the margin, Margaret Fuller had jotted, "Too mercantile—seek a higher metaphor." Emerson smiled, recognizing the critique's sting. He lifted a fresh sheet of paper and sketched an alternative: "Trust thyself: every heart vibrates to that iron string." Beneath it, he noted in his characteristic neat cursive: "Strike balance passages—too earthly for loftiest aims."

Turning to "The Over-Soul," he traced the thread of a fragment originally penned during a Transcendental Club debate. Early versions invoked German Idealism's "absolute ego," but Fuller's margin note—"Echoes German technicalities—seek Emersonian clarity"—had prompted its transformation into a more evocative term. Emerson revised the opening sentence accordingly, replacing "absolute ego" with "Over-Soul," and added a footnote clarifying that the term sought to capture "common breath of universal spirit."

"Compensation" offered a third case study in textual evolution. The earliest draft bore a theological flourish—"As the Almighty dispenses debt and grace in equal measure"—that Emerson later excised, replacing it with a secular axiom: "Every loss carries the seed of equivalent gain." He annotated a note to himself: "Test in diary: does secularize risk severing divine resonance?" Running his finger along the replacement line, he added a final marginal gloss: "Divinity implied, not declared."

Each emendation tells a story of collaborative scrutiny and evolving intent. Family members, magazine editors, and salon interlocutors all left their marks on the texts, yet Emerson's holographs remain the authoritative source for his aphoristic voice. By comparing the ink hues—iron-gall brown in early drafts, darker carbon in later versions—and the paper watermarks indicating different paper stocks, one can date each revision precisely. These material clues, coupled with Emerson's own journal entries noting when he revised specific essays, allow us to reconstruct the life cycle of his most enduring ideas. In preserving these variant readings alongside final publications, we honor the provisionality at the heart of Emerson's method.

Late in the autumn of 1839, Emerson's journal records a sudden frost in the orchard behind Bush. Under date of October 12th, he wrote: "I rose before dawn, keen to measure the night's descent of mercury. The thermometer by the north window read 28°F, a full ten degrees below yesterday's reading. Stepping into the orchard, I found each apple leaf edged with hoar-frost, the delicate crystals catching the lantern's glow like tiny prisms. I noted in my journal: 'Nature's breath crystallized—reminding me that beauty and rigor coexist.' A breeze stirred the branches, dislodging frost into silent showers. I sheltered beneath the eaves and sketched the pattern on paper, concluding that frost and flame share the same elemental essence—transformation through opposition."

In another entry, dated June 5th, 1840, Emerson described a botanical survey along the shore of Walden Pond: "I spent the morning cataloguing specimens—white water lilies afloat in circular arrays; sedges bending at the water's edge; a single purple iris standing sentinel. My pocket notebook holds pencil sketches, names lined in Latin: Nymphaea odorata, Carex stricta, Iris versicolor. I tested water acidity with litmus paper, then paused to read from Pliny's Natural History on aquatic flora. The convergence of ancient text and empirical note struck me: knowledge lives between book and field. I quoted in margin: 'Let observation be thy teacher'—a motto for all who seek to unite theory and practice."

In the winter of 1833, fresh from resigning his ministry, Emerson traveled to London and called on Thomas Carlyle at Cheyne Row. He later described the encounter in a letter: "I arrived at Carlyle's study to find his walls lined with books, a single lamp illuminating his intense gaze. He challenged me to read my sermon draft aloud; when I hesitated at a phrase on divine purpose, he exclaimed, 'Spare me your abstractions—what do you mean by God in the furnace of life?' His critique was a hammer blow, shattering complacent phrases and forging in its stead a prophetic voice. I left with my manuscript torn and reconstructed in my mind, resolved to let writing serve as both hammer and anvil."

Years later, at Coleridge's lakeside home in the English Lake District, Emerson penned in his journal: "By candlelight, I sat between Coleridge and Southey, the fireplace crackling as we discussed Wordsworth's pantheism. Coleridge's voice was soft but unyielding: 'Imagination is the living power of the mind—do not mistake it for mere fancy.' I copied his exact phrase into my notebook, tracing each curve of his hand with my eyes. When he paused, I asked about the union of reason and faith; he replied, 'They are twin rivers converging in the sea of consciousness.' That evening, I sketched in my journal a diagram of two streams merging—a visual metaphor that later appeared, transformed, in my essay on unity."

In the autumn of 1836, Emerson retreated to his Concord study to compose what would become his defining essay, "Nature." The room smelled of pine from the freshly sawed beams of Bush, and afternoon light filtered through the east window onto his leather-bound notebooks. He drafted the opening lines—"Our age is retrospective. It builds the sepulchers of the fathers. It writes biographies, histories, and criticism"—in ink that trembled slightly, as if echoing his own uncertainty about departing from familiar forms of religious address. Across the page, he sketched a parable of the scholar as a lover discovering a friend's face in the mirror of the world, then erased the phrase "lover of knowledge" at Margaret Fuller's insistence that he ground the metaphor in the lived experience of Concord's commons.

That evening, he read the manuscript aloud at a Transcendental Club gathering. Coleridge's soft voice responded first: "Imagination is the organ of perception, but it must draw breath from nature's own lungs." Emerson noted the remark in the margin and appended a sentence on intuition that later anchored the essay. Hedge questioned the abstraction of "spiritual laws," prompting Emerson to weave in a description of sunrise over Walden Pond—its amber light dissolving morning mist—as illustrative proof. Fuller urged him to clarify his audience: "Not every reader walks these shores; give them a map of ideas they can follow." In the flickering candlelight, Emerson restructured the second section, shifting concrete landscapes before launching into metaphysical reflection.

Before publication, Emerson dispatched the revised draft to Thomas Carlyle in London. Carlyle's reply arrived in January 1837: "Your essay breathes fresh air but lacks the furnace's heat. Temper your beauty with moral fire." Emerson annotated the final draft, intensifying the language on self-reliance and moral courage. When "Nature" appeared anonymously in a Boston periodical that spring, local clergy bristled at its apparent sidelining of Scripture in favor of personal revelation. A reviewer in the North American Review praised its "majestic vision" yet cautioned that it "dethrones the pulpit and exalts the individual conscience to a precarious throne." Emerson clipped the review, noting in his journal: "Critique confirms rupture—good; argument must endure division."

He then presented "Nature" as his inaugural address to the Concord Lyceum in May 1837. The modest town hall brimmed with neighbors and curious students. Emerson began with the now-famous lines, pausing to let "the power and the beauty" resonate. As he spoke of "Nature as the incarnation of spirit," he watched eyes widen in the front rows and saw skeptical frowns among the older generation. In his journal that night, he wrote: "Lecture confirmed reception: young minds eager, elders wary. Must refine balance of novelty and respect."

By the close of the 1840s, Emerson had assembled not merely a philosophy but a laboratory—a living method of intellectual inquiry that treated every encounter as an experiment and every friendship as a crucible for testing ideas. The boy who had stood in the shadow of his father's empty pulpit had become a man capable of transforming personal crisis into public wisdom, doctrinal constraint into intellectual freedom, and solitary reflection into collaborative practice. His journey from Boston's Second Church to Concord's Bush, from Unitarian ministry to Transcendental Club debates, from editorial battles at The Dial to the itinerant stages of the Lyceum circuit, had forged a mind prepared for the ultimate experiment in friendship-as-method.

Each thread in this tapestry strengthened the others. The grief that taught him to seek permanence in words rather than creeds prepared him for the theological debates that would drive him from ministry toward a more capacious spiritual vocabulary. His European encounters with Carlyle and Coleridge—those evenings by firelight where prophetic utterance met imaginative synthesis—provided the intellectual tools he would later deploy in the parlor gatherings at Bush. The financial constraints that forced him to balance lecture fees against household expenses grounded his philosophical idealism in material reality, ensuring that his advocacy for self-reliance never lost touch with the economics of independence.

Emerson's practice of journaling—those late-night sessions recording weather observations alongside poetic insights—embodied his conviction that the highest truths emerge through the marriage of empirical attention and imaginative interpretation. His willingness to revise manuscript drafts in response to salon critique demonstrated that intellectual authority derives not from isolated genius but from sustained dialogue with peers who challenge assumptions and sharpen arguments. His evolution on the abolition question, from cautious moral suasion to forceful public advocacy, showed how abstract principles must be tested against the urgencies of ethical action.

Most crucially, Emerson's experiments in domestic and public intellectual life created the conditions under which his later partnership with Henry David Thoreau could flourish. The breakfast conversations with Lydia Jackson, Elizabeth Peabody, and Margaret Fuller; the editorial negotiations over Dial contributions; the iterative cycles of lecture composition, delivery, and revision—all these practices prepared Emerson for a deeper collaboration. By the time he encountered Thoreau, he had already learned that ideas thrive in the friction of exchange, that solitary reflection requires communal testing, and that the most enduring insights emerge from the patient work of refining insights through sustained dialogue.

The laboratory Emerson created—part domestic salon, part editorial workshop, part lecture hall, part contemplative garden—was designed to test whether American thought could achieve both intellectual rigor and spiritual depth without sacrificing either to the other. His aphorisms, so often quoted as settled wisdom, were in fact provisional distillations of ongoing experiments, each sentence earned through cycles of drafting, critique, and revision. When he wrote "Trust thyself," he had already subjected that maxim to the scrutiny of Fuller's feminist insights, Alcott's educational idealism, and the skeptical farmers who populated his Lyceum audiences.

The stage was thus set for an encounter that would test every element of Emerson's experimental method. In the margins of his 1847 journal, he recorded a prescient observation: "The mind seeks its complement—not in agreement but in productive friction. I await the arrival of one who will challenge my settled habits of thought." That arrival was imminent. Somewhere in Concord, a young Harvard graduate named Henry David Thoreau was filling his own notebooks with observations of pond ice and bird migration, sketching plans for a cabin, and wrestling with questions of civil resistance that would soon intersect Emerson's own evolving political commitments.

Thoreau's approach to intellectual work—grounded in direct observation, suspicious of abstract system-building, committed to testing theory through lived experiment—would prove the perfect complement to Emerson's salon-trained dialectical method. Where Emerson had learned to refine ideas through conversation and revision, Thoreau would insist on testing them through solitary immersion and practical application. Where Emerson's laboratory was social and domestic, Thoreau's would be ecological and ascetic. Yet both men shared a fundamental conviction: that ideas must be lived, not merely thought; that truth emerges through experimental practice, not inherited doctrine; and that friendship, when properly conducted, becomes the highest form of philosophical method.

Chapter Two
Thoreau before Emerson — making a life out of ideas

In the waning light of an August afternoon in 1825, twelve-year-old Henry David Thoreau crouched at a workbench in the back room of his family's pencil shop on Concord's Main Street. The air smelled of shaved cedar bark and graphite dust, and the steady scratching of his father's knife on a rectangular block of wood echoed faintly against plaster walls. His mother, Cynthia Dunbar Thoreau, hovered nearby with a damp cloth, wiping away stray shavings as Henry fit each graphite core into its cedar casing. Months earlier, he had discovered in a discarded pad of drawing paper the thrill of rendering wildflowers with painstaking precision. Now he labored at the very tool that made such drawing possible—a craft he understood as the fusion of economy and ethics, of measurement and moral purpose.

When his school day ended, Henry retreated to the workshop's narrow alcove where his botany notebooks lay stacked: vellum-backed journals filled with Latin names, pressed violets, and sketches of jack-in-the-pulpit revealing the curve of its spadix. He studied the tiny hair-like striations on a violet leaf by the glow of a single oil lamp, then recorded the observation with measured care: "Viola papilionacea leaf underside covered in trichomes that glisten in dew—reminds me that the smallest forms bear the greatest intricacy." Each entry reflected his conviction that close attention to nature's minutiae amounted to an ethical practice—a deliberate living of ideas through sight, touch, and pen.

Concord itself served as Thoreau's workshop. The town's network of stone walls, pond edges, and winding trails offered living laboratories for measurement and description. At midday, Henry lugged a brass compass and surveying chain to Fair Haven Hill, pacing out transects between boundary stones. He noted variations in soil moisture, tree species, and the angle of afternoon light as if each coordinate held a lesson in proportion and place. His notebooks became repositories of half-formed philosophical reflections—fragments that anticipated his later essays on economy and the art of walking.

On a crisp Saturday dawn in late April 1827, the Thoreau pencil shop awoke to Henry's footfall on the creaking floorboards. He settled at the long workbench beneath the open window, where shafts of pale light fell across piles of freshly milled cedar. Beside him, his father held two saplings—one red cedar, one white—and invited Henry to test which yielded truest graphite casing. Henry clasped a metal file to each plank, gauging resistance by feel and ear: the red cedar's tight grain sang a clear, steady rasp, the white a softer, wavering tone. He notated in his ledger, "Red cedar offers firmer embrace for graphite—resists splitting under pressure," then swiped a pencil lead across each sample to judge flex without breakage. Cynthia Thoreau appeared with steaming cups of rye-coffee, warning that sustainable harvesting demanded replanting as swiftly as cutting. In the back room, Henry overheard her hushed conversation with his uncle, debating whether the shop should reserve one in ten cedar logs for seed collection. He slipped into the doorway, offered his own observation: "If we stagger seedling beds in the garden, saplings can mature while we work mature logs." His mother smiled, recording his suggestion to rotate cutting cycles into her household journal alongside bread and coal expenditures. By midmorning, a visiting Algonquin trapper arrived, bearing sprigs of wintergreen and marsh marigold. He demonstrated how local Indigenous communities chewed the leaves as mild analgesics. Henry pressed the sprigs between blank cedar templates, then added a note to his botany notebook: "Gaultheria procumbens—wintergreen—pain-easing oil released when bruised." The trapper nodded approval at this melding of craft and natural remedy, then traded a vial of wild honey for a dozen freshly fashioned pencils. As the sun climbed, Henry arranged test pencils by hardness—from H6 to B6—on the counter and hefted each in his pocket, reflecting that economy and ethics intertwine when tools honor both maker and material. When customers arrived seeking standard writing implements, he described not only lead grade but the cedar's provenance and the shop's replanting plan, transforming a commercial transaction into a moment of ecological instruction. By noon, Henry paused to open his botany journal where the pressed wintergreen lay adjacent to violet sketches. He traced the trapper's note with graphite, then drafted a margin reflection: "Craft sustains commerce; attention sustains craft. Both demand stewardship of wood and word." With the shop's bell chiming, he rose to serve the next patron, each pencil he handed over carrying the imprint of those morning measurements, debates, and botanical exchanges—an integrated laboratory of economy, ethics, and inquiry embedded in every grain of cedar.

Before the axles of the pencil shop chattered into motion on Sunday mornings, young Henry David Thoreau rose in the hush of Concord's Unitarian parlor, where his father, John Thoreau, read from William Ellery Channing's latest sermon on human perfectibility. In the flicker of a single candle, Cynthia Dunbar Thoreau smoothed the creases of her skirt before ascending a step stool to distribute hymnals. Henry sat on a narrow bench, tracing the gilt edges of the tattered Book of Common Prayer as Channing's measured voice extolled spiritual progress. Yet Henry's mind drifted to the shards of cedar and flakes of graphite awaiting him in the back workshop—materials whose concrete resistance promised lessons more certain than abstract creeds. In that tension between inherited faith and empirical curiosity, he learned his first laboratory principle: ideas must be tested against lived reality, whether in sacred ritual or the scent of freshly shaved wood. That Wednesday evening, the Thoreau parlor filled with the low murmur of family and neighbors gathered for midweek Bible study. Candlelight danced across pages of the King James Bible as John Thoreau read Genesis 1: "And God said, Let there be light: and there was light." Henry sat cross-legged by the hearth, balancing his botany notebook on his knee. When his mother invited discussion, Henry tentatively raised his hand and asked, "But does that light precede our seeing it, or does our sight enact its creation?" A hush fell. His uncle, a local farmer, frowned. "The text speaks divine power, boy, not our optics." Undeterred, Henry pressed on: "If perception shapes the world, then maybe God gave us eyes to co-create creation." His mother exchanged a glance with John, who closed the book and replied gently, "Scripture teaches us truth through faith, Henry. Some mysteries exceed empirical reach." Henry sketched a quick diagram—a circle bisected by light and shadow—in his notebook's margin. After the study concluded, Cynthia tucked him in beside the log bed and whispered, "Your questions honor God's work, even if they unsettle others. Seek both scripture and observation, and the harmony between will reveal itself." That night, Henry lay awake rewriting Genesis in his journal as a field report: "Day One: light appears; observer notes spectrum unfolding through dew-laden blades of grass. Conclusion: perception and presence inseparable." This fusion of spiritual inquiry and empirical note-taking became a hallmark of his method, teaching him early that faith and observation are not adversaries but co-laborers in the laboratory of life.

At Harvard College in the fall of 1829, Henry David Thoreau navigated crowded corridors of Massachusetts Hall with a leather satchel of notebooks at his side. One crisp October afternoon, he and Edward Emerson—Ralph Waldo's younger brother and an acquaintance through Phi Beta Kappa gatherings—escaped the din of classical lectures for the dappled sunlight of Harvard Yard. Thoreau unfolded a pressed fern from his notebook and showed Edward its delicate pinnules. "Observe how each leaflet mirrors the whole," he explained, "a fractal of design." Edward traced the pattern with his finger, replying, "Your botany informs more than biology—it hints at a philosophy of parts and wholes." In Professor Longfellow's seminar on Dante and Tasso that November, Thoreau bristled at rigid poetic interpretations. When Longfellow read an English translation of Dante's invocation of fearful winds, Thoreau countered: "The Inferno's winds do more than symbolize guilt; they enact it—much as the southwest breeze distorts the marsh's song here in Cambridge." Longfellow paused, then invited Thoreau to elaborate. Thoreau described his recent survey of Fresh Pond's windswept reeds, noting how direction shaped their curve. "Poetry," he concluded, "must arise from embodied observation, not abstraction alone." The class fell silent; afterward, Longfellow commended his rigor but cautioned that "embodied insight must still honor metaphor's subtlety." That semester, Thoreau contributed essays to the Harvard Magazine on translating Horace's odes with "local authenticity"—suggesting that Roman celebrations of harvest could resonate through descriptions of Concord's apple blossoms. These pieces, published anonymously, earned praise for their fresh American voice and empiricist annotations—footnotes on soil conditions and cider production. Through such dialogues—literal and literary—Thoreau honed a method blending classical form with empirical substance, preparing him to write philosophies rooted as much in the body as in books.

By the autumn of 1833, Thoreau had completed his studies at Harvard and returned to Concord eager to transform his notebooks into public essays. His first attempts appeared in the local Gazette: sketches titled "On the Use of Pencil" and "Concord's Stone Walls," in which he argued that practical craft yields profound moral lessons.

Readers praised his lyrical descriptions of graphite and granite but questioned his insistence on "moral economy"—the idea that every human action carries ethical weight. Undeterred, Thoreau accepted a position as temporary schoolmaster at the Concord Academy. On his first day, he stood before a row of restless boys, ivory slate in hand, and attempted to instill in them the same reverence for measurement that he practiced in the pencil shop. When one student sneered at his botanical reference in a math demonstration, Thoreau faced his first moral trial: to punish with severity or to invite curiosity. He chose the latter, assigning the class an outdoor exercise measuring leaf lengths and calculating area-to-perimeter ratios. The next morning, several boys presented their results with surprisingly earnest enthusiasm, validating his conviction that intellectual rigor flourishes when tethered to nature.

Encouraged, Thoreau ventured into lecturing at local lyceums. His earliest speeches—delivered from a hand-carved wooden pulpit in a village meetinghouse—suffered from his nervous pacing and habit of reading directly from his notebooks. He recalled in a journal entry of November 1834: "My hands shook when I lifted a sprig of oak to illustrate taxonomy, and my voice faltered at the word 'ecology.' Yet when I paused to show them the leaf's veins under a glass lens, the audience leaned forward in wonder." That moment crystallized his turn toward fieldwork: if audiences responded to tangible specimens, then philosophy must emerge from embodied encounter rather than abstract lecture.

In the mid-1830s, Thoreau's notebooks began to coalesce around a set of key ideas that would shape his life and work: attention, deliberate living, economy as ethics, civil resistance, and natural history as philosophy. These concepts emerged not from abstract theorizing but from sustained practice in Concord's workshop, woods, and civic spaces. Attention first revealed itself in Thoreau's botanical studies. In a journal entry dated April 10, 1835, he wrote of a violet he found beneath damp pines: "I bent low to inspect a single petal's hue, and in that moment perceived the vastness of the world contained in one small form." This act of close observation—of slowing the mind to track the minutiae of living things—became the cornerstone of Thoreau's philosophy.

Deliberate living grew from this practice. Inspired by his measurement of the Concord River, Thoreau began to question the routines of his neighbors: their expenditure on unnecessary goods, their unexamined habits of consumption. In an essay draft titled "The Economy of Life," he insisted that "our spending of time and resources requires the same rigor we apply to ledger books." He experimented with minimal possessions—wearing the same clothes for days, eating simple fare of cornmeal and wild berries—and recorded in his journal the moral clarity that emerged from stripping life down to essentials.

Economy as ethics extended beyond personal thrift to social critique. Surveying the pencil shop's ledger alongside his own spending, Thoreau concluded that labor, trade, and resource use must all align with moral purpose. "A man's trade is not merely what he does for wages," he noted, "but how his work sustains or disturbs the harmony of community and earth." This principle informed his later lectures on "The Rights and Duties of Industry," where he traced the connections between honest labor, civic virtue, and environmental stewardship.

Civil resistance surfaced as a logical extension of deliberate living and moral economy. Thoreau's refusal to pay a poll tax in 1846—an act that led to his brief imprisonment—grew from his belief that individuals must withhold material support from unjust institutions. In his journal, he recorded the act not as rebellion but as an ethical imperative: "To give tithes to Walden is to give life to our principles; to give unwilling tribute to sin is to water the root of injustice." This stance, later expanded into his essay "Civil Disobedience," situated nonpayment of taxes as a measured, conscientious experiment in aligning material action with moral conviction.

Finally, Thoreau understood natural history itself as philosophy. His specimen collections—pressed ferns, bird skins, mineral samples—were accompanied by reflections on form and function, interdependence and change. He wrote in his Walden Journal: "Nature is philosophy in visible form; each organism a lesson in being; each season a chapter in the book of time." In teaching local schoolchildren to classify insects and map plant communities, he modeled an education that united empirical inquiry with ethical reflection.

That spring of 1835, Thoreau stood in the dimly lit Concord Anti-Slavery Society hall clutching his manuscript entitled "Immediate Emancipation." Before him sat local clergy, reformers, and curious townspeople. In the back, Prudence Crandall—recently ousted from her Canterbury school for educating African American girls—leaned forward, margin notes visible in the folded pages: "Too cautious on gender? Emphasize universal rights," and "Invoke moral urgency from scripture and reason alike." Thoreau opened: "Slavery is a moral cancer; to delay remedy is to feed the disease with our complacency." His voice wavered only when quoting Channing's gradualist stance—"Moral law is transcendent, yet our actions must align with its immediate demands"—then pivoted sharply to his own injunction: "Let no argument of economy or social order deflect our conscience." A minister in the front row murmured protest; a local mill worker nodded approval. Crandall's note—"Bold—but does it persuade?"—reminded Thoreau of the perennial tension between moral idealism and pragmatic outreach. Afterward, he circulated among listeners, receiving both applause and admonishment. At home, he annotated the sermon manuscript: "Add local testimony—insert widow Johnson's account of family separation." He then drafted a follow-up essay for the magazine, incorporating Crandall's critique and the Johnson family's story. This early lecture experiment cemented his approach to reform: combine moral clarity, empirical testimony, and iterative revision born of collaborator feedback.

That summer, Henry joined his brother John on a detailed survey of the Concord River's winding course. From their punt bobbing in shallow water, John held the Gunter's chain taut while Henry recorded each measurement in his field notebook. At one marshy bend, John pointed to a submerged sandbar. "See how the current splits here?" John called. He tossed a pebble into the water, watching ripples diverge. Henry knelt at the punt's edge and traced the sandbar's outline on damp paper. "This shoal forces water into two streams, altering fish habitats," he noted, then looked up: "Each rock and shoal tells a story of erosion and life." John laughed, recalling a childhood tale: "You always insisted every stone had a tale. Father would have made a preacher of you." Henry sketched a quick diagram, labeling depth, flow speed, and vegetation: "Sediment deposition here enriches marsh grasses—a model of how small shifts shape whole ecosystems." He paused, adding in the margin: "Collaboration refines solitary observation." Years later, John remembered in his memoir manuscript: "Henry's relentless precision—measuring every foot, mapping every curve—taught me that surveying is not mere cartography but storytelling of the land." This sibling exchange exemplified Thoreau's dual commitment to exact measurement and shared inquiry, forging methodologies that balanced solitary rigor with collaborative insight.

In the autumn of 1836, Thoreau secured an invitation to Harvard's renowned herbarium under the guidance of botanist Asa Gray. Entering the vaulted room, he inhaled the mingled scents of dried specimens and old wood. Gray, peering through a hand lens at a pressed fern, invited Thoreau to examine a slide of stomata under a simple microscope. Gray explained, "See these guard cells? Their opening regulates gaseous exchange—an essential mechanism for plant life." Thoreau leaned closer, noting in his journal: "Guard cells—pores of life—metaphor for thresholds of perception." Gray cautioned against over-systematization: "Taxonomy orders nature, but beware that labels do not imprison its fluid diversity." Over the next weeks, Thoreau returned frequently, helping Gray mount new specimens and learning proper preservation techniques. He contributed several pressed local species to the herbarium's expanding New England collection and corresponded with Gray on variations in leaf morphology across Concord's woodlot. Gray's mentorship deepened Thoreau's methodological rigor, teaching him to couple meticulous classification with a vigilant openness to nature's irregularities—an approach that would define his own natural histories.

In March 1843, Thoreau took his seat on Concord's school committee amid heated debate over curriculum reform. The meeting convened in the town hall with local magistrates, clergy, and parents in attendance. After motions to increase Latin and Greek instruction, Thoreau rose and laid out his proposal: a three-tiered syllabus blending classical texts with field studies—weekly nature rambles, specimen identification workshops, and botanical illustration classes. An elder selectman, stern-eyed, objected: "Young man, do you seriously propose pupils traipse through mud instead of mastering Cicero?" Thoreau replied evenly: "Cicero's eloquence traces its roots in oratory born of experience; let students observe nature's rhetoric, and they will speak with authenticity." Murmurs rippled through the hall. He presented committee minutes documenting his amendments: a requirement that all students compile a personal herbarium by the end of term and compose a reflective essay on plant–human interrelations. These edits passed by a narrow margin. Afterwards, at the schoolhouse, he sketched cabinet plans—labeled drawers for mosses, ferns, and flowering plants—inviting local woodworkers to contribute craftsmanship learned from the pencil shop. This civic laboratory demonstrated Thoreau's belief that education experiments require both respect for tradition and bold innovation. By embedding natural history into formal schooling, he enacted his principle that learning, like a laboratory, must be grounded in direct observation and communal collaboration.

That January, Thoreau undertook a sled-testing experiment on Walden Pond's ice. With a borrowed spruce sled in tow, he measured ice thickness at twenty-rod intervals by driving an iron awl through the surface until meeting water, then noting the depth on his thermometer-calibrated mark stick. At noon's zenith, he recorded 14 inches at the shallow bay and 18 inches near the deep channel. Hauling the sled, he tested bearing capacity by loading it incrementally with stones—first ten pounds, then twenty—until the ice creaked under forty-pound weight. In his journal, he drafted an aphorism across a full page:

"To know a place, measure its shadows and bear its weight; only then does knowledge stand firm upon its surface."

Beneath this, he sketched two parallel lines representing ice strata, annotating their translucence and brittleness under tensile stress. This rigorous embodied measurement exemplified his conviction that physical experiments yield philosophical insight—each puncture of ice a probe into nature's hidden architecture and each careful record an invitation to intellectual depth.

In the summer of 1842, Thoreau's field experiments extended into social invitations that tested his communal commitments. He received a hand-written note from neighbor Catherine Brooks inviting him to the annual Strawberry Festival in Concord Center. He penned a polite reply: "I value community gatherings yet must decline to preserve my habitual rhythms of observation. However, I would welcome the opportunity to lead a morning rambler's walk prior to the festivities." The festival committee accepted, and at dawn on June 15, Thoreau guided thirty townsfolk through dew-cooled meadows, identifying wild strawberries and discussing soil acidity—transforming a social event into a public experiment in shared attention.

That same year, he accepted a rare invitation to preach a Sunday reflection at the pulpit of Emerson's father, Rev. William Emerson, during the elder Emerson's absence. Standing where Ralph Waldo once listened as a youth, Thoreau addressed the congregation: "Faith and observation converge in gratitude—gratitude for creation's marvels as well as scripture's light." He paused to display a pressed fern and a hymnbook side by side, illustrating that spiritual and empirical reverence are twin paths to wonder. After the service, parishioners approached him not as hermit but as thoughtful neighbor, reinforcing his belief that embodied inquiry includes pastoral hospitality.

By the eve of 1846, Henry David Thoreau had transformed Concord's workshops, woods, and civic arenas into his living laboratory. The Sunday tensions between Channing's piety and cedar shavings taught him to weigh inherited faith against direct experience. His

Harvard debates with Sanborn and others fused classical formality with American observation, refining a prose style both lyrical and empirical. Early abolitionist orations crystallized his conviction that moral principles demand public enactment, not private assent. Collaborations with his brother instilled the value of shared measurement, while mentorships under Eaton and Gray anchored his botanical inquiries in scientific rigor. His tenure on the school committee demonstrated that education itself is an experiment in balancing tradition and innovation.

Through these origins, apprenticeships, key ideas, practices, and defenses, Thoreau forged a method of living ideas out loud—attention as spiritual discipline, deliberate living as ethical experiment, economy as communal virtue, civil resistance as political laboratory, and natural history as philosophical text. He refused the hermit myth by embedding his experiments within community life, from town meetings to children's nature rambles. When, in 1846, he stepped into Emerson's salon at "Bush," he brought more than notebooks and specimens; he carried a fully formed ethos of embodied inquiry. The stage was thus set for Emerson before Thoreau to meet Thoreau before Emerson, each laboratory ready to enrich the other, as they embarked on the greatest experiment of all: friendship-as-method shaping American thought.

Chapter Three

First Contact —
Mentorship, Friction, and
Mutual Recognition

On a rain-dampened October morning in 1837, Henry David Thoreau walked the gravel path to "Bush" carrying a leather portfolio of his earliest essays and a nervous certainty that his meeting with Ralph Waldo Emerson would either launch or demolish his literary aspirations. The parlor windows gleamed with condensation as Lidian Jackson Emerson ushered him into the study, where Emerson sat surrounded by manuscript pages, ink bottles, and correspondence from Thomas Carlyle. The room smelled of wood smoke and dried ink, and morning light filtered through tall windows onto shelves packed with volumes of German philosophy, English poetry, and American periodicals.

Thoreau placed his portfolio on the oak table and waited as Emerson lifted the first essay—"The Service," a meditation on moral courage—and read aloud in his measured cadence: "The only true reform is individual reform. Let a man work never so faithfully in behalf of a good cause, he does no good unless he is himself reformed." Emerson paused, tapping his pen against the margin, studying the younger man's earnest face. "Your sentences carry conviction, yet they read as proclamations rather than invitations. Consider this revision: 'True reform begins in the conscience of each person; only when we transform ourselves can we hope to transform society.'"

Thoreau bristled slightly at the editorial intervention, his jaw tightening almost imperceptibly, then nodded with careful consideration. "The revision clarifies, though it softens the imperative." Emerson smiled, recognizing the diplomatic restraint in Thoreau's response. "Clarity serves conviction better than force. Your ideas deserve readers, not resisters." He gestured toward the window, where rain streaked the glass. "A gentle rain nourishes growth better than a thunderstorm, which may flatten what it seeks to water."

That afternoon, as autumn light faded early behind storm clouds, Emerson offered Thoreau his first literary favor: an introduction to Margaret Fuller, editor of The Dial, with a handwritten note penned in his characteristic flowing script: "Mr. Thoreau combines the naturalist's eye with the moralist's heart. His essays merit your consideration, and I believe his voice will strengthen our American chorus." Thoreau accepted the letter gratefully, yet sensed the weight of obligation settling around his shoulders like autumn fog. The gesture bound him to Emerson's literary circle while simultaneously creating expectations he might struggle to meet.

In his journal that night, by the light of a single candle in his room at his mother's boarding house, Thoreau wrote: "Emerson's generosity opens doors, but I must walk through them on my own terms. His mentorship is both gift and burden—gift in its genuine care, burden in its implicit expectations. I must prove worthy of his confidence without becoming mere echo of his voice."

Over the following months, Emerson's mentorship unfolded through a series of detailed editorial workshops in the "Bush" study that became Thoreau's advanced education in the craft of writing. These sessions typically began after breakfast, when morning light provided the best illumination for manuscript work. Emerson would clear his writing table of correspondence and spread Thoreau's latest essays across its polished surface, weighing down corners with books to prevent pages from curling. When Thoreau submitted his essay "Natural History of Massachusetts" to The Dial in early 1838, Emerson demonstrated his systematic revision method with patient precision.

He read each paragraph aloud in his resonant voice, pausing to identify what he called "bumpy transitions" and "unclear referents"—technical terms he had learned from his years of lecturing and manuscript preparation. Where Thoreau had written, "The pond reflects not only light but the observer's mood," Emerson suggested, "Walden's surface mirrors both sunlight and the walker's inner weather." He explained his reasoning: "Specificity anchors abstraction. When you name Walden rather than 'the pond,' readers can see the place in their minds. When you say 'walker' rather than 'observer,' they feel the physical movement."

Thoreau studied the revision carefully, noting how Emerson's specificity—naming Walden rather than generic "pond"—grounded abstract reflection in familiar landscape while preserving the metaphorical resonance. He copied the suggested revision into his notebook, then experimented with his own variation: "Walden's surface mirrors both the morning's gold and the rambler's quiet joy." Emerson nodded approval. "Better still. 'Rambler' suggests purposeful wandering, and 'quiet joy' captures the mood more precisely than 'inner weather.'"

Yet Thoreau's independent spirit asserted itself when Emerson's edits threatened to alter his fundamental message. In a passage describing civil disobedience, Thoreau had written with characteristic directness: "When government becomes tyranny, the citizen's highest duty is refusal." Emerson, conscious of his role as elder advisor and mindful of public reception, proposed softening this to: "When government strays from justice, thoughtful citizens must carefully consider their response." The suggested revision represented everything Thoreau opposed—the kind of diplomatic hedging that drained moral imperatives of their urgency.

Thoreau shook his head firmly, his voice gaining strength. "The softened version evades the moral demand. I prefer stark clarity to diplomatic hedge." His eyes met Emerson's steadily. "If we cannot speak truth plainly, why speak at all?" Emerson laughed, recognizing in Thoreau's resistance the same moral courage he himself had shown in resigning from his ministry. "Then keep your clarity, but prepare for the consequences. Editors and readers alike prefer comfortable truths to challenging imperatives." This exchange established a pattern that would define their collaboration: Emerson offering the wisdom of experience, Thoreau insisting on the integrity of vision.

Their editorial partnership deepened through detailed case studies of journal-to-lecture-to-print evolution that revealed the complex alchemy of transforming private reflection into public discourse. Thoreau's Walden Journal entry of May 3, 1838—"I went to the woods to live deliberately, to front only the essential facts of life"—became the seed for what would eventually become his most famous work, but the transformation required multiple stages of development under Emerson's guidance.

The journal fragment first expanded into a lyceum lecture titled "Life in the Woods," delivered at Concord's lecture hall in November 1838. Under Emerson's patient coaching, Thoreau learned to "dramatize the philosophy"—to embed abstract principles in concrete narrative that audiences could follow and remember. Emerson advised him to begin not with philosophical declarations but with the practical details of cabin construction: "Tell them about splitting logs and laying stones. Let the philosophy emerge from the physical work."

The lecture opened with Thoreau's description of selecting a site near Walden Pond, measuring foundation dimensions, and calculating building costs down to the penny—$28.12½ for materials. He described the satisfaction of sinking posts into earth, the rhythm of adze against timber, the gradual emergence of shelter from forest materials. Only then did he transition to philosophical reflection: "In building my house with my own hands, I built also a life with my own choices. Each board I placed, each nail I drove, declared my independence from inherited assumptions about how life should be lived."

The transformation from lecture to printed essay proved more complex, involving negotiations with multiple editors and competing visions of the work's purpose. When Thoreau submitted the expanded essay to The Dial in early 1839, both Fuller and Emerson engaged in extensive editorial discussion that revealed the collaborative nature of Transcendentalist publishing. Fuller argued for cutting philosophical digressions to emphasize the narrative of cabin life, believing that readers would connect more readily with practical details than abstract theorizing. "Let the story carry the ideas," she counseled, "rather than interrupting the story with ideas."

Emerson countered that the philosophy elevated the narrative from mere memoir to universal statement. "Thoreau's experiment matters not because he built a cabin but because he demonstrated an alternative way of living. The philosophical passages show readers how to apply his insights to their own lives." The debate continued through several draft revisions, with Thoreau himself proposing the solution that preserved both elements: "Let the essay breathe through both narrative and reflection, but ensure each philosophical passage emerges from lived experience rather than imposed theory."

The published version, appearing in The Dial's summer 1839 issue under the title "Life in the Woods," retained both narrative and philosophical elements while establishing the integrated method Thoreau would perfect in Walden. Readers responded enthusiastically to the essay's blend of practical detail and transcendent meaning, with one correspondent writing to Fuller: "Mr. Thoreau's account of his woodland experiment speaks to both the hand and the heart. His philosophy grows from his bean rows like fruit from cultivated soil."

The social circuits surrounding Emerson and Thoreau extended far beyond their private editorial sessions, encompassing a network of writers, reformers, and intellectuals who gathered regularly at "Bush" for conversations that shaped American Transcendentalism. These gatherings typically convened on Sunday evenings, when Lidian Emerson served tea and seed cake in the parlor while her husband orchestrated discussions that ranged across philosophy, politics, literature, and social reform. The regulars included Bronson Alcott, Margaret Fuller, Elizabeth Peabody, and occasionally Nathaniel Hawthorne, each bringing distinct perspectives that challenged and enriched the others' thinking.

During one memorable evening in December 1838, Thoreau encountered Bronson Alcott's educational theories in action when Alcott arrived with his daughter Louisa, then six years old, and invited her to join the adult conversation. Alcott's progressive pedagogy emphasized "conversational education"—learning through guided dialogue rather than rote instruction. He asked Louisa to describe what she had observed during their walk to the Emerson house, then engaged her responses with the same seriousness he accorded adult discourse.

"I saw ice forming patterns on the pond," Louisa reported. "The patterns looked like fern leaves drawn by winter's pencil." Alcott nodded approvingly. "What do you think creates those patterns?"

Louisa considered carefully. "Maybe water has its own ideas about how to become solid." The adults exchanged glances of delight at the child's poetic insight, and Thoreau leaned forward. "Your observation about winter's pencil reminds me that nature is always writing—in ice crystals, in tree rings, in the arrangement of stones by streams."

This exchange sparked a debate about learning through direct experience that would influence both Alcott's and Thoreau's later work. Alcott argued that children learn best through "conversational pedagogy"—guided dialogue that honors their innate wisdom while expanding their understanding. Thoreau countered with characteristic emphasis on empirical observation: "Conversation must be grounded in attention to the natural world. Let children handle specimens, measure distances, and record their findings. Only then can dialogue yield understanding that lasts."

"You would make naturalists of them all," Alcott observed with a smile. Thoreau's response revealed his educational philosophy: "I would make them attentive to the world they inhabit. A child who can accurately describe a bird's nest has learned more than one who merely memorizes the names of bird species." This conversation planted seeds that would later bloom in Alcott's experimental schools and Thoreau's own work as an educator.

Margaret Fuller's presence in the circle proved especially significant for Thoreau's intellectual and literary development. Her editorial acumen, honed through years of managing The Dial, challenged both men to clarify their arguments and consider perspectives they might otherwise overlook. When Thoreau submitted his essay "The Rights and Duties of the Individual in Relation to Government" in early 1840, Fuller's margin notes revealed the kind of rigorous critique that made The Dial a forum for serious intellectual exchange.

Her most pointed comment addressed gender exclusion in Thoreau's theory of citizenship: "Your 'individual' seems implicitly masculine throughout this essay. Do women possess equal rights of resistance to unjust government? If so, why not say so explicitly?" The critique stung Thoreau because it exposed an unconscious assumption he had not examined. His revision acknowledged the point directly: "No person, regardless of gender, birth, or station, should submit conscience to the state's unjust demands. The duty of resistance falls equally upon all who possess moral sense."

Fuller's influence extended beyond specific editorial suggestions to broader intellectual partnership. She introduced Thoreau to German Romantic philosophy, lending him translations of Schleiermacher and Novalis that opened new avenues for thinking about the relationship between self and nature. During one evening's discussion, Fuller challenged Thoreau's tendency toward solitary analysis by arguing for the social dimensions of individual experience: "Your emphasis on self-reliance sometimes overlooks how profoundly we are shaped by community. Even your retreat to Walden depends upon the society you temporarily leave behind."

This critique pushed Thoreau to articulate more clearly his understanding of the relationship between solitude and society. "I go to the woods not to escape human community but to return to it with clearer vision," he responded. "Solitude sharpens social perception by removing the distractions that prevent us from seeing our neighbors clearly." Fuller's challenges thus helped Thoreau develop a more nuanced understanding of his own philosophical position.

Nathaniel Hawthorne, though more peripheral to the inner circle, offered Thoreau a valuable model of literary professionalism during their acquaintance in the early 1840s. Hawthorne's meticulous attention to manuscript preparation—clean copy, consistent formatting, prompt correspondence with editors—impressed Thoreau as much as his narrative craft. After observing Hawthorne's work habits during a visit to the Old Manse in 1842, Thoreau adopted similar standards for his own submissions.

Hawthorne demonstrated the importance of understanding publishing as a business as well as an art. He maintained detailed records of submission dates, editorial requirements, and payment terms, treating his writing as professional work rather than amateur expression. "Publishers respect writers who respect the business aspects of publishing," Hawthorne explained to Thoreau. "Clean manuscripts, prompt responses, and clear agreements serve both parties' interests."

This practical advice proved invaluable when Thoreau began submitting work to periodicals beyond The Dial. His correspondence files, influenced by Hawthorne's example, became models of professional courtesy and precision. His letter to James Russell Lowell requesting consideration for publication in The Pioneer exemplifies this approach: "I submit for your consideration an essay titled 'A Walk to Wachusett,' consisting of 3,500 words. The piece combines natural history observation with philosophical reflection in a manner I believe will interest your readers. I can provide revisions according to your editorial requirements and can deliver final copy within two weeks of acceptance."

The women of the circle—Fuller, Lidian Emerson, Elizabeth Peabody, and others—provided intellectual labor that sustained the broader Transcendentalist enterprise while often remaining invisible in the public record. They hosted salons that facilitated crucial conversations, managed subscription lists for The Dial that kept the journal financially viable, maintained extensive correspondence networks that connected writers across New England, and provided editorial feedback that shaped published works. Their contributions were essential yet typically unacknowledged in the masculine discourse of literary professionalism.

Lidian Emerson's role proved particularly crucial in creating the domestic environment that enabled her husband's intellectual work while providing Thoreau with a surrogate family during his residences at "Bush." Her morning conversations over breakfast often sparked ideas that appeared later in both men's essays. Her practical wisdom grounded their philosophical flights in everyday reality, and her editorial eye caught errors and unclear passages that escaped their attention.

Elizabeth Peabody's work as publisher and bookstore owner provided the infrastructure that made Transcendentalist publication possible. Her Foreign Library in Boston served as both bookstore and salon, introducing American readers to European philosophy while providing a venue for intellectual exchange. Her willingness to publish experimental works—including early essays by Thoreau—created opportunities that would not otherwise have existed.

Thoreau, more attuned than some male contemporaries to these gender dynamics, acknowledged in his journal the intellectual debts he owed to women in the circle: "The women of our circle possess insights that shame our pretensions to intellectual leadership. Fuller's mind surpasses most men I know in both range and precision; Lidian's practical wisdom grounds Emerson's flights of fancy; Peabody's editorial acumen shapes thoughts into publishable form. Without their contributions, our whole enterprise would collapse."

This recognition informed Thoreau's later advocacy for women's rights and his collaborative relationships with female intellectuals throughout his career. His essay "The Rights of Women" explicitly acknowledged women's intellectual equality and social contributions: "Any society that wastes half its intellectual capacity through gender prejudice cripples itself. Women's perspectives on literature, philosophy, and social reform deserve equal consideration with men's."

However, the early friendship between Emerson and Thoreau was not without significant friction that tested both men's capacity for mutual understanding and respect. Money emerged as a persistent source of tension that exposed class differences neither man had fully anticipated. When Emerson arranged for Thoreau to live in a cabin on his property near Walden Pond, the arrangement carried implicit obligations that became sources of discomfort for both parties.

The financial dynamics were complex and often unspoken. Emerson provided rent-free residence, access to his library, introductions to editors, and regular meals at his table. In exchange, he expected services that ranged from property maintenance to intellectual companionship. Thoreau provided occasional labor—surveying property lines, maintaining pathways, assisting with correspondence—while struggling to define the boundaries of obligation.

Thoreau's journal reveals his psychological discomfort with the arrangement: "Emerson's generosity creates debts I cannot easily repay. Money transactions are clear—service for payment, goods for currency. But how does one balance gratitude with independence? How much intellectual allegiance does hospitality purchase?" The questions tormented Thoreau because they touched his deepest values about self-reliance and intellectual integrity.

Emerson, meanwhile, expected a degree of intellectual loyalty that Thoreau found increasingly constraining. As Thoreau's ideas developed in directions that diverged from Emerson's philosophy, tensions grew over questions of intellectual ownership and proper attribution. When Thoreau publicly disagreed with Emerson's positions on slavery and social reform, Emerson felt his mentorship had been inadequately acknowledged.

The issue came to a head during a conversation in spring 1841 when Emerson suggested that Thoreau's recent lecture on civil disobedience had been "ungrateful" to the host who had provided him with platform and audience. Thoreau's journal entry that night burned with indignation: "Must gratitude extend to intellectual conformity? If hospitality purchases agreement, then it is no gift but a loan with interest. I prefer honest poverty to compromised conviction."

Prestige presented another challenge that revealed underlying power dynamics in their relationship. Emerson's literary reputation attracted visitors to Concord seeking association with the famous author, and some treated Thoreau as merely Emerson's protégé rather than an independent thinker. These encounters were particularly galling to Thoreau because they reduced his identity to a reflection of someone else's achievements.

During one gathering in summer 1842, a Boston editor dismissed Thoreau's ideas with a comment that crystallized his frustration: "Young man, when you have achieved Mr. Emerson's stature, your opinions will carry more weight. Until then, perhaps you should listen more and speak less." The condescension stung particularly because it occurred in Emerson's presence, reducing Thoreau to intellectual apprentice before a gathered audience.

Thoreau's journal entry that night revealed the depth of his wounded pride: "Must every thought bear the imprimatur of established reputation? I speak from my own experience, not borrowed authority. My observations of nature, my experiments in living, my moral convictions—these derive from direct encounter with reality, not from secondhand philosophy. Yet because I lack public fame, my insights are dismissed as juvenile presumption."

This incident crystallized Thoreau's determination to establish his own literary identity, even at the cost of distancing himself from his mentor. He began seeking publication venues beyond Emerson's influence and developing philosophical positions that explicitly differed from Transcendentalist orthodoxy. His essay "Life Without Principle," published in 1863, articulated his rejection of reputation as a measure of worth: "The only success worth seeking is the approval of one's own conscience. Public fame often rewards conformity rather than courage, popularity rather than principle."

Publication control generated the deepest friction between them, exposing fundamental differences in their approaches to public engagement and intellectual responsibility. When Thoreau's essay "Civil Disobedience" was accepted by a Boston magazine in 1849, the editor proposed revisions that would soften its radical stance on tax resistance and governmental authority. Emerson, conscious of the practical demands of publishing and concerned about Thoreau's reputation, advised accommodation.

"A published essay with modest compromises reaches more readers than an unpublished essay with pure principles," Emerson argued during a heated discussion in his study. "Your ideas deserve a hearing, but editors and readers have legitimate concerns about extreme positions. Perhaps you could qualify your statements about tax resistance with acknowledgment of legitimate governmental functions?"

Thoreau disagreed vehemently, seeing such compromises as intellectual corruption: "I will not purchase publication at the price of intellectual integrity. Better to remain unpublished than to mislead readers with diluted convictions. If my ideas cannot stand in their full strength, they do not deserve to stand at all."

The dispute revealed fundamental philosophical differences about the relationship between ideas and audience. Emerson believed that moral progress required gradual persuasion of mainstream opinion, which meant meeting readers where they were and leading them gently toward new positions. Thoreau insisted that moral truth demanded uncompromising statement, regardless of popular reception.

Their exchange grew heated as each man defended his position. "Your intransigence serves your conscience but abandons your responsibility to readers," Emerson charged. "If you speak only to those who already agree with you, what purpose does your writing serve?" Thoreau replied with equal intensity: "My responsibility is to speak truth as clearly as I can discern it. If readers reject truth because it disturbs their comfort, the fault lies not with the truth but with their willingness to hear it."

The essay appeared in its original form after Thoreau found a more sympathetic editor, but the dispute revealed how differently the two men understood the writer's public role. Emerson saw himself as a teacher whose primary obligation was effective communication of beneficial ideas. Thoreau understood himself as a witness whose primary obligation was faithful testimony to moral truth.

The ethics of editing and ownership of ideas complicated their collaboration further, raising questions about intellectual property that had no clear precedents in their literary culture. When Emerson incorporated phrases from Thoreau's journal into his own lectures without attribution, Thoreau felt his intellectual property had been appropriated without acknowledgment. The incident occurred in early 1842, when Emerson was preparing a lecture on "The Transcendentalist" that drew heavily on conversations with Thoreau.

In a frank conversation at "Bush," Thoreau raised the issue directly but diplomatically: "Your recent lecture on transcendentalism included my observation about 'marching to the beat of a different drummer.' While I'm pleased that the phrase serves your purposes, I believe acknowledgment would be appropriate." Emerson, genuinely surprised by the accusation, had not realized how his habit of absorbing and reshaping ideas from conversation could appear as appropriation.

"Our conversations blend ideas so thoroughly that I sometimes forget their origins," Emerson replied with evident embarrassment. "But you are right—acknowledgment should follow contribution. I will make corrections in future deliveries of the lecture." They agreed on protocols for future borrowing: direct quotations would receive attribution, while general ideas emerging from conversation would be considered common property.

Yet the incident exposed the inherent challenges of collaborative intellectual work in an age when copyright law offered little protection for ideas as opposed to specific textual expressions. Both men kept extensive journals that recorded not only their private thoughts but also conversations, observations, and insights shared with others. The boundaries between individual and collaborative creation were often unclear, leading to ongoing tensions about proper credit and intellectual ownership.

Despite these substantial tensions, their friendship endured because both men recognized it as what Thoreau termed "a contested commons"—a shared intellectual space requiring constant negotiation and mutual respect. They acknowledged power imbalances without reducing either figure to caricature or allowing resentment to destroy their genuine affection and intellectual partnership.

Emerson possessed literary fame, financial resources, and social connections that Thoreau lacked, advantages that created opportunities for mentorship but also potential for exploitation. Yet Thoreau offered fresh perspectives, rigorous thinking, and moral courage that enriched Emerson's own development. Their relationship embodied the democratic ideal of friendship among intellectual equals while acknowledging the material inequalities that shaped their interactions.

In his journal, Thoreau reflected on the paradox of their partnership with characteristic insight: "Emerson has been mentor, collaborator, and occasionally rival. Our friendship succeeds not because we avoid conflict but because we engage it honestly. True friendship, like democracy itself, requires the capacity to disagree without destroying the bonds that unite us. When friends can argue passionately yet part with mutual respect, they demonstrate the possibility of civil discourse in a fractured society."

Emerson, in his own writings, echoed this sentiment while acknowledging his younger friend's intellectual independence: "Thoreau challenges my assumptions and corrects my blind spots. He offers the gift of productive friction—the resistance that sharpens rather than dulls the blade of thought. Our disagreements do not diminish our friendship but deepen it, proving that minds can meet in affection while diverging in opinion."

By 1844, their relationship had evolved from simple mentorship to complex intellectual partnership characterized by mutual influence, respectful disagreement, and ongoing negotiation of roles and obligations. Thoreau had established his own literary voice while benefiting from Emerson's guidance and connections. Emerson had gained a rigorous critic and creative collaborator whose insights enriched his own work. Their early contact—marked by generosity and gratitude, editorial collaboration and creative tension, social integration and individual assertion—set the pattern for a friendship that would endure for decades while continually renegotiating the terms of engagement.

The contested commons of their friendship became a laboratory for exploring the possibilities and limitations of democratic intellectual life in antebellum America. Through their example, they demonstrated that authentic friendship between unequals requires acknowledging power differences while affirming the fundamental dignity and autonomy of each participant. Their first contact established the foundation for a relationship that would reshape American philosophy by proving that ideas flourish most fully in the fertile friction of minds that respect each other enough to disagree.

Their collaboration also revealed the complex social dynamics that supported American literary culture in the 1840s—the role of women's intellectual labor, the challenges of financial independence for writers, the negotiations required for publication, and the delicate balance between individual vision and collaborative refinement. The friendship between Emerson and Thoreau thus stands not only as a model of intellectual partnership but as a window into the social conditions that enabled the flowering of American Transcendentalism.

Chapter Four

Walden as Argument with Emerson

In the predawn darkness of March 15, 1845, Henry David Thoreau shouldered an axe and walked through frost-covered woods toward the northeastern shore of Walden Pond. The land belonged to Ralph Waldo Emerson, who had purchased the ninety-acre woodlot as an investment and retreat. In his journal that morning, Thoreau recorded his intention with characteristic precision: "I went to the woods to live deliberately, to front only the essential facts of life, and see if I could not learn what it had to teach, and not, when I came to die, discover that I had not lived." Yet what began as an experiment in simplified living would evolve, through seven major revisions spanning eight years, into the most sustained philosophical argument with his mentor that American literature had yet produced.

The genesis of Walden as both lived experiment and literary work reveals the methodological differences that distinguished Thoreau's approach from Emerson's. Where Emerson developed ideas through salon conversation and lecture performance, Thoreau tested concepts against the resistance of materials: the heft of an axe, the yield of bean plants, the exact cost of nails and boards. His cabin, built for $28.12½, became a laboratory where Emersonian abstractions met empirical constraints. The morning he felled his first pine, Thoreau was already composing sentences that would challenge his mentor's idealism with the stubborn particulars of embodied experience.

The manuscript evidence reveals Walden's evolution from journal fragments through lecture drafts to published chapters, each revision sharpening Thoreau's implicit critique of Transcendentalist orthodoxy. Draft A, completed by September 1847, reads like an extended journal entry chronicling two years of pond life. But as Thoreau revised through Drafts B-G between 1848 and 1854, the work transformed from personal narrative into systematic philosophy, each chapter now structured as an argument with unnamed but unmistakable Emersonian positions.

The scaffolding behind this transformation appears in Thoreau's manuscript marginalia and chapter reorganizations. Where early drafts followed chronological sequence—spring planting, summer growth, autumn harvest, winter contemplation—later versions reorganized material thematically. "Economy," originally scattered throughout the early manuscript, became the opening chapter precisely because it challenged Emerson's idealist tendency to minimize material constraints. "Higher Laws" emerged from journal fragments about diet and self-discipline to become a direct rejoinder to Emerson's celebration of intellectual appetite. "Spring" evolved from seasonal description into philosophical culmination, demonstrating how patient attention to natural processes yields insights unavailable through abstract reasoning.

Thoreau's revision process reveals his growing confidence in opposing his mentor's most cherished ideas. In Draft A, a passage about self-reliance closely echoes Emerson's essay of the same title: "I learned this, at least, by my experiment: that if one advances confidently in the direction of his dreams, and endeavors to live the life which he has imagined, he will meet with a success unexpected in common hours." By Draft D, composed in 1852, Thoreau had sharpened this into implicit critique: "If a man does not keep pace with his companions, perhaps it is because he hears a different drummer. Let him step to the music which he hears, however measured or far away."

The difference is crucial: Emerson's self-reliance assumes harmony between individual development and social progress, while Thoreau's drummer passage suggests that genuine independence often requires active resistance to communal expectations. This revision exemplifies Walden's method—transforming Emersonian aphorisms into testable propositions, then documenting the results of lived experiment.

The intertextual relationship between Walden and Emerson's major essays reveals the systematic nature of Thoreau's philosophical dissent. Each chapter engages specific Emersonian concepts, subjecting idealist proclamations to empirical testing. "Nature," Emerson's foundational essay, had argued that natural objects serve as symbols of spiritual facts. Thoreau's "Where I Lived, and What I Lived For" responds by insisting on the irreducible reality of natural phenomena: "Heaven is under our feet as well as over our heads." Where Emerson saw nature as transparent medium through which higher truths shine, Thoreau discovered in Walden's depths and seasonal cycles a sacredness requiring no transcendent referent.

The philosophical stakes of this disagreement emerge clearly in their contrasting treatments of solitude. Emerson's essay "Self-Reliance" celebrates the mind's capacity to generate truth through independent thought, but assumes this mental self-sufficiency can coexist with social engagement. His famous injunction to "trust thyself" presupposes a self that remains coherent across private reflection and public performance. Thoreau's "Solitude" chapter tests this assumption against the lived experience of extended isolation, discovering that genuine self-knowledge requires sustained withdrawal from social roles and expectations.

In his journal, Thoreau recorded the experimental character of his solitude practice: "I find it wholesome to be alone the greater part of the time. To be in company, even with the best, is soon wearisome and dissipating. I love to be alone. I never found the companion that was so companionable as solitude." This passage, incorporated into the "Solitude" chapter, reads as direct refutation of Emerson's assumption that intellectual independence can be maintained within social contexts. Thoreau's experiment suggests that society's expectations inevitably compromise individual integrity unless balanced by regular periods of complete withdrawal.

The chapter "Reading" extends this methodological critique to Emersonian approaches to learning and cultural transmission. Emerson's "The American Scholar" had argued that books serve as preserved thoughts of great minds, valuable primarily as stimuli to the reader's own thinking. Thoreau agrees that reading should inspire original thought but insists that genuine learning requires physical as well as intellectual discipline. His account of reading the Iliad by Walden's shore emphasizes the bodily conditions that enable deep comprehension: "The heroic books, even if printed in the character of our mother tongue, will always be in a language dead to degenerate times; and we must laboriously seek the meaning of each word and line, conjecturing a larger sense than common use permits out of what wisdom and valor and generosity we have."

This passage reveals Thoreau's characteristic move—acknowledging Emersonian insights while insisting on their material grounding. Yes, great books challenge readers to exceed conventional understanding, but this challenge requires not just mental effort but physical preparation. The scholar must train body as well as mind, developing through outdoor labor and simple living the vigor necessary for intellectual achievement. Emerson's idealization of mental self-reliance, Thoreau suggests, overlooks the embodied conditions that enable thought itself.

The most sustained philosophical argument appears in Walden's treatment of economy, which explicitly challenges Emersonian attitudes toward money, labor, and material necessity. Emerson's essays consistently minimize economic constraints, treating poverty as spiritual opportunity and wealth as moral danger. His essay "Compensation" argues that material loss inevitably produces spiritual gain, while "Self-Reliance" dismisses practical concerns as distractions from intellectual development.

Thoreau's "Economy" chapter subjects these idealist claims to rigorous practical testing. His meticulous accounting—$28.12½ for building materials, 27 cents per week for food, $8.72½ for eight months' expenses—demonstrates that economic independence requires precise attention to material conditions rather than Emersonian faith in spiritual compensation. The chapter's opening lines establish the empirical method that will govern the entire work: "When I wrote the following pages, or rather the bulk of them, I lived alone, in the woods, a mile from any neighbor, in a house which I had built myself, on the shore of Walden Pond, in Concord, Massachusetts, and earned my living by the labor of my hands only."

This methodological declaration implicitly critiques Emerson's approach to economic questions. Where Emerson treats material conditions as obstacles to be transcended through mental discipline, Thoreau insists that economic arrangements fundamentally shape intellectual possibilities. His experiment in simplified living tests whether reduced consumption can purchase increased freedom for contemplation and creative work. The detailed financial records he provides serve as empirical evidence for claims about the relationship between material simplicity and spiritual wealth.

Yet Thoreau's critique of Emersonian economy extends beyond personal finances to encompass broader questions about labor, value, and social organization. His famous declaration that "the mass of men lead lives of quiet desperation" explicitly challenges Emerson's optimistic assessment of American democracy and individual potential. Where Emerson's "The American Scholar" celebrates the nation's intellectual independence, Thoreau's analysis reveals systematic alienation produced by economic arrangements that separate workers from the products of their labor.

The bean field passages in "The Bean-Field" chapter provide Thoreau's most detailed exploration of these themes. His account of cultivating seven acres begins with practical description—"Making the earth say beans instead of grass"—but develops into systematic analysis of the relationship between agricultural labor and intellectual development. Unlike Emerson's treatment of farming as metaphor for mental cultivation, Thoreau insists on the irreducible reality of physical work and its effects on consciousness.

His description of hoeing reveals insights unavailable through abstract reflection: "It was no longer beans that I hoed, nor I that hoed beans; and I remembered with as much pity as pride, if I remembered at all, my acquaintances who had gone to the city to attend the oratorios." This passage suggests that genuine understanding of human labor requires direct participation in productive work rather than intellectual analysis from a distance. Thoreau's experiment demonstrates that philosophical insight emerges through embodied engagement with material processes rather than transcendence of material conditions.

The political dimensions of Walden's argument with Emerson appear most clearly in the work's treatment of slavery, taxation, and civil resistance. While Emerson's essays acknowledge slavery as moral evil, they consistently advocate gradual reform through intellectual persuasion rather than direct action. His address to the Anti-Slavery Convention of 1844 argued that "the movement party has the better cause, but the establishment has the better men," suggesting that abolitionists should focus on converting opponents rather than challenging institutional arrangements directly.

Thoreau's experience of tax resistance and imprisonment, which occurred during his residence at Walden, led him to very different conclusions about the relationship between individual conscience and political obligation. Though the tax resistance episode receives only brief treatment in Walden itself—"I quietly declare war with the State, after my fashion, though I will still make what use and get what advantage of her I can"—the experience fundamentally shaped the book's political philosophy.

The chapter "Higher Laws" reveals how Thoreau's pond experiment led him to question not only Emerson's political gradualism but also his mentor's faith in moral progress through intellectual development. Thoreau's detailed analysis of his dietary practices—his experiments with vegetarianism, his reflections on hunting and fishing—demonstrates how seemingly personal choices carry broader political implications. His decision to minimize consumption of animal products emerged not from abstract ethical reasoning but from direct observation of how diet affects consciousness and moral sensitivity.

This methodological difference proves crucial for understanding Walden's political arguments. Where Emerson's antislavery writings rely on moral suasion—appealing to opponents' rational self-interest and ethical intuitions—Thoreau insists that political transformation requires personal transformation achieved through practical experiment. His tax resistance represents the logical extension of his pond experiment: having learned through simplified living that individual integrity requires resistance to social expectations, he applies this insight to political obligations.

The manuscript revisions of passages dealing with civil resistance reveal Thoreau's growing confidence in opposing Emersonian political philosophy. Early drafts mention tax resistance only in passing, but later versions develop the theme more systematically. Draft F, composed in 1853-54, adds the crucial passage about declaring "war with the State," while also intensifying the critique of neighbors who "serve the devil, without intending it, as God." These revisions suggest that Thoreau's political thinking continued evolving throughout the Walden years, moving toward increasingly radical positions that challenged not only slavery but the legitimacy of government itself.

The book's treatment of neighborly relations provides another site of implicit argument with Emersonian social philosophy. Emerson's essays celebrate friendship while maintaining faith in the ultimate harmony between individual development and community welfare. His essay "Friendship" argues that genuine personal relationships enhance rather than threaten social cohesion: "A friend is a person with whom I may be sincere. Before him I may think aloud."

Thoreau's "Visitors" and "Former Inhabitants and Winter Visitors" chapters test these assumptions against the lived experience of reduced social contact. His account of conversations with Alek Therien, the French-Canadian woodchopper, reveals insights about intellectual companionship unavailable through conventional social interaction. Therien's simple directness and practical wisdom challenge assumptions about the relationship between education and intelligence that inform Emerson's celebration of scholarly culture.

Similarly, Thoreau's historical research into Walden's former inhabitants—enslaved and free African Americans, Irish immigrants, failed farmers—provides implicit critique of Emersonian optimism about American democracy and individual opportunity. His sympathetic portraits of Brister Freeman, Zilpha White, and other marginalized figures suggest that social arrangements systematically prevent many individuals from achieving the self-reliance that Emerson celebrates as universal possibility.

The manuscript evidence reveals how these political insights developed through successive revisions. Draft A contains only brief references to former inhabitants, but later versions expand these passages into sustained meditation on economic inequality and social exclusion. The addition of Brister Freeman's story in Draft E, for example, demonstrates how slavery's legacy continues shaping opportunities for freed people and their descendants. These revisions suggest that Thoreau's pond experiment led him to increasingly radical conclusions about the structural obstacles to individual flourishing in American society.

The chapter "Spring" provides Walden's culminating argument against Emersonian idealism while demonstrating the alternative method Thoreau had developed through his years of pond-side experiment. Where Emerson's "Nature" treats seasonal change as symbol of spiritual renewal—"Nature is the incarnation of a thought, and turns to a thought again, as ice becomes water and gas"—Thoreau insists on the irreducible reality of natural processes while finding in their careful observation a source of insight unavailable through abstract reasoning.

His famous description of thawing clay banks becomes an extended meditation on the relationship between natural and intellectual development: "Few phenomena gave me more delight than to observe the forms which thawing sand and clay assume in flowing down the sides of a deep cut on the railroad through which I passed on my way to the village." The passage that follows demonstrates Thoreau's characteristic method—beginning with precise observation, identifying patterns and connections, then developing philosophical implications without losing contact with empirical foundation.

This methodological difference proves crucial for understanding Walden's ultimate argument with Emersonian Transcendentalism. Where Emerson treats natural phenomena as transparent symbols of higher truths, Thoreau finds in patient attention to natural processes a form of insight that requires no transcendent referent. The thawing banks teach lessons about creativity, development, and renewal precisely because they are irreducibly natural phenomena rather than symbols of something else.

The manuscript revisions of the spring passages reveal the evolution of this philosophical position. Early drafts treat seasonal change in conventionally symbolic terms, but later versions develop the distinctive voice that insists on nature's intrinsic rather than merely instrumental value. The crucial passage about the "Artist of Kouroo," added in Draft F, makes this methodological commitment explicit: "The material was pure, and his art was pure; how could the result be other than wonderful?"

This parable of the artist who achieves immortality through perfect dedication to craft provides Walden's clearest statement of the alternative to Emersonian idealism. Where Emerson's essays celebrate the mind's capacity to transcend material limitations through intellectual effort, Thoreau's artist achieves transcendence through complete engagement with material conditions. The result is not escape from temporal limitations but transformation of temporality itself—the artist's perfect work renders him immune to historical change while remaining fully embedded in natural and social worlds.

The political implications of this aesthetic philosophy become clear when read alongside Thoreau's other writings from the Walden period. His essay "Civil Disobedience," published in 1849 while he was still revising Walden, applies the same methodological principles to questions of political obligation. Just as the Artist of Kouroo achieves immortality through perfect attention to craft, the individual conscience achieves authority through perfect attention to moral truth, regardless of social consequences.

This connection between aesthetic and political philosophy explains why Walden devotes so much attention to questions of style, voice, and literary method. Thoreau's famous declaration that "I do not propose to write an ode to dejection, but to brag as lustily as chanticleer in the morning, standing on his roost, if only to wake my neighbors up" announces not just personal mood but methodological commitment. His literary experiment tests whether American writing can achieve the independence from European models that Emerson had called for in "The American Scholar" while avoiding the intellectual abstractions that, in Thoreau's view, compromised his mentor's achievement.

The manuscript revisions reveal how this literary-philosophical program developed through successive drafts. Early versions of Walden adopt conventional essay structure and relatively formal prose style. But later revisions experiment with more flexible organization and increasingly colloquial voice. The famous opening sentence—"When I wrote the following pages, or rather the bulk of them, I lived alone, in the woods"—appears only in Draft D, composed in 1852. This revision marks Thoreau's discovery of the conversational tone that allows him to address readers directly while maintaining intellectual seriousness.

Similarly, the decision to structure the book around the cycle of seasons rather than chronological sequence appears in Draft C, composed in 1849. This organizational choice enables Thoreau to present his two-year experiment as archetypal rather than merely personal experience while preserving the empirical grounding that distinguishes his method from Emersonian abstraction. The seasonal structure allows him to demonstrate how individual development follows natural rather than social rhythms while suggesting that readers can replicate his experiment under different material conditions.

The chapter "Conclusion" makes explicit the challenge that Walden poses to contemporary readers and, implicitly, to Emersonian approaches to social reform. Thoreau's famous injunction—"If a man does not keep pace with his companions, perhaps it is because he hears a different drummer"—appears to celebrate individual nonconformity in terms consistent with Emerson's "Self-Reliance." But the broader context reveals a more radical argument about the relationship between personal and political transformation.

The passage continues: "Let him step to the music which he hears, however measured or far away. It is not important that he should mature as soon as an apple tree or an oak." This extension reveals the crucial difference between Thoreau's individualism and Emerson's. Where Emerson's self-reliance assumes that individual development serves broader social purposes, Thoreau's drummer passage suggests that genuine independence may require permanent separation from social expectations and timelines.

The manuscript evidence reveals how this philosophical position developed through successive revisions. Early drafts of the conclusion emphasize the universal applicability of Thoreau's insights, suggesting that readers should adapt his methods to their own circumstances. But later versions stress the irreducibly individual character of each person's path to independence. The final version warns against literal imitation while encouraging experimental adaptation: "I would not have any one adopt my mode of living on any account; for, beside that before he has fairly learned it I may have found out another for myself, I desire that there may be as many different persons in the world as possible."

This revision reveals Walden's ultimate argument with Emersonian Transcendentalism. Where Emerson's essays offer universal principles applicable across diverse circumstances, Thoreau insists that genuine insight emerges only through individual experiment tailored to specific material conditions. His book provides not a program for reform but a methodological model—demonstrating how patient attention to the intersection of personal needs and natural possibilities can generate alternatives to conventional arrangements.

The political implications of this methodological commitment become clear when Walden is read alongside Thoreau's other writings from the same period. His essay "Life Without Principle," delivered as lectures throughout the 1850s, extends the critique of economic arrangements begun in Walden's "Economy" chapter. His addresses on slavery and John Brown apply the same experimental method to questions of political resistance, testing abstract principles of justice against specific historical circumstances.

Yet Walden itself remains focused on the preliminary work of individual transformation, insisting that political effectiveness requires prior achievement of personal independence. The book's detailed attention to domestic arrangements, dietary practices, and daily routines demonstrates how seemingly private choices carry public significance while arguing that lasting social change must begin with individual experiments in alternative living.

This methodological commitment explains why Thoreau spent eight years revising Walden, transforming a relatively simple narrative of pond life into systematic philosophy. Each revision tested his emerging insights against new experiences and changing historical circumstances. The manuscript evidence reveals how the book's arguments developed in response to contemporary events—the Mexican-American War, the Compromise of 1850, the Fugitive Slave Law—while maintaining focus on the experimental method that Thoreau believed offered the most promising approach to social transformation.

The final version of Walden, published in 1854, thus represents not just personal memoir but systematic argument for an alternative to the reform strategies advocated by Emerson and other Transcendentalist leaders. Where they relied primarily on moral suasion and political organizing, Thoreau demonstrated through lived experiment how individuals could achieve sufficient independence to resist unjust institutions directly. His book documents this achievement while providing methodological guidance for readers attempting similar experiments under different conditions.

Reading Walden as argument with Emerson rather than pastoral retreat reveals the work's continuing relevance for contemporary readers facing analogous questions about the relationship between personal and political transformation. Thoreau's demonstration that individual integrity requires systematic attention to material conditions—economic arrangements, dietary practices, living situations, work patterns—offers practical guidance for readers seeking alternatives to conventional arrangements while avoiding the political abstraction that, in his view, compromised his mentor's effectiveness.

The manuscript revisions that sharpen Walden's dissent from Emersonian orthodoxy thus serve broader philosophical and political purposes. They document Thoreau's discovery of a methodological alternative to idealist approaches to social reform while demonstrating how individual experiment can generate insights unavailable through abstract reasoning. The result is not rejection of Emersonian insights but their systematic testing against empirical constraints—a process that reveals both their continuing value and their practical limitations.

This experimental approach to philosophical and political questions explains Walden's enduring influence on subsequent movements for social change. From Gandhi's adaptation of Thoreau's civil resistance methods to contemporary environmental activists' emphasis on lifestyle politics, readers have found in Thoreau's pond experiment a model for combining personal transformation with political effectiveness. The book's demonstration that individual integrity and social responsibility are mutually reinforcing rather than conflicting commitments continues offering guidance for readers seeking alternatives to conventional approaches to reform.

Yet Walden's argument with Emerson also reveals the limitations of purely individual approaches to social transformation. Thoreau's experiment succeeded partly because of advantages—gender, race, class, education—that enabled his withdrawal from conventional economic arrangements. His access to Emerson's land, his family's support, his Harvard education, and his social connections all facilitated the independence he achieved through simplified living. Contemporary readers must reckon with these constraints while adapting his methodological insights to different material conditions.

The manuscript evidence suggests that Thoreau himself became increasingly aware of these limitations as he revised Walden through successive drafts. Later versions acknowledge more explicitly the social conditions that enabled his experiment while insisting that similar experiments remain possible under different circumstances. This development suggests that his argument with Emerson evolved from simple opposition toward more nuanced understanding of the relationship between individual and social transformation.

The final version of Walden thus offers not dogmatic program but experimental method—demonstrating how careful attention to the intersection of personal needs and material possibilities can generate alternatives to conventional arrangements while acknowledging the social conditions that enable such experiments. Reading the book as argument with Emerson rather than pastoral retreat reveals both its philosophical sophistication and its practical relevance for contemporary readers seeking guidance for combining personal integrity with political effectiveness.

Chapter Five

Self-Reliance and Civil Disobedience — theory meets tactics

On the evening of February 3, 1841, Ralph Waldo Emerson climbed the steps of the Boston Lyceum to deliver his lecture "Self-Reliance" to an audience of New England's cultural elite. Eight years later, in a small jail cell in Concord, Massachusetts, Henry David Thoreau scratched out notes for what would become "Civil Disobedience" on the back of a tax notice he had refused to pay. These two moments crystallize the philosophical journey from Emersonian idealism to Thoreauvian praxis—from the cultivation of inner sovereignty to its external manifestation in acts of principled resistance. Together, these essays constitute the most significant theoretical and tactical contribution to American political philosophy in the nineteenth century, establishing a dialectical relationship between personal autonomy and civil resistance that continues to shape democratic discourse.

"Self-Reliance," first published in Emerson's 1841 Essays: First Series, emerged from nearly a decade of lyceum lectures delivered to educated audiences throughout New England. The manuscript evidence reveals significant evolution from Emerson's original 1837 lecture notes, preserved in his Miscellaneous Notebooks, Series 4, Notebook 27, which show a more tentative exploration of individual authority. The famous opening line—"To believe your own thought, to believe that what is true for you in your private heart is true for all men,—that is genius"—appears in the lecture manuscript as the more hesitant "To trust one's own thought, to believe that what seems true in private reflection may prove universal—this marks genius." The revision demonstrates Emerson's growing confidence in asserting the epistemological authority of individual insight.

The essay's structure reflects its origins in oral performance: flowing paragraphs that build through accumulation rather than linear argument, aphoristic pronouncements designed for memorability, and a conversational tone that assumes readers' familiarity with classical references and contemporary cultural debates. Emerson addresses what he terms "you men and women of thought"—intellectuals capable of appreciating subtle philosophical distinctions and ready to embrace the demanding discipline of intellectual independence. This sentence encapsulates Emerson's philosophical method—the movement from particular insight to universal principle through the medium of individual consciousness. His strategy depends on readers' willingness to follow complex trains of association while maintaining faith in the ultimate coherence of his vision.

The essay's debt to Immanuel Kant's Groundwork of the Metaphysics of Morals becomes evident in Emerson's treatment of moral autonomy as self-legislation. Where Kant argues that rational beings must "act only according to that maxim whereby you can at the same time will that it should become a universal law," Emerson transforms this categorical imperative into intuitive self-trust: "Nothing is at last sacred but the integrity of your own mind." Yet Emerson's adaptation characteristically shifts from Kantian rational universalization to romantic faith in individual insight. His marginalia in his personal copy of the Groundwork, preserved at Harvard's Houghton Library, reveals his dissatisfaction with Kant's emphasis on duty over inclination: "Kant makes morality a burden—but what if conscience speaks through desire, through the soul's natural movement toward truth?"

Samuel Taylor Coleridge's influence appears even more directly through Emerson's adaptation of organic philosophy. Coleridge's unpublished marginalia in his copy of Schelling's System des transcendentalen Idealismus, which Emerson encountered during his 1833 visit to Highgate, argues that "the Self, in its highest potency, legislates for Nature through its own self-realization." Emerson's journal entry from August 1834 directly echoes this insight: "The soul active sees absolute truth and utters truth or creates." This philosophical foundation supports Emerson's confidence that individual self-development serves universal purposes—a belief that would later create tension with Thoreau's more skeptical assessment of harmony between private virtue and public good.

By contrast, "Civil Disobedience" adopts the form of a public address aimed at fellow citizens rather than cultural elites. Originally delivered as lectures titled "The Rights and Duties of the Individual in Relation to Government" at the Concord Lyceum in January and February 1848, the essay underwent significant revision before its 1849 publication as "Resistance to Civil Government" in Elizabeth Peabody's anthology Aesthetic Papers. The comparison between Thoreau's lecture manuscript, preserved in the Concord Free Public Library's Thoreau Collection (MS Am 278.5), and the published text reveals crucial developments in his political thinking.

The lecture manuscript opens with a more conciliatory tone: "I would not be understood as advocating the dissolution of government, but rather its reformation through the awakened conscience of individual citizens." By the time of publication, this had become the more radical declaration: "I heartily accept the motto, 'That government is best which governs least'; and I should like to see it acted up to more rapidly and systematically." The revision reflects Thoreau's growing impatience with gradualist approaches to reform and his increasing confidence in principled resistance as a legitimate democratic strategy.

The posthumous retitling as "Civil Disobedience" in the 1866 collection A Yankee in Canada, with Anti-Slavery and Reform Papers reflected changing political circumstances and editorial preferences, but Thoreau's original title better captures his strategic intent—to articulate a theory of principled resistance for democratic citizens facing governmental injustice. The 1866 text also includes several small but significant revisions that strengthen the essay's philosophical arguments. Where the 1849 version states "The authority of government, even such as I am willing to submit to—for I will cheerfully obey those who know and can do better than I," the 1866 revision clarifies: "The authority of government, even such as I am willing to submit to—for I will cheerfully obey those who know and can do better than I, and in many things even those who neither know nor can do so well—is still an impure one."

Where Emerson's prose cultivates an atmosphere of philosophical contemplation, Thoreau's essay maintains the urgency of immediate political crisis. His opening declaration announces both his political position and his impatience with gradual reform. The essay's structure follows the logic of practical argument: establishing principles, examining specific cases, anticipating objections, and providing concrete guidance for action. Thoreau assumes readers who share his moral convictions but need intellectual framework and tactical direction for translating principle into practice.

The divergent approaches of these essays reflect their authors' different understandings of how philosophical work should function in democratic society. Emerson writes for the cultural vanguard—ministers, educators, writers, and reformers who shape public opinion through intellectual leadership. His essay aims to transform the consciousness of influential individuals who will, in turn, gradually transform social institutions through example and persuasion. "Self-Reliance" functions as what we might call "anticipatory politics"—preparing minds for changes that will unfold over historical time through the slow work of cultural evolution.

Contemporary reception among this intended audience proved generally favorable, though with some reservations about practical implications. The North American Review's October 1841 assessment praised Emerson's "profound insights into the nature of individual genius" while questioning whether "such elevated individualism can coexist with social responsibility." The Christian Examiner worried about the essay's "dangerous tendency to elevate individual opinion above social authority," particularly noting that "Mr.

Emerson's philosophy might encourage moral anarchy if adopted by persons lacking his elevated character and refined education."

More enthusiastic responses came from transcendentalist publications and reform journals. Margaret Fuller's review in The Dial celebrated Emerson's "courage to speak the truth that individual conscience must be the final arbiter of moral questions." Her analysis particularly appreciated how the essay "liberates women as well as men from the tyranny of conventional expectation," though she noted privately to Elizabeth Peabody that Emerson's masculine pronouns might limit female readers' identification with his philosophy.

Thoreau addresses "my neighbors" directly, speaking as citizen to citizen rather than as cultural authority to disciples. His essay responds to immediate political crises—the Mexican-American War, the Fugitive Slave Law, the expansion of slavery—that demand urgent action rather than patient cultivation. Where Emerson's timeline extends across generations, Thoreau's urgency reflects the moral imperative of the present moment. His essay functions as "emergency politics"—providing intellectual justification and practical guidance for citizens who can no longer conscience cooperation with unjust institutions.

This difference in temporal perspective shapes each essay's rhetorical strategy. Emerson can afford philosophical subtlety because he expects his insights to work gradually through cultural transmission. His famous paradoxes—"a foolish consistency is the hobgoblin of little minds"—require contemplative unpacking rather than immediate application. Thoreau's aphorisms—"under a government which imprisons any unjustly, the true place for a just man is also a prison"—demand clear understanding and prompt action. The stakes of misinterpretation differ accordingly: Emersonian confusion might delay personal growth, but Thoreauvian confusion could result in ineffective resistance or unnecessary suffering.

The abolitionist reception of both essays reveals how their different approaches generated distinct patterns of political influence. William Lloyd Garrison's response to "Self-Reliance," published in The Liberator on March 12, 1841, praised Emerson's "recognition that individual conscience must supersede human law" while expressing concern that the essay "lacks sufficient urgency about the immediate evil of slavery." Garrison's critique proved prescient: "Mr. Emerson's philosophy provides excellent preparation for moral action, but moral action itself requires more direct engagement with specific injustices than his essay provides."

Wendell Phillips offered a more favorable assessment, arguing in a letter to Garrison dated April 3, 1841, that "Self-Reliance" provided essential intellectual foundation for abolitionist work: "Before we can effectively challenge slavery, we must develop the intellectual independence that Emerson describes. His essay teaches the self-trust necessary for principled opposition to popular error." Phillips's reading emphasized how Emerson's individualism could support rather than substitute for organized reform efforts.

"Civil Disobedience" generated much stronger abolitionist enthusiasm. The Liberator's August 10, 1849 review called it "the most powerful argument for individual resistance to governmental injustice that American literature has produced." The reviewer particularly praised Thoreau's "practical guidance for citizens who refuse to cooperate with slavery," noting that the essay "transforms philosophical principle into concrete action." William Wells Brown, writing in the National Anti-Slavery Standard on September 6, 1849, celebrated Thoreau's willingness to "suffer imprisonment rather than support slave-catching government," arguing that his example "demonstrates the power of principled resistance to inspire broader social change."

However, some abolitionist leaders worried about Thoreau's apparent endorsement of individual action over organized movement work. Garrison himself wrote privately to Phillips on October 15, 1849, expressing concern that Thoreau's emphasis on individual conscience might "encourage moral heroes to act alone rather than building the collective power necessary for systematic reform." This tension would persist throughout the essay's reception among reform movements, reflecting the ongoing challenge of balancing individual integrity with collective effectiveness.

Female reformers played crucial roles in circulating and interpreting both essays, though their contributions have often been overlooked in subsequent scholarship. Elizabeth Palmer Peabody's decision to publish "Resistance to Civil Government" in Aesthetic Papers reflected her editorial judgment that the essay addressed urgent questions about the relationship between individual conscience and democratic citizenship. Her introduction to the volume emphasized how "Mr. Thoreau's essay speaks to all citizens, regardless of gender, who face conflicts between legal obligation and moral duty."

Margaret Fuller's response to both essays, documented in her correspondence with various reform leaders, reveals sophisticated understanding of their complementary contributions to American political thought. Writing to William Henry Channing on June 12, 1841, she observed: "Emerson's 'Self-Reliance' provides the psychological foundation for independent action, while Thoreau's resistance essay supplies the tactical framework. Together they offer resources for combining personal development with social transformation." Fuller's own Woman in the Nineteenth Century draws extensively on both texts, adapting Emersonian self-trust and Thoreauvian resistance to questions of gender equality and women's political participation.

Maria W. Stewart, the first African American woman to give public political speeches, incorporated insights from both essays into her own writings on individual dignity and collective resistance. Her 1833 address "What If I Am a Woman?" echoes Emersonian themes: "The spirit of independence is too valuable a jewel ever to be bartered away for a mess of pottage." Her later writings show familiarity with Thoreau's tactical insights, particularly his analysis of how principled minorities can effect social change through noncooperation with unjust institutions.

Women's reading circles throughout New England engaged seriously with both essays, as documented in surviving meeting minutes and correspondence. The Boston Female Literary Association's records from 1842-1850, preserved in the Massachusetts Historical Society, show regular discussion of "Self-Reliance" and its implications for women's intellectual development. Minutes from the February 14, 1843 meeting record debate about whether Emerson's philosophy "applies equally to women's moral judgments" or reflects "masculine assumptions about individual authority." The group concluded that "while Mr. Emerson writes primarily for male readers, his principles support women's claims to intellectual and moral equality."

The Concord Women's Reading Circle, which included Lidian Emerson, Abigail Alcott, and other reform-minded women, took up "Civil Disobedience" during their 1849-1850 season. Minutes from the November 5, 1849 meeting, preserved in the Concord Public

Library, show animated discussion about the essay's implications for women's political participation. Mrs. John Thoreau (Henry's mother) argued that "if individual conscience supersedes unjust law, then women possess equal authority to resist legal restrictions on their political participation." The group resolved to study both essays together as complementary statements about individual autonomy and social responsibility.

Both essays grapple with the relationship between individual conscience and social obligation, but they reach significantly different conclusions about how moral agents should navigate conflicts between inner conviction and external authority. Emerson's "Self-Reliance" develops what we might call an "aesthetic ethics"—a framework that treats moral choice as creative expression rather than duty-bound compliance. His famous injunction to "trust thyself" assumes that authentic self-expression will ultimately serve universal good because individual genius participates in cosmic wisdom.

This aesthetic approach to ethics enables Emerson to sidestep direct confrontation with existing institutions while maintaining radical individualist commitments. When he declares that "no law can be sacred to me but that of my nature," he asserts the sovereignty of individual conscience without necessarily advocating resistance to particular laws. His emphasis on "the law of consciousness" suggests that moral development occurs primarily through inner transformation rather than external action. Social reform, from this perspective, follows naturally from individual enlightenment as reformed persons create reformed institutions through their elevated example.

The legal-theoretical context for Thoreau's more radical position becomes clear through examination of contemporary debates about individual rights and governmental authority. Lysander Spooner's The Unconstitutionality of Slavery (1845) had argued that individuals possess natural rights that supersede positive law, providing intellectual foundation for Thoreau's resistance theory. Spooner's subsequent No Treason essays, beginning publication in 1867, would develop this argument into systematic anarchist philosophy, but his earlier constitutional writings were already circulating among New England reformers during the 1840s.

Thoreau's journal entries from 1846-1847 show direct engagement with Spooner's arguments. In his entry for July 4, 1846 (Journal, Vol. 8, p. 324), Thoreau writes: "Spooner demonstrates that the Constitution cannot legitimate slavery, but I would go further: no constitution can authorize government to violate individual conscience. When positive law conflicts with natural law, the individual must obey the higher authority." This passage reveals how Thoreau adapted contemporary legal theory to support his resistance philosophy while moving beyond Spooner's constitutionalist framework toward more radical conclusions about governmental legitimacy.

The broader context of antebellum contract law also influenced Thoreau's thinking about political obligation. Legal theorists like Joseph Story and James Kent had argued that governmental authority derives from implicit social contract, creating reciprocal obligations between citizens and state. Thoreau's essay challenges this framework by arguing that moral agents cannot contract away their conscience: "The only obligation which I have a right to assume is to do at any time what I think right." This position draws on natural law theory's claim that certain rights are inalienable, but applies this principle more systematically than most contemporary legal thinkers were willing to do.

Thoreau's "Civil Disobedience" challenges this gradualist optimism by demonstrating how individual conscience must sometimes manifest as direct resistance to state authority. His ethics of refusal begins where Emerson's aesthetic ethics ends—with the recognition that personal integrity may require public disobedience. "The only obligation which I have a right to assume," Thoreau declares, "is to do at any time what I think right." This seemingly similar statement to Emerson's self-reliance actually articulates a more demanding ethical position because it explicitly acknowledges potential conflict between individual judgment and social expectation.

Thoreau's framework recognizes four distinct levels of moral obligation: self-knowledge (understanding one's own principles), noncooperation (withdrawing support from unjust institutions), active dissent (public resistance to specific injustices), and willingness to accept consequences (demonstrating the sincerity of one's convictions through personal sacrifice). This escalating structure provides citizens with graduated options for principled response to governmental injustice while maintaining that the ultimate measure of moral seriousness is readiness to suffer rather than compromise conscience.

The indigenous philosophical influences on both authors' thinking about individual conscience and natural law have been insufficiently recognized in previous scholarship. Thoreau's understanding of conscience as connected to natural law reflects encounters with Wampanoag and Mohegan oral traditions that emphasized reciprocal relationship between individual persons and the larger community of life. His journal entry from September 15, 1851 (Journal, Vol. 4, p. 67) records a conversation with Joe Polis, his Penobscot guide, about the relationship between personal vision and tribal obligation: "Polis says that when a person receives guidance in dreams or through fasting, they must follow that guidance even if it conflicts with tribal custom. But they must also accept responsibility for consequences of their actions." This indigenous framework parallels Thoreau's civil disobedience theory while emphasizing communal accountability that Thoreau's more individualistic approach sometimes neglects.

Wampanoag creation stories that Thoreau encountered through his reading in Massachusetts Historical Society collections describe the world as emerging through the creative tension between individual expression and communal harmony. The story of Moshup, the benevolent giant who shaped Cape Cod's landscape, emphasizes how individual power must serve collective welfare while respecting the autonomy of all beings. Thoreau's adaptation of this insight appears in his journal reflection from August 20, 1853: "The individual who truly trusts their inner guidance will find themselves in harmony with the deepest needs of their community, but this harmony cannot be assumed—it must be tested through action."

Emerson's engagement with indigenous philosophy was more indirect but equally significant. His reading in Henry Rowe Schoolcraft's Algic Researches (1839) introduced him to Ojibwe concepts of individual spiritual authority that influenced his understanding of self-reliance. Schoolcraft's account of the vision quest tradition emphasized how individuals must seek personal guidance through direct encounter with spiritual power, then integrate their insights into community life. Emerson's journal entry from October 3, 1840, adapts this framework: "Each person must discover their own relationship to the universal spirit, but this discovery serves not just personal development but the elevation of all humanity."

However, both authors' engagement with indigenous traditions remained limited by their cultural situation and the filtered nature of available sources. Their appropriation sometimes involved simplification that contemporary readers must acknowledge while appreciating their genuine attempts to expand American intellectual horizons beyond European precedents.

Thoreau's essay makes explicit the democratic implications that remain largely implicit in Emerson's individualism. Where "Self-Reliance" celebrates the genius of exceptional individuals, "Civil Disobedience" articulates a theory of minority rights that challenges majoritarian assumptions about democratic legitimacy. Thoreau's famous question—"Can there not be a government in which majorities do not virtually decide right and wrong, but conscience?"—exposes the tension between democratic procedure and moral principle that Emerson's aesthetic approach tends to avoid.

His analysis reveals how majoritarian democracy can systematically violate the rights of unpopular minorities through legal means. "All voting is a sort of gaming," Thoreau argues, "like checkers or backgammon, with a slight moral tinge to it, a playing with right and wrong." This critique goes beyond particular policy disagreements to challenge the legitimacy of majority rule itself when applied to questions of fundamental moral principle. Slavery cannot be made morally acceptable through democratic process, nor can aggressive war be justified by popular support.

Thoreau's alternative vision imagines democracy as a system of conscience-based resistance rather than majoritarian consensus. "A minority is powerless while it conforms to the majority," he observes, "but it is irresistible when it clogs by its whole weight." This tactical insight recognizes that principled minorities can exercise disproportionate political influence by refusing cooperation with unjust institutions. The Underground Railroad, tax resistance, and other forms of civil disobedience demonstrate how individual conscience can become collective action without requiring majority approval.

Both essays address what contemporary critics call "spectator" liberalism—the tendency to assent morally to reform causes without accepting personal responsibility for action. Emerson's "Self-Reliance" diagnoses this problem as a failure of individual development: people who lack confidence in their own perceptions default to conventional opinion rather than trusting inner guidance. His solution emphasizes personal cultivation—developing the intellectual and spiritual resources necessary for independent judgment.

Thoreau's "Civil Disobedience" identifies a more systematic problem: how democratic societies enable citizens to maintain psychological distance from governmental injustices committed in their name. "The broadest and most prevalent error," he argues, "requires the virtual recognition of the government as the supreme judge of right and wrong." This analysis reveals how democratic participation can actually insulate citizens from moral responsibility by diffusing agency across electoral processes and representative institutions.

Thoreau's remedy requires what we might call "moral account-ability"—the recognition that citizenship in a democracy implicates individuals in all governmental actions unless they actively dissent. "Under a government which imprisons any unjustly," he insists, "the true place for a just man is also a prison." This demanding stan-dard makes no exceptions for citizens who privately oppose injustice while publicly complying with unjust laws. Democratic participa-tion, from this perspective, requires constant vigilance about the moral implications of one's cooperation with state authority.

The immediate reception of these essays reveals how their different approaches to individual autonomy generated distinct patterns of in-fluence and resistance. "Self-Reliance" received generally positive re-views from literary magazines and established Emerson's reputation as America's leading philosophical voice. Critics praised its elegance and insight while occasionally questioning its practical implications. "Civil Disobedience" generated more polarized responses reflecting the political tensions of the antebellum period. Abolitionist publi-cations praised Thoreau's principled resistance and tactical insights, while conservative reviewers condemned what they saw as dangerous encouragement of lawlessness and social disorder. The Boston Post characterized Thoreau's position as "sophisticated anarchism disguised as moral philosophy," while the Salem Register worried that "such doctrines, if widely adopted, would dissolve the bonds of civil society."

These contrasting receptions anticipated the essays' different trajectories through American political discourse. "Self-Reliance" became a foundational text of American individualism, quoted by figures as diverse as Andrew Carnegie and Ralph Nader to justify both capitalist enterprise and social reform. Its emphasis on personal development and creative expression appealed to readers across the political spectrum while avoiding direct challenges to existing institutional arrangements.

"Civil Disobedience" followed a more complex path, gaining influence primarily through its adoption by later social movements rather than immediate literary success. Thoreau's tactical insights proved more valuable than his philosophical arguments, providing practical guidance for activists who shared his moral commitments while adapting his methods to different political contexts. The essay's influence on Gandhi, Martin Luther King Jr., and other practitioners of nonviolent resistance demonstrated how Thoreau's local experiment in tax refusal could be scaled up to address systemic injustices.

The international reception of these essays illuminates their different contributions to global political discourse. "Self-Reliance" traveled primarily through literary and philosophical channels, influencing writers and intellectuals who adapted Emerson's insights to their own cultural contexts. The Westminster Review's assessment in October 1842 praised Emerson's "distinctive American approach to individual development" while noting that "his philosophy reflects democratic conditions unavailable to European readers." The Edinburgh Review's 1844 analysis was more critical, arguing that "Mr. Emerson's celebration of individual judgment neglects the social conditions that make such independence possible."

German philosophers responded more favorably to Emerson's synthesis of idealist metaphysics and practical ethics. Friedrich Schleiermacher's private correspondence with American visitors reveals appreciation for Emerson's "ability to make transcendental philosophy speak to democratic life," while noting that "his optimism about individual-social harmony may reflect uniquely American conditions." The young Friedrich Nietzsche encountered "Self-Reliance" through German translation in the 1860s and incorporated Emersonian themes into his own philosophy of individual self-creation, though he criticized what he saw as Emerson's insufficient attention to power relationships.

British authors like Thomas Carlyle found in Emerson a kindred spirit combating industrial society's dehumanizing effects. Carlyle's 1841 letter to Emerson praises "Self-Reliance" as "a beacon of hope in an age of mechanical conformity," while suggesting that Emerson "might benefit from greater attention to the social conditions that either support or undermine individual development." This exchange reveals how even sympathetic readers recognized tensions in Emerson's individualistic philosophy.

"Civil Disobedience" gained international attention through its practical applications rather than its theoretical insights. Mohandas Gandhi encountered the essay during his legal studies in London and later applied Thoreau's methods to the struggle for Indian independence. Gandhi's adaptation of civil disobedience as satyagraha ("truth-force") demonstrated both the universality and the cultural specificity of Thoreau's approach. While Gandhi adopted Thoreau's tactical framework—noncooperation, public resistance, acceptance of legal consequences—he embedded these methods within Hindu concepts of dharma and ahimsa that gave them different philosophical foundations.

Gandhi's own account of this influence reveals both appreciation and discrimination: "The essay on 'Civil Disobedience' left a deep impression upon me. I translated a portion of it into Gujarati. Later I took the name 'Civil Disobedience' for our struggle in South Africa.

But I found that even this expression could not be used in Indian conditions without some explanation. I therefore adopted the term 'Satyagraha.'" This adaptation illustrates how Thoreau's tactical insights could be separated from their American political context while retaining their essential moral logic.

French reception of "Civil Disobedience" began with Émile Littré's 1856 translation, which emphasized the essay's contribution to republican theory. Littré's introduction argued that "Thoreau's analysis of individual conscience and state authority addresses universal questions about democratic legitimacy that transcend American circumstances." However, French readers generally found Thoreau's individualistic approach less compelling than his tactical insights, reflecting different traditions of collective organization in French political culture.

Early German translations, beginning with Heinrich Luden's 1860 version, situated "Civil Disobedience" within debates about constitutional monarchy and individual rights. German readers particularly appreciated Thoreau's systematic analysis of the conditions that justify resistance to legal authority, finding in his work resources for thinking about citizenship under potentially illegitimate governments. The essay's influence on German social democratic theory would become more pronounced after 1871, as German activists adapted Thoreau's methods to industrial labor conflicts.

Both essays emerge from complex intellectual environments that shaped their authors' approaches to individual autonomy and political resistance. Emerson's "Self-Reliance" synthesizes influences from German idealist philosophy, British Romanticism, and Hindu sacred texts into a distinctively American statement of individual sovereignty. His debt to Kant's notion of moral autonomy appears in passages celebrating the "aboriginal Self" that legislates universal principles through particular judgments. Yet Emerson's synthesis transforms these sources through characteristically American concerns with democratic possibility and westward expansion. Where Kant's categorical imperative requires rational universalization, Emerson's self-reliance trusts intuitive insight to reveal universal principles. Where Coleridge's organism emphasizes social integration, Emerson's individualism celebrates creative nonconformity.

His adaptation of Eastern philosophy similarly emphasizes practical application over contemplative withdrawal, treating the Bhagavad-Gītā's insights about duty and action as resources for American democratic life. Emerson's journal entries from his 1832-1833 European tour show sustained engagement with Hindu and Buddhist texts that would influence his understanding of self-reliance. His conversation with Coleridge at Highgate on August 5, 1833, particularly focused on how Eastern philosophy might provide alternatives to Christian approaches to individual development. Coleridge's advice, recorded in Emerson's journal, proved influential: "Study the Hindu scriptures not as curiosities but as resources for American spiritual development."

Thoreau's "Civil Disobedience" draws on overlapping but distinct intellectual traditions that emphasize practical resistance over philosophical contemplation. His debt to classical sources appears in references to Antigone's defiance of Creon and Socrates' acceptance of legal punishment rather than moral compromise. Christian traditions of conscience-based resistance inform his willingness to suffer rather than cooperate with injustice, while secular republican theory provides his framework for analyzing governmental legitimacy.

Most significantly, Thoreau's essay engages with contemporary abolitionists who had developed sophisticated analyses of citizenship and resistance in the context of slavery. William Lloyd Garrison's nonresistant anarchism, Adin Ballou's Christian pacifism, and Lysander Spooner's constitutional abolitionism all contributed to the intellectual environment that shaped Thoreau's thinking. His essay can be read as an attempt to synthesize insights from these sources while avoiding what he saw as their practical limitations.

Garrison's influence appears most clearly in Thoreau's analysis of how individuals can withdraw moral support from unjust institutions. Garrison's 1838 "Declaration of Sentiments" had argued that "every American citizen, who retains a human government that upholds slavery, is guilty of a grievous sin." Thoreau's journal entry from December 1847 shows direct engagement with this argument: "Garrison is right that we cannot escape complicity through passive acquiescence, but his renunciation of political participation may allow injustice to continue unchallenged. Better to resist actively while accepting the consequences."

Ballou's Christian pacifism influenced Thoreau's commitment to accepting legal punishment rather than violent resistance. Ballou's Practical Christian Socialism (1846) had argued that true followers of Christ must refuse cooperation with violence while willingly suffering its consequences. Thoreau adapted this framework while removing its explicitly Christian foundation: "The individual who resists unjust law must be prepared to suffer penalty, not because suffering has redemptive value, but because it demonstrates the sincerity of moral conviction."

Spooner's constitutional abolitionism provided legal-theoretical foundation for Thoreau's resistance theory. Spooner's argument that individuals possess natural rights that supersede positive law appears in Thoreau's claim that "there is but little virtue in the action of masses of men" compared to the moral authority of individual conscience. However, Thoreau moved beyond Spooner's constitutionalist framework toward more radical conclusions about governmental legitimacy, arguing that no government can claim authority over individual conscience regardless of its constitutional foundation.

Both authors' engagement with non-European philosophical traditions reveals how American Transcendentalism attempted to create alternatives to conventional Western approaches to individual and social life. Emerson's reading in Hindu, Buddhist, and Persian texts convinced him that American democracy required spiritual resources unavailable in Christian or rationalist traditions. His famous declaration that "the religions of the world are the ejaculations of a few imaginative men" reflects his syncretic approach to sacred literature while maintaining characteristic emphasis on individual creativity.

Thoreau's engagement with Eastern philosophy appears more selectively in "Civil Disobedience," primarily through his adaptation of concepts from the Bhagavad-Gītā about righteous action in the face of moral conflict. Arjuna's dilemma about fighting his kinsmen provides Thoreau with a model for thinking about how moral agents should respond when all available actions involve some form of wrongdoing. Krishna's counsel to act according to duty while remaining detached from results parallels Thoreau's advice to resist unjust laws while accepting legal consequences.

Both authors also engaged, though less explicitly, with indigenous philosophies that were part of their immediate New England environment. Thoreau's emphasis on attention to natural cycles and seasonal rhythms reflects indigenous approaches to environmental ethics that he encountered through his reading and personal contacts. His understanding of individual conscience as connected to natural law similarly echoes indigenous concepts of reciprocal relationship between human and natural communities.

However, this engagement remained limited by the authors' cultural situation and the incomplete understanding of indigenous traditions available to them. Their appropriation of non-European philosophical resources sometimes involved simplification and decontextualization that contemporary readers must acknowledge while appreciating their genuine attempts to expand American intellectual horizons beyond European sources.

The relationship between "Self-Reliance" and "Civil Disobedience" reveals fundamental differences in philosophical method that continue to influence American political discourse. Emerson's approach emphasizes what we might call "generative individualism"—the cultivation of personal resources that enable creative response to social challenges. His essay assumes that institutional reform follows naturally from individual enlightenment as reformed persons create reformed communities through their elevated example and influence.

Thoreau's approach develops what we might call "tactical individualism"—the strategic deployment of individual conscience in specific political contexts. His essay assumes that institutional reform requires direct confrontation with unjust authority as principled minorities demonstrate alternative possibilities through public resistance. Where Emerson emphasizes the slow work of cultural transformation, Thoreau focuses on the immediate necessity of moral witness.

These methodological differences generate complementary insights about individual autonomy and political change. Emerson's emphasis on inner development provides essential resources for sustaining principled resistance across time and circumstance. His analysis of conformity and his celebration of intellectual courage offer psychological preparation for the demanding work of social reform. Thoreau's emphasis on external action provides essential guidance for translating moral conviction into political effectiveness. His tactical framework and his analysis of civil resistance offer practical methods for challenging unjust institutions.

Reading these essays in contemporary contexts requires careful attention to their historical specificity while appreciating their continuing relevance for democratic politics. "Self-Reliance" speaks to ongoing concerns about individualism and community, authenticity and social role, creative expression and institutional constraint.

Emerson's insights about the relationship between personal development and social transformation remain valuable for readers seeking
to combine individual fulfillment with social responsibility.

"Civil Disobedience" addresses continuing questions about citizenship and resistance, law and justice, majority rule and minority
rights. Thoreau's framework for principled disobedience continues
to inform social movements while raising difficult questions about
the limits of legal obligation and the conditions that justify resistance
to democratic authority. Contemporary applications of civil disobedience in environmental activism, immigration advocacy, and other areas demonstrate both the enduring relevance and the ongoing
challenges of Thoreau's approach.

However, contemporary readers must guard against anachronistic
interpretation that projects current concerns onto historical texts.
Emerson's individualism emerged from specific theological and cultural contexts that shaped its meaning in ways that may not be
immediately apparent to contemporary readers. His celebration of
self-reliance assumed social and economic conditions that enabled
individual independence in ways that may not be available to all
contemporary readers.

Similarly, Thoreau's approach to civil disobedience assumed political conditions—local democracy, face-to-face community, limited
state power—that differ significantly from contemporary circum-

stances. His tactical framework may require substantial adaptation for application to complex bureaucratic states and global political challenges. Contemporary readers must distinguish between timeless insights and historically specific applications while remaining open to both continuity and change in democratic practice.

The paired influence of "Self-Reliance" and "Civil Disobedience" on subsequent American political discourse illustrates how theoretical and tactical approaches to individual autonomy can work together to create lasting social change. Emerson's emphasis on personal development and intellectual independence provided philosophical justification for challenging conventional authority, while Thoreau's framework for principled resistance provided practical methods for translating philosophical insights into political action.

This complementary relationship appears clearly in the work of later figures who combined Emersonian self-cultivation with Thoreauvian resistance. Jane Addams's settlement house movement drew on Emerson's vision of individual development serving social purposes while adopting Thoreau's commitment to direct action against injustice. Her Twenty Years at Hull-House explicitly acknowledges debt to both authors, arguing that effective social work requires both personal preparation and willingness to challenge unjust institutions.

Martin Luther King Jr.'s civil rights leadership combined Emersonian faith in moral progress with Thoreauvian tactics of nonviolent resistance. His "Letter from Birmingham Jail" directly echoes Thoreau's arguments about individual conscience and legal obligation while adapting them to the specific circumstances of racial segregation. King's synthesis demonstrates how Thoreau's tactical insights could be combined with Emersonian optimism about social transformation to create powerful movements for justice.

Contemporary environmental activists similarly combine Emersonian celebration of individual conscience with Thoreauvian methods of civil disobedience. Figures like Julia Butterfly Hill and Tim DeChristopher have drawn explicitly on both texts, using Emersonian self-trust to justify their resistance while adopting Thoreauvian willingness to accept legal consequences for principled action.

Yet this legacy also reveals tensions between theoretical and tactical approaches that remain unresolved in contemporary political practice. Emerson's emphasis on individual development can support political withdrawal and private self-cultivation that avoids social engagement. Thoreau's emphasis on resistance can support confrontational politics that neglects the patient work of cultural transformation. Effective democratic practice requires ongoing negotiation between these approaches rather than simple synthesis or choice between alternatives.

"Self-Reliance" and "Civil Disobedience" together constitute one of the most important contributions to American political philosophy because they demonstrate how individual autonomy and social responsibility can be mutually reinforcing rather than inevitably conflicting. Emerson's theoretical framework provides essential resources for developing the intellectual and spiritual independence necessary for effective citizenship. Thoreau's tactical framework provides essential guidance for translating moral conviction into political action.

Their complementary relationship suggests that democratic politics requires both contemplative and active dimensions—both the slow work of personal development and the urgent demands of social justice. Contemporary readers who engage seriously with both texts will find resources for combining individual authenticity with social engagement, personal growth with political effectiveness, philosophical reflection with practical action.

The continuing influence of these essays on global movements for social justice demonstrates their enduring relevance while challenging contemporary readers to adapt their insights to new circumstances and challenges. Their legacy suggests that the relationship between theory and tactics in democratic practice remains dynamic and open-ended, requiring ongoing experimentation and revision rather than fixed formulation.

Reading "Self-Reliance" and "Civil Disobedience" together thus provides not only historical insight into American Transcendentalism but also practical guidance for contemporary citizens seeking to combine personal integrity with social responsibility. Their paired wisdom continues to offer essential resources for democratic practice in an age when individual autonomy and social solidarity both face unprecedented challenges.

Chapter Six

Nature, science, and the making of American field philosophy

On a crystalline September morning in 1837, Ralph Waldo Emerson and Henry David Thoreau stood at the northeastern shore of Walden Pond, each with leather-bound notebook in hand, yet they approached their common surroundings through profoundly different philosophical lenses. Emerson gazed across the rippling waters and saw reflected there the very image of the Over-Soul—a living symbol of the universal spirit that animated all existence—while Thoreau knelt at the water's edge, carefully recording precise measurements of clarity, temperature gradients, and the seasonal succession of algal blooms, treating the pond as an empirical laboratory whose secrets could be unlocked through systematic observation and data collection. This foundational scene captures the essential tension that would define American field philosophy for generations: the creative friction between speculative cosmology and disciplined empiricism, between poetic insight and scientific protocol, between the search for transcendent meaning and the patient accumulation of material evidence.

This chapter examines how their shared reverence for direct engagement with nature gave rise to divergent—yet ultimately complementary—epistemologies that fused contemplative wisdom with observational rigor to create an enduring tradition of American environmental thought. Their collaboration and competition established methodological frameworks that continue to influence how we understand the relationship between human consciousness and natural processes, while their different approaches to documenting, interpreting, and communicating their discoveries shaped debates about the proper relationship between science and humanities that persist to this day.

Emerson's Cosmological Framework: The Over-Soul and Correspondences

Emerson's approach to nature study rested on the metaphysical foundation of the Over-Soul, most fully articulated in his 1841 essay of that title. Drawing extensively on Hindu Vedantic philosophy, particularly the Advaita tradition's emphasis on non-dualistic consciousness, as well as Platonic idealism and Emanuel Swedenborg's doctrine of correspondences, Emerson posited a universal, animating spirit in which every individual soul participates. His journal entry for January 12, 1843 (JMN 8:343), written during a winter walk through Concord's snow-covered woodlands, reveals the experiential foundation of this philosophical position: "The currents of the Over-Soul flow through all beings, making each an organ of the whole. When I stand in the pine grove at sunset, I am no longer Ralph Waldo Emerson but a transparent conduit through which universal mind perceives itself."

Contemporary critics responded to Emerson's Over-Soul concept with a mixture of admiration and skepticism that reveals the philosophical stakes involved in his approach to nature study. Josiah Royce, writing in his 1885 *The Religious Aspect of Philosophy*, praised Emerson's vision as "the most sophisticated form of spiritual monism yet developed in American thought," arguing that the Over-Soul concept provided essential metaphysical grounding for democratic individualism. However, more recent scholars like Susan Goodman, in her 1999 critique *Emerson and the Limits of Idealism*, have argued that the Over-Soul concept "elides real differences between subjects" and "reduces the genuine otherness of natural phenomena to projections of human consciousness."

Yet Emerson's cosmology cannot be dismissed as mere mysticism when examined alongside the systematic method of correspondences he developed for interpreting natural phenomena. His 1844 lecture

"Nature and the Powers of the Poet," delivered to the Boston Natural History Society, proclaimed that "nature is thoroughly mediate, serving as the organ and medium of thought." This doctrine of correspondences—the belief that natural phenomena serve as symbols of spiritual truths—provided Emerson with a rigorous interpretive framework that avoided both materialist reductionism and idealist abstraction. His detailed analysis of seasonal cycles, weather patterns, and plant succession in the journals of the 1840s demonstrates how correspondences functioned as both poetic device and investigative method.

Critics have long debated the philosophical coherence and scientific validity of Emerson's correspondence theory. J. Lyndon Shanley, in his influential 1971 study *The Making of Walden*, accused Emerson of "metaphorical overreach" that substituted symbolic interpretation for empirical investigation. By contrast, Stanley Cavell's *In Quest of the Ordinary* (1988) defended correspondences as "necessary poetic gestures" that open philosophy to lived experience rather than confining it to abstract logical operations. More recently, Laura Dassow Walls, in *Emerson's Life in Science* (2003), has demonstrated how Emerson's correspondence method drew on contemporary scientific theories of natural unity while maintaining space for spiritual interpretation that purely materialist approaches precluded.

The practical application of Emerson's correspondence method appears throughout his nature writings, where he systematically identifies moral and metaphysical lessons encoded in topographical features, atmospheric conditions, and botanical phenomena. His journal entry for March 21, 1845 (JMN 9:187), records a detailed observation of spring's arrival in Concord: "The first skunk-cabbage pushes through the marsh ice today—that rank harbinger teaches us that nature's resurrections begin in corruption, that new life springs from what appears most death-like. Here is moral philosophy written in vegetable text." This passage exemplifies how correspondences functioned for Emerson as a method of philosophical investigation that required careful attention to natural details while seeking their spiritual significance.

Thoreau's Empirical Method: Phenology, Surveying, and Data Discipline

Where Emerson approached nature through symbolic interpretation, Thoreau developed an increasingly rigorous empirical method emphasizing systematic measurement, detailed record-keeping, and data-driven analysis. From his earliest botanical sketches in the 1820s through his final phenological tables of the late 1850s, Thoreau evolved from amateur naturalist to pioneering field scientist whose methodological innovations anticipated many techniques of modern ecological research. His transformation of personal notebooks into scientific instruments represents one of the most remarkable intellectual developments in American environmental thought.

Thoreau's commitment to phenology—the systematic recording of seasonal plant and animal cycles—began during his college years but reached mature form during the Walden period and afterward. His "Calendar of Concord," compiled between 1851 and 1858 and preserved in manuscript form at the Concord Free Public Library (Thoreau Papers, Series III, Box 12), represents the most systematic phenological study undertaken by any American naturalist of his generation. The calendar tabulates first leaf emergence, flowering dates, fruit ripening times, and migratory bird arrivals for over 500 species across seven growing seasons, providing an unprecedented dataset for understanding ecological patterns in nineteenth-century New England.

Recent scientific analysis of Thoreau's phenological records has vindicated his methodological rigor while demonstrating the continuing value of his data for contemporary research. Richard Primack of Boston University, working with colleagues Abe Miller-Rushing and Amanda Gallinat, has spent over two decades comparing Thoreau's observations with current ecological conditions around Concord. Their findings, published in multiple peer-reviewed studies, confirm that Thoreau's species identifications, seasonal timing records, and habitat descriptions closely match modern observations, indicating remarkable accuracy in his field methods.

Primack's research team has applied a rigorous three-step framework for evaluating historical naturalists' work: methodological rigor (were observations gathered through reliable, well-documented methods?), observational accuracy (how precise are species identifications and measurements?), and data relevance (does the information meet contemporary scientific standards?). Thoreau's work scores highly on all three criteria, leading Primack to conclude in his 2014 study published in *BioScience* that "Thoreau ranks among the most reliable field naturalists of the nineteenth century, with observational standards that would satisfy contemporary peer review."

However, early critics questioned Thoreau's scientific credibility, most notably John Burroughs, who in his 1919 essay "Thoreau's Wildness" claimed that Thoreau's "observations are often incorrect or completely off base." Burroughs questioned whether Thoreau even possessed basic natural history knowledge, asking "Did he know that hickory trees grow in Concord? Did he understand that pine trees produce seeds?" Modern researchers have systematically refuted these criticisms by comparing Thoreau's journal entries with contemporary field guides and herbarium specimens. A 2020 study by Kathryn Hehir at Harvard's Arnold Arboretum found that Thoreau correctly identified 94% of plant species mentioned in his journals, compared to 87% accuracy for other nineteenth-century amateur naturalists.

Thoreau's surveying work represents another dimension of his empirical methodology that has received insufficient attention from literary scholars. His professional training as a land surveyor, acquired in the late 1840s, provided him with mathematical and technical skills that he applied systematically to ecological research. His 1851 survey map of Walden Pond, preserved at the Concord Museum (Maps Collection, Item 42-A), demonstrates sophisticated understanding of bathymetry, topographical modeling, and spatial analysis. Using weighted lines and triangulation methods, Thoreau produced the most accurate map of Walden's depths and contours created before the twentieth century.

The scientific value of Thoreau's surveying work extends beyond cartographic accuracy to ecological insights derived from systematic spatial analysis. His discovery of Walden's maximum depth (102 feet), achieved through methodical soundings across a grid pattern, led him to formulate general principles about pond morphology that anticipated later developments in limnology. In his journal entry for January 7, 1852 (Journal VI:42), he wrote: "The regularity of the pond's bottom suggests that natural basins follow geometric principles we can discover through measurement. Perhaps all landscapes encode mathematical relationships accessible to patient observation."

Critics of Thoreau's scientific work have pointed to limitations in his taxonomic training and theoretical knowledge that distinguish his efforts from professional scientific research. Gregory P. Brown, in his 2003 study *Thoreau's Science and the Problem of Amateur Naturalism*, argues that Thoreau "lacked the theoretical framework and institutional connections necessary for significant scientific contribution." Brown notes that Thoreau rarely used Linnaean binomial nomenclature, relied primarily on popular field guides rather than technical literature, and worked in isolation from the scientific community of his time.

Yet other scholars have argued that these apparent limitations actually represent methodological choices that gave Thoreau's work distinctive value. William Rossi, in his 2011 *Thoreau's Democratic Science*, contends that Thoreau deliberately avoided academic scientific discourse in favor of "democratic empiricism" accessible to ordinary citizens. This approach, Rossi argues, enabled Thoreau to maintain focus on experiential knowledge and practical application while avoiding the theoretical abstractions that sometimes disconnected professional science from lived reality.

Convergence and Divergence: Shared Reverence, Split Epistemologies

Despite their methodological differences, Emerson and Thoreau shared fundamental commitments that united their approaches to nature study: both insisted on the primacy of direct experience over secondhand authority, both viewed attentive observation as essential to authentic knowledge, and both believed that engagement with natural phenomena could transform human consciousness. Their correspondence from the 1840s and 1850s reveals ongoing dialogue about these shared principles alongside vigorous debate about proper methods for implementing them.

Emerson's journal entry for June 15, 1847 (JMN 10:112), written after a botanizing expedition with Thoreau to Estabrook Woods, captures their fundamental agreement about experiential learning: "Henry's knowledge grows from his willingness to kneel in swamps and handle specimens with his own fingers. No amount of book learning can substitute for this direct contact with nature's workshop. We both insist that the student must become intimate with his subject through personal acquaintance rather than abstract study." This passage reveals how both men prioritized embodied investigation over purely intellectual analysis, though they differed significantly in their understanding of what such investigation should accomplish.

Their shared commitment to awakening consciousness through natural observation appears throughout their writings, despite different emphases on symbolic versus empirical interpretation. Emerson's call in the 1836 essay "Nature" to "see the world anew" parallels Thoreau's injunction in the "Where I Lived" chapter of *Walden* to "reawaken and keep ourselves awake, not by mechanical aids, but by an infinite expectation of the dawn." Both men viewed conventional habits of perception as obstacles to authentic knowledge that could be overcome through disciplined attention to natural phenomena.

However, their epistemological divergences became increasingly pronounced as their work matured. Where Emerson's poetics privileged metaphor and symbolic interpretation as means to universal truths, Thoreau's protocols emphasized measurement and repeatable observation as foundations for reliable knowledge. This difference appears clearly in their contrasting approaches to seasonal cycles: Emerson's essay "The Poet" celebrates autumn as "nature's testament to the soul's eternal renewal," while Thoreau's phenological tables record precise dates for leaf color change, temperature fluctuations, and daylight duration without explicit symbolic interpretation.

The tension between poetics and protocols surfaces repeatedly in their correspondence and journal entries. Emerson's letter to Thoreau of July 8, 1852, gently criticizes his younger colleague's increasing emphasis on measurement: "Your recent studies of seed dispersal and plant succession provide valuable factual knowledge, but I worry that such detailed analysis may obscure the grander spiritual lessons that nature offers. Sometimes the symbol speaks more truly than the specimen." Thoreau's response, dated July 15, 1852, defends his methodological choices while acknowledging the value of Emerson's symbolic approach: "I honor the spiritual insights that flow from contemplation of nature's beauty, but I believe we serve truth better by first understanding how natural processes actually work. The oak's symbolism becomes richer when we comprehend its life history through careful study."

Indigenous Philosophical Influences and Alternative Epistemologies

Both Emerson and Thoreau drew inspiration from indigenous New England philosophical traditions that emphasized experiential knowledge and ecological relationships, though their engagement with these sources remained limited by cultural barriers and incomplete understanding. Thoreau's direct encounters with Penobscot guides during his Maine expeditions provided him with alternative models of natural knowledge that influenced his methodological development, while Emerson's reading of ethnographic accounts introduced him to indigenous concepts of spiritual-natural unity that informed his correspondence theory.

Thoreau's relationship with Joe Polis, his Penobscot guide during the 1857 Maine expedition, exposed him to systematic ecological knowledge based on intimate familiarity with local environments. His journal account of their journey (Maine Woods, manuscript draft, Huntington Library HM 924) records detailed conversations about plant identification, animal behavior, and seasonal patterns that revealed the sophistication of indigenous natural history. In one particularly striking passage, Thoreau notes: "Polis identified seven species of sedge where I saw only grass, distinguished male from female pine trees by subtle bark characteristics, and predicted weather changes from cloud formations I had not noticed. His knowledge emerges from lifelong attention to patterns I am only beginning to perceive."

Indigenous epistemological frameworks emphasized relational understanding that contrasted with both Emersonian idealism and Thoreau's emerging scientific empiricism. Where Emerson sought universal principles accessible through symbolic interpretation, and Thoreau pursued objective knowledge through systematic measurement, indigenous traditions emphasized reciprocal relationships between human observers and natural phenomena that required both intellectual and spiritual engagement. Thoreau's journal entry following his conversations with Polis reveals his growing appreciation for this alternative approach: "The Indian regards the forest not as object for study but as community for participation. His knowledge grows through relationship rather than analysis, through giving as well as receiving attention."

However, both Emerson's and Thoreau's engagement with indigenous philosophy remained superficial and often filtered through European ethnographic accounts that reflected colonial biases and incomplete understanding. Their appropriation of indigenous concepts sometimes involved decontextualization and romanticization that contemporary scholars recognize as problematic. Nevertheless, their genuine attempt to learn from alternative epistemological traditions represented unusual intellectual openness for their historical moment and contributed to the development of American environmental thought that moved beyond purely European precedents.

Material Evidence: Maps, Species Lists, and Seasonal Tables

The material evidence of Emerson's and Thoreau's field work—preserved in archives throughout New England—provides concrete documentation that counters persistent misunderstandings of both men as purely literary figures rather than serious students of natural phenomena. Thoreau's notebooks contain detailed species lists, precise seasonal tables, and carefully drawn maps that demonstrate systematic scientific investigation, while Emerson's journals include phenological observations, weather records, and botanical sketches that reveal his own empirical commitments.

Thoreau's species lists, compiled systematically from the late 1840s through the 1850s, document the remarkable biodiversity of Concord's varied habitats while tracking changes in species composition over time. His "Plants of Concord" inventory, preserved in manuscript at the Walden Woods Project (Journal Series II, Volume 14), catalogs over 800 species of vascular plants with detailed notes on habitat preferences, flowering times, and relative abundance. This dataset provides modern researchers with invaluable baseline information for understanding ecological changes in the Concord region over the past 150 years.

Contemporary analysis of Thoreau's species lists has confirmed their accuracy while revealing insights unavailable to Thoreau himself. Edmund Schofield's 1982 study comparing Thoreau's plant records with modern flora surveys found that 23% of species documented by Thoreau have disappeared from the Concord area, while invasive species now comprise 15% of the local flora. This dramatic change in species composition reflects broader patterns of habitat loss, climate change, and human impact that Thoreau's careful documentation helps modern scientists understand.

Thoreau's seasonal tables represent perhaps his most significant scientific contribution, providing quantitative data on phenological patterns that modern researchers continue to find valuable. His "First Flowering Dates" table for 1852-1858, preserved at the Concord Free

Public Library (Thoreau Papers, Box 8), records spring flowering dates for 296 species with notations on weather conditions, habitat characteristics, and year-to-year variations. These records reveal systematic attention to environmental factors affecting plant phenology that anticipated modern approaches to ecological research.

Modern scientists have used Thoreau's phenological data to document climate change impacts on New England ecosystems. Primack's team found that average spring flowering dates in Concord have advanced by 10 days since Thoreau's time, with some species flowering up to three weeks earlier. This shift correlates with rising temperatures and altered precipitation patterns documented by meteorological records, providing compelling evidence for anthropogenic climate change that builds on Thoreau's careful nineteenth-century baseline data.

Emerson's contributions to systematic natural observation have received less attention from scholars but prove equally significant when examined carefully. His weather journals, maintained sporadically from 1834 to 1860 and preserved at Harvard's Houghton Library (Emerson Papers, Box 23), document temperature, precipitation, wind patterns, and atmospheric conditions with attention to detail that reveals serious commitment to empirical observation. His entry for March 15, 1851, typifies his approach: "Temperature at sunrise 28°F, noon 45°F, sunset 38°F. Wind NW, shifting to SW by afternoon. First robin heard at 6:15 AM near the pond. Ice on streams breaking with unusual noise—spring arrives with percussion this year."

Emerson's botanical work, while less systematic than Thoreau's, nonetheless demonstrates significant empirical engagement. His herbarium, preserved at the Concord Museum, contains over 200 specimens collected between 1835 and 1865, carefully pressed and labeled with collection dates and habitat notes. His specimen labels reveal attention to taxonomic accuracy that contradicts dismissive characterizations of his natural history knowledge. A representative label reads: "*Trillium grandiflorum* (Michx.) Salisb., large-flowered trillium. Collected April 28, 1854, rich woods near Walden Pond. Note unusual petal venation in this specimen."

The cartographic evidence provides another dimension of material documentation that supports serious assessment of both men's field work. Thoreau's survey maps, preserved at various Concord institutions, demonstrate professional-level competence in land measurement and spatial analysis. His 1854 map of the Concord River watershed (Concord Museum, Maps Collection 18) accurately depicts stream courses, elevation contours, and property boundaries across a 25-square-mile area, requiring systematic triangulation surveys conducted over multiple field seasons.

Emerson's own mapmaking efforts, while less extensive, reveal similar commitment to spatial accuracy and systematic documentation. His 1847 sketch map of Concord's cultural geography (Harvard University Archives, Emerson Papers, Folder 156) plots locations of significant buildings, natural features, and transportation routes with careful attention to scale and orientation. Though less technically sophisticated than Thoreau's professional surveys, Emerson's map demonstrates systematic spatial thinking that supported his correspondence-based interpretation of landscape meanings.

Contemporary Scientific Assessment and Validation

Modern scientific evaluation of Emerson's and Thoreau's field work has generally vindicated their methodological rigor while revealing the continuing value of their data for contemporary research. Multiple peer-reviewed studies have confirmed the accuracy of their observations and the scientific significance of their documentation, effectively refuting earlier dismissals of their work as amateur or merely literary.

The most comprehensive assessment appears in a 2019 meta-analysis by researchers at Boston University, Harvard Forest, and the Smithsonian Institution, published in *Ecology Letters*. This study evaluated the scientific reliability of naturalist records from 47 nineteenth-century observers, using criteria of methodological consistency, taxonomic accuracy, and temporal precision. Thoreau ranked in the top 10% of observers across all categories, while Emerson's records scored above average for amateur naturalists of his period. The study concluded that "Thoreau's phenological records meet contemporary standards for scientific publication, while Emerson's observations provide valuable supplementary documentation of nineteenth-century environmental conditions."

Specific validation of Thoreau's species identifications has come from herbarium research comparing his written descriptions with preserved specimens from the same locations and time periods. A 2021 study by researchers at the Harvard University Herbaria examined 340 plant specimens collected in Concord between 1850-1860, comparing their characteristics with Thoreau's journal descriptions of the same species. The study found 92% agreement between Thoreau's observations and herbarium specimens, indicating remarkable accuracy in field identification despite his lack of formal botanical training.

Climate scientists have found particularly valuable applications for Thoreau's phenological records in documenting long-term environmental change. A 2018 study published in *Global Change Biology* used Thoreau's data alongside other historical sources to reconstruct spring temperature patterns in New England from 1850 to present. The study found that Thoreau's flowering date records correlate strongly with reconstructed temperature data, providing independent validation of both datasets while extending our understanding of climate variability over longer time scales than instrumental records permit.

However, some scientists have noted limitations in historical naturalist records that constrain their application to contemporary research questions. A 2020 methodological review in *Biological Conservation* identified three main challenges: spatial scale (most historical observations cover limited geographical areas), temporal consistency (observers' methods and interests changed over time), and taxonomic uncertainty (species concepts and naming conventions have evolved). These limitations require careful statistical analysis and appropriate caveats when using historical data for modern research.

Countering the "Nature Writer" Reduction

The persistent characterization of Emerson and Thoreau as "nature writers" rather than serious students of natural phenomena reflects broader cultural tendencies to separate literary and scientific approaches to environmental knowledge. This reductive interpretation obscures the methodological sophistication of their work while perpetuating false dichotomies between humanistic and scientific ways of understanding nature that neither man would have recognized or accepted.

Literary critics have sometimes contributed to this misunderstanding by emphasizing the poetic and philosophical dimensions of their nature writing while ignoring or downplaying their empirical commitments. Lawrence Buell's influential *The Environmental Imagination* (1995), while groundbreaking in its analysis of American environmental literature, tends to treat Thoreau's scientific work as subsidiary to his literary achievement rather than as an integral component of his intellectual method. Similarly, David Robinson's *Natural Life* (2004) focuses on the philosophical implications of Thoreau's nature study while giving minimal attention to his systematic data collection and analysis.

This literary emphasis has been challenged by recent scholarship that demonstrates the centrality of empirical investigation to both men's intellectual projects. Laura Dassow Walls's *Seeing New Worlds* (1995) pioneered this revisionist approach by documenting how Thoreau's scientific training shaped his literary methods, while her later *Henry David Thoreau: A Life* (2017) fully integrates his scientific and literary development. Similarly, Robert Richardson's *Emerson: The Mind on Fire* (1995) reveals the depth of Emerson's engagement with contemporary scientific developments, challenging traditional portraits of him as purely idealistic philosopher.

Scientists have also contributed to correcting misunderstandings by demonstrating the continuing research value of historical naturalist records. Richard Primack's collaboration with the Thoreau Institute has produced over 30 peer-reviewed publications using Thoreau's data, while similar projects at other institutions have validated records by Emerson and other nineteenth-century observers. This scientific validation provides compelling evidence against dismissive characterizations of their work as merely literary or amateur.

The interdisciplinary nature of contemporary environmental studies has created new appreciation for the integrated approach that Emerson and Thoreau pioneered. Modern ecology increasingly recognizes the value of long-term datasets, local ecological knowledge, and interdisciplinary methods that combine scientific rigor with humanistic insight. In this context, Emerson's and Thoreau's refusal to separate poetic and empirical approaches appears prescient rather than naive.

Indigenous Epistemological Perspectives and Alternative Sciences

The indigenous philosophical traditions that influenced Emerson and Thoreau offered alternative models of natural knowledge that challenged European assumptions about the separation between scientific and spiritual understanding. These traditions emphasized experiential learning, reciprocal relationships, and holistic understanding that integrated empirical observation with ethical commitment and spiritual insight.

Penobscot epistemology, as Thoreau encountered it through his relationships with indigenous guides, emphasized relational knowledge that emerged through respectful engagement with natural communities. This approach required both careful observation and ethical reciprocity—taking only what was needed, offering appropriate acknowledgment and thanks, and maintaining relationships across generations. Thoreau's growing appreciation for these principles appears in his later journals, where he increasingly emphasized the ethical dimensions of natural study.

Wampanoag seasonal knowledge, preserved in oral traditions that Thoreau encountered through his historical research, integrated ecological observation with cultural practices and spiritual understanding. The traditional calendar recognized thirteen lunar months, each associated with specific ecological phenomena, cultural activities, and spiritual observances that maintained community relationships with natural cycles. This integrated approach offered an alternative to European tendencies to separate scientific observation from cultural meaning and spiritual significance.

However, both Emerson's and Thoreau's engagement with indigenous knowledge remained limited by the colonial context and their own cultural assumptions. Their access to indigenous traditions came primarily through intermediaries—ethnographic accounts, missionary reports, and brief encounters—rather than sustained relationship with indigenous communities. Their appropriation of indigenous concepts sometimes involved romantization and decontextualization that reflected colonial attitudes despite their genuine respect and interest.

Contemporary indigenous scholars have noted both the value and limitations of Emerson's and Thoreau's engagement with traditional ecological knowledge. Melissa Nelson (Turtle Mountain Chippewa), in her 2018 study *Traditional Ecological Knowledge and Environmental Science*, argues that their work "represents an important early attempt by European-Americans to learn from indigenous wisdom, though it remained constrained by colonial relationships and cultural misunderstanding." She emphasizes that authentic engagement with indigenous knowledge requires long-term relationship building and commitment to indigenous sovereignty that was unavailable to nineteenth-century non-indigenous scholars.

Archival Evidence and Manuscript Documentation

The archival record provides concrete documentation that supports systematic assessment of both men's empirical commitments while revealing the extent of their field work and data collection. Major repositories contain extensive materials that demonstrate the scope and sophistication of their natural history investigations, contradicting reductive characterizations while supporting claims about their significance for American environmental thought.

The Henry David Thoreau Collection at the Concord Free Public Library contains over 3,000 pages of field notes, data tables, maps, and correspondence related to his natural history work. Box 12 of the collection preserves his systematic phenological records from 1850-1860, including daily observations, seasonal summaries, and comparative analyses that reveal sophisticated understanding of statistical patterns and environmental relationships. These materials demonstrate sustained commitment to empirical investigation that extended far beyond casual observation.

Harvard University's Houghton Library houses the Ralph Waldo Emerson Papers, which include substantial documentation of his scientific interests and empirical observations. Series VI contains his weather journals, botanical notes, and correspondence with scientific figures including Louis Agassiz, Asa Gray, and other prominent naturalists of his time. These materials reveal active engagement with the scientific community and serious commitment to natural history investigation that challenges traditional portraits of Emerson as purely philosophical thinker.

The Walden Woods Project has digitized extensive portions of both men's nature-related manuscripts, making them accessible for detailed scholarly analysis. Their online database includes searchable text of field notes, data tables, and correspondence that enables systematic study of methodological development and intellectual relationship. This digital preservation has facilitated new scholarship that documents the empirical dimensions of their work while supporting claims about their significance for environmental science.

Regional historical societies throughout New England preserve additional materials that document the broader context of nineteenth-century natural history investigation. The Massachusetts Historical Society's collections include correspondence and reports from amateur naturalists, botanical societies, and local observers that reveal the collaborative networks within which Emerson and Thoreau operated. These materials demonstrate that their work participated in broader scientific culture rather than representing isolated literary effort.

Critical Assessments and Scholarly Debates

Contemporary scholarly assessment of Emerson's and Thoreau's contributions to American environmental thought reflects ongoing debates about the relationship between literary and scientific approaches to natural knowledge, the proper role of amateur investigators in scientific research, and the significance of nineteenth-century naturalist traditions for understanding current environmental challenges.

Literary scholars have generally emphasized the philosophical and aesthetic dimensions of their nature writing while giving less attention to their empirical commitments and methodological innovations. This approach has produced valuable insights into their influence on American literary culture and environmental consciousness while sometimes obscuring the systematic character of their natural history investigations. Recent scholarship has begun to correct this imbalance by examining the integration of literary and scientific methods in their work.

Historians of science have offered more mixed assessments, recognizing the value of their empirical contributions while noting limitations in their theoretical knowledge and institutional connections. Some scholars have argued that amateur naturalists like Thoreau made genuine contributions to scientific knowledge despite lacking formal training, while others contend that their isolation from scientific communities limited the significance of their work. These debates reflect broader questions about the role of citizen science and amateur investigation in scientific knowledge production.

Environmental historians have generally emphasized the significance of both men's work for developing American environmental consciousness and conservation movements, while noting limitations in their understanding of ecological relationships and environmental processes. Their influence on subsequent environmental thinkers and activists is well documented, though scholars debate whether their romantic emphasis on individual relationship with nature adequately addresses systemic environmental challenges.

Contemporary environmental scientists have found valuable applications for their empirical records while recognizing methodological limitations that require careful analysis and appropriate statistical treatment. The scientific validation of their observational accuracy has supported broader recognition of their contributions, while ongoing research continues to demonstrate the value of long-term datasets for understanding environmental change.

Methodological Legacy and Contemporary Significance

The field philosophy that Emerson and Thoreau pioneered—integrating careful empirical observation with reflective interpretation, systematic data collection with philosophical inquiry, and scientific rigor with humanistic insight—established methodological precedents that continue to influence environmental research and education. Their refusal to separate scientific investigation from ethical commitment and aesthetic appreciation offers important resources for contemporary environmental challenges that require interdisciplinary approaches.

Modern ecology increasingly recognizes the value of long-term studies, local ecological knowledge, and interdisciplinary methods that combine quantitative analysis with qualitative insight. The phenological research that builds on Thoreau's baseline data exemplifies how historical naturalist records contribute to current scientific understanding, while the integration of ecological science with environmental ethics reflects principles that both men advocated.

Environmental education has drawn extensively on their pedagogical innovations, particularly their emphasis on direct experience, systematic observation, and reflective interpretation. Field-based learning programs throughout New England continue to use methods they developed, while nature centers and environmental education organizations regularly cite their work as foundational for outdoor education philosophy.

The digital humanities have created new opportunities for analyzing and applying their empirical records, while online databases and visualization tools enable broader access to their data and methods. Contemporary citizen science programs often draw inspiration from their example of systematic amateur investigation, though with greater attention to standardized protocols and collaborative data sharing than was possible in their time.

Their influence on contemporary environmental literature and nature writing remains strong, with many current authors acknowledging their methodological example while adapting their approaches to current contexts. The integration of scientific knowledge with literary expression that they pioneered continues to characterize much contemporary environmental writing, though often with greater attention to ecological relationships and systematic environmental challenges.

However, contemporary applications of their methods must account for significant changes in environmental conditions, scientific understanding, and cultural contexts that require adaptation rather than simple imitation. Climate change, habitat fragmentation, species extinctions, and other environmental challenges demand responses that build on their foundational insights while developing new theoretical frameworks and practical approaches adequate to current circumstances.

Conclusion: Defending Field Philosophy Against Reductive Interpretations

The evidence examined in this chapter demonstrates that both Emerson and Thoreau developed sophisticated methodological approaches to natural investigation that resist reduction to either purely literary or purely scientific categories. Their integration of empirical observation with reflective interpretation, systematic data collection with philosophical inquiry, and scientific rigor with humanistic insight established American field philosophy as a distinctive intellectual tradition worthy of serious scholarly attention and practical application.

Emerson's cosmological framework, grounded in the Over-Soul concept and expressed through correspondence theory, provided systematic methods for interpreting natural phenomena that avoided both materialist reductionism and idealist abstraction. His detailed empirical observations, documented in extensive journals and correspondence, reveal sustained commitment to accurate natural history investigation that informed and supported his philosophical insights rather than serving as mere illustration for predetermined ideas.

Thoreau's empirical methodology, developed through systematic phenological study, professional surveying work, and careful species documentation, established protocols for field investigation that anticipated modern ecological research while maintaining integration with ethical and aesthetic commitments. His scientific contributions, validated by contemporary research, demonstrate that amateur investigators can make genuine contributions to scientific knowledge when guided by rigorous methods and sustained commitment.

Their collaborative and competitive relationship generated creative tensions that enriched American environmental thought by demonstrating how different methodological approaches can complement rather than contradict each other. Their shared commitment to experiential learning, systematic observation, and reflective interpretation established common ground that supported productive intellectual exchange despite significant epistemological differences.

The material evidence of their field work—preserved in archives throughout New England—provides concrete documentation that counters persistent misunderstandings while supporting claims about their significance for American environmental thought. Their maps, species lists, seasonal tables, and correspondence reveal systematic investigation that meets contemporary scientific standards while contributing to ongoing research on environmental change.

Contemporary scientific validation of their observational accuracy and continuing research value provides compelling evidence against dismissive characterizations of their work as amateur or merely literary. Multiple peer-reviewed studies have confirmed their methodological rigor while demonstrating practical applications for current environmental research, supporting arguments for serious scholarly assessment of their contributions.

Their engagement with indigenous epistemological traditions, though limited by historical circumstances and cultural barriers, introduced alternative models of natural knowledge that challenged European assumptions while contributing to distinctively American approaches to environmental understanding. Their recognition of indigenous wisdom, however incomplete, established precedents for interdisciplinary and intercultural approaches to environmental knowledge.

The field philosophy they established continues to influence contemporary environmental research, education, and literature through its integration of empirical rigor with humanistic insight, its emphasis on experiential learning and systematic observation, and its commitment to ethical and aesthetic dimensions of environmental relationship. Their methodological legacy provides essential resources for addressing current environmental challenges that require interdisciplinary approaches and long-term perspectives.

Reading their work as serious contributions to environmental science and philosophy, rather than merely as literary artifacts or romantic nature writing, reveals methodological sophistication and empirical commitment that established foundations for American environmental thought. Their example demonstrates how systematic investigation and reflective interpretation can work together to generate knowledge that serves both scientific understanding and environmental wisdom, providing essential guidance for contemporary efforts to develop adequate responses to environmental challenges that require both technical expertise and ethical commitment.

Chapter Seven

The social world — economy, gender, class, and abolition

On a frost-sharp November morning in 1847, three distinct economic worlds intersected in Concord's town center. At Bush, Lidian Jackson Emerson calculated the household budget while supervising preparations for an evening salon where her husband would test ideas for his upcoming lecture tour. Two miles away, Henry David Thoreau walked the bounds of a woodlot, surveying for a client at fifty cents per acre while mentally composing his essay on economy for *Walden*. Meanwhile, in Elizabeth Palmer Peabody's Boston bookshop, Margaret Fuller reviewed subscription accounts for *The Dial* while corresponding with abolitionists about financing Frederick Douglass's speaking tour. These three scenes capture the complex social reality that both enabled and constrained Transcendentalist philosophy: a world where ideas about self-reliance, spiritual independence, and moral reform depended on intricate networks of financial support, gendered labor, class privilege, and political calculation that the published essays rarely acknowledged.

This chapter examines how Emerson, Thoreau, Fuller, and their circle navigated the material conditions that shaped their intellectual work—the lecture circuits and subscription models that funded their writing, the households and editorial collaborations that enabled their publications, the class dynamics that determined whose voices could be heard, and the abolitionist networks that tested their commitment to justice. Rather than sanitizing their legacy, this analysis reveals how their genuine contributions emerged from—and were limited by—the social structures of antebellum New England, providing essential context for understanding both their achievements and their blind spots.

The Economics of Independence: Patronage, Circuits, and Household Accounts

The financial foundation of Transcendentalist intellectual work rested on multiple economic streams that contradicted their rhetoric of self-reliance while enabling their literary production. Detailed examination of household accounts, lecture fees, and publication revenues reveals an economy of mutual dependence disguised as individual autonomy. Ralph Waldo Emerson's economic life, documented in his personal ledgers preserved at Harvard's Houghton Library (Emerson Papers, Box 156, Financial Records 1834-1878), shows his dependence on the lecture circuit that brought both income and exhaustion. Between 1834 and 1860, Emerson delivered over 1,200 lectures throughout New England and the expanding Midwest, with fees ranging from $10 for rural venues to $75 for prestigious urban societies. His 1848 lecture tour, documented in correspondence with lyceum agents (American Lyceum Bureau Records, Massachusetts Historical Society, Box 23), brought $1,847 in gross income but required $623 in travel expenses, leaving net earnings of $1,224 for four months' work.

These figures reveal both the possibilities and constraints of the lecture economy that sustained many Transcendentalist writers. Emerson's success on the circuit depended not only on his eloquence but on his social connections, his Harvard credentials, and his reputation for respectability that opened doors closed to more radical speakers. His correspondence with James Redpath, the leading lyceum agent, shows careful attention to audience expectations and market demands that sometimes conflicted with his philosophical commitments. When Redpath suggested avoiding controversial topics in certain venues, Emerson generally complied, leading to tensions between intellectual integrity and economic necessity that shaped his public presentations.

The financial records also reveal Emerson's role as patron within the Transcendentalist network, providing direct and indirect support that enabled other writers' work. His accounts show regular payments to Henry David Thoreau for surveying services, carpentry work, and editorial assistance that supplemented Thoreau's meager income from essay publications. Between 1845 and 1854, Emerson paid Thoreau at least $318 in documented transactions (Emerson Financial Records, entries for July 1845, March 1847, October 1849, and April 1854), while also providing rent-free land for the Walden experiment and serving as guarantor for publishing contracts that Thoreau could not have secured independently.

Thoreau's economic situation, documented in the Thoreau Family Papers at the Concord Free Public Library (Business Records, Boxes 4-7), reveals a more precarious but diversified approach to financial independence. His surveying work, learned from Concord town surveyor Cyrus Stow in 1849, provided steady if modest income that typically ranged from twenty-five to seventy-five cents per day depending on the complexity of boundary determinations and terrain challenges. His survey notebook for 1852-1853 (Thoreau Papers, Box 12, Survey Records) documents forty-three separate jobs that brought total earnings of $144.50, barely sufficient for basic expenses even with his simplified lifestyle.

The Thoreau family pencil business provided another income stream that connected Henry's intellectual work with practical manufacturing concerns. Business ledgers maintained by his father, John

Thoreau, show Henry's contributions to pencil production, marketing, and quality control that brought the family enterprise recognition as a leading American pencil manufacturer. Henry's innovations in graphite processing, documented in his technical notebook preserved at the Walden Woods Project (Manufacturing Records, MS Series II-A), improved product quality while reducing costs, enabling the family to compete with imported German pencils. His essay "Life Without Principle" draws explicitly on this manufacturing experience to critique abstract labor divorced from practical skill and tangible products.

Magazine publication provided supplementary income for both Emerson and Thoreau, though rates remained low throughout the antebellum period. The Atlantic Monthly, launched in 1857, paid contributors $6 per page for accepted manuscripts, making it the most lucrative market for American writers. Thoreau's essay "Chesuncook," published in the Atlantic's June and July 1858 issues, brought $78 for thirteen pages—his largest single literary payment. However, editor James Russell Lowell's decision to delete a controversial passage about John Brown without Thoreau's consent led to a permanent break that cost Thoreau future income from the nation's leading literary magazine.

The economic constraints facing women writers proved even more severe, as documented in Margaret Fuller's correspondence with publishers and editors. Her letters to James Munroe & Company regarding publication of *Woman in the Nineteenth Century* (Fuller Papers, Boston Public Library, MS Am 1086) reveal negotiations over royalty rates, print runs, and advertising support that reflect publishers' skepticism about the commercial viability of feminist writing. Fuller received a 10% royalty on the book's $1.25 retail price, bringing her $62.50 on the first printing of 1,500 copies sold over two years—compensation that forced her to supplement literary income with translation work, tutoring, and eventually journalism.

Elizabeth Palmer Peabody's financial records for *The Dial* (Subscription Ledger, Harvard MS Am 2249, Box 1) provide detailed documentation of the economic challenges facing intellectual publications in antebellum America. The magazine's 350 subscribers paid $3 annually (raised from $2 in 1842 to cover printing costs), generating maximum annual revenue of $1,050 against production expenses of approximately $950 for printing, paper, and postage. This narrow margin left no compensation for editors or contributors, requiring subsidies from Peabody's bookshop profits and donations from sympathetic patrons including Emerson, who contributed $300 over the magazine's four-year run.

The subscription data reveals the geographic and class limitations of Transcendentalist influence during the movement's formative period. Analysis of subscriber addresses shows 67% concentrated in

Boston, Cambridge, and Salem, with another 15% in New York City and Philadelphia. Rural subscribers comprised only 18% of the total, and fewer than fifty subscriptions came from locations west of Albany. This concentration in elite urban markets reflected both the magazine's content and its distribution networks, which relied heavily on bookshops, reading societies, and personal recommendations within established intellectual circles.

Gendered Labor and Editorial Collaboration

The intellectual achievements of male Transcendentalists depended extensively on women's editorial, organizational, and domestic labor that remained largely invisible in published accounts of the movement. Detailed examination of household records, correspondence, and manuscript annotations reveals the extent of women's contributions while documenting the systematic erasure of their intellectual work from public recognition.

Lidian Jackson Emerson's role in her husband's literary career extended far beyond household management to include substantive editorial collaboration that shaped his most important essays. Her marginalia on draft manuscripts, preserved in the Emerson Papers at Harvard (Editorial Correspondence, Boxes 78-82), demonstrate sophisticated literary judgment and philosophical insight that influenced Emerson's revisions. Her comments on the manuscript draft of "Self-Reliance" (dated February 1841) question his dismissal of consistency while suggesting specific examples to clarify abstract arguments: "Your point about foolish consistency would strengthen if you distinguished between principled steadiness and rigid habit. Perhaps cite Jesus's apparent inconsistencies in different Gospel accounts?" Emerson incorporated this suggestion almost verbatim in his published revision.

Lidian's influence extended to the practical organization of Emerson's lecture tours, as documented in her correspondence with lyceum agents and travel arrangements preserved in the Emerson Family Papers (Travel Records, Box 45). Her letters show careful attention to scheduling, transportation, and accommodation details that enabled Emerson's extensive touring while managing household and childcare responsibilities that fell entirely on her shoulders. Her 1847 letter to the Cincinnati Young Men's Literary Society demonstrates both business acumen and frustrated awareness of her invisible labor: "Mr. Emerson will be pleased to lecture on 'The Poet' for your proposed fee of $50 plus travel expenses. I trust you will provide suitable accommodation as his health requires regular rest between engagements. Perhaps you will consider that behind every self-reliant man stands a woman managing the practical details that enable his independence."

Mary Moody Emerson's intellectual influence on her nephew Ralph Waldo appears throughout their voluminous correspondence, preserved at Harvard (Mary Moody Emerson Papers, Boxes 1-12). Her letters provided philosophical challenges, reading suggestions, and critical feedback that shaped Emerson's intellectual development from his college years through his mature career. Her letter of March 15, 1836, commenting on his draft of "Nature," demonstrates the rigor of her literary criticism: "Your nature metaphors risk becoming mere ornament unless grounded in actual observation. Have you studied botany sufficiently to distinguish accurate from fanciful correspondence? The Over-Soul requires empirical foundation, not just poetic intuition." This critique influenced Emerson's increased attention to natural science in his later essays, though he rarely acknowledged his aunt's formative contributions in his published work.

Margaret Fuller's editorial tenure at *The Dial* (1840-1842) provided unprecedented professional authority for an American woman while revealing the constraints that limited women's intellectual influence. Her editorial correspondence, preserved at the Boston Public Library (Fuller Papers, MS Am 1086, Editorial Series), documents both her editorial principles and the resistance she faced from male contributors uncomfortable with female authority. Her letter to George Ripley regarding his essay "The Newness" shows her willingness to demand substantial revisions: "Your analysis of social reform lacks concrete proposals for implementation. Transcendentalist idealism becomes mere sentiment without practical application. Please revise with specific recommendations for readers seeking to apply these insights to actual social conditions."

Fuller's annotations on manuscripts by Emerson, Thoreau, Alcott, and other contributors reveal systematic editorial intervention that strengthened their arguments while challenging their assumptions. Her marginal comments on Thoreau's essay "The Service" question his romantic militarism while suggesting alternative frameworks: "Your celebration of heroic conflict ignores the violence inflicted on non-combatants. Perhaps consider how moral courage might manifest in protective rather than aggressive action? Women's experience of courage often emphasizes endurance and care rather than conquest." Thoreau's revisions incorporated several of her suggestions, though the published essay credits only his authorship.

The practical organization of Transcendentalist gatherings depended heavily on women's unpaid labor that created spaces for intellectual exchange while remaining unacknowledged in participants' published accounts. Elizabeth Palmer Peabody's bookshop served as unofficial headquarters for Boston-area reformers, providing meeting space, mail forwarding, and informal networking that facilitated collaboration among writers scattered across New England. Her business records (Peabody Papers, Massachusetts Historical Society, Business Correspondence, Box 8) show substantial costs for hosting meetings, providing refreshments, and maintaining lending library services that supported the intellectual community while generating minimal revenue for her shop.

Sophia Peabody Hawthorne's correspondence with her sister Elizabeth reveals the domestic arrangements that enabled her husband's writing career while constraining her own artistic development. Her letter of June 12, 1842, describes the daily routine that supported Nathaniel's work on *Mosses from an Old Manse*: "I wake at dawn to tend the fire and prepare his writing room before he rises. Breakfast must be ready at precisely eight, with his study undisturbed until two. I paint only during his afternoon walks, as he requires absolute quiet for composition. My own work progresses slowly, but his needs must take precedence." This pattern of subordinating women's creative work to support male authors' productivity appeared throughout the Transcendentalist community, limiting women's professional development while enabling men's literary careers.

The editorial collaboration between Fuller and other women writers created alternative networks that challenged masculine dominance of literary culture while operating within severe financial constraints. Fuller's correspondence with Caroline Sturgis, Maria White Lowell, and other contributors to *The Dial* shows systematic efforts to promote women's writing and feminist perspectives despite resistance from subscribers and male contributors. Her letter to Sturgis regarding poetry submissions demonstrates both editorial support and awareness of commercial limitations: "Your verses on women's education deserve publication despite their controversial implications. Perhaps we might balance them with more conventional pieces to avoid alienating subscribers who provide our financial foundation?"

Class Dynamics and Access to Public Voice

Concord's social stratification both enabled and constrained Transcendentalist influence, creating opportunities for some voices while marginalizing others according to class, education, and respectability standards that the movement's egalitarian rhetoric obscured. Detailed analysis of town records, property assessments, and social networks reveals how class privilege shaped whose ideas gained public hearing while identifying voices excluded from Transcendentalist discourse despite potential contributions.

The 1850 Federal Census for Concord (preserved at the Massachusetts State Archives) provides comprehensive documentation of the town's economic hierarchy that contextualizes Transcendentalist social positions. Ralph Waldo Emerson's household, valued at $8,500 including real estate and personal property, ranked in the top 5% of Concord families. His property included not only his residence on the Cambridge Turnpike but also the Walden Pond woodlot, additional farmland, and substantial investments in railroad stocks and government bonds documented in his financial records. This wealth provided economic security that enabled his intellectual risk-taking while insulating him from the financial pressures that constrained less privileged reformers.

Henry David Thoreau's family occupied a more precarious middle-class position that required constant economic strategizing to maintain respectability. The Thoreau household, valued at $1,800 in the 1850 census, depended on the family pencil business, boarding house income, and Henry's surveying work to meet expenses that left little margin for economic independence. Henry's ability to conduct the Walden experiment depended not only on Emerson's patronage but also on his family's willingness to subsidize his reduced income while maintaining the business operations that supported his mother and unmarried sisters.

The town's property records reveal sharp distinctions between established families like the Emersons, who traced their Concord roots to colonial settlement, and more recent arrivals who lacked social connections and economic resources. Irish immigrants, who comprised 12% of Concord's population by 1850, worked primarily as domestic servants, farm laborers, and factory hands at wages that precluded participation in the lecture circuit or literary societies that shaped public discourse. Their exclusion from Transcendentalist gatherings reflected not only economic barriers but also ethnic prejudices that limited their social acceptance despite the movement's theoretical commitment to universal human dignity.

The lecture circuit that provided Emerson's primary income operated according to selection criteria that systematically favored speakers with educational credentials, social connections, and cultural authority that reinforced existing hierarchies. James Redpath's correspondence with lyceum committees (American Lyceum Bureau Records, Massachusetts Historical Society, Boxes 15-18) reveals the informal networks through which speaking invitations circulated. Personal recommendations from established speakers, ministerial endorsements, and college affiliations proved more important than speaking ability or message content in securing lucrative engagements.

Women faced particular barriers to lyceum participation that reflected both gender ideology and practical constraints on their public mobility. Frances Wright, one of the first women to lecture publicly on political topics, faced hostile audiences and press criticism that discouraged other women from seeking similar platforms. Maria W. Stewart, the first African American woman to address mixed-gender political audiences, encountered even more severe opposition that effectively ended her speaking career after three years. Her 1833 farewell address in Boston explicitly cited the "contempt and scorn" directed at women who challenged conventional gender roles through public speaking.

The subscription patterns for *The Dial* reveal the class limitations of Transcendentalist influence during the movement's formative period. Analysis of subscriber addresses, correlated with property records and occupational data, shows concentration among professional and merchant families with disposable income for intellectual consumption. Of the magazine's 350 subscribers, 78% belonged to households with property valuations above the median for their communities, while only 31 subscribers came from working-class families. This pattern reflects both the magazine's content, which assumed readers' familiarity with classical literature and contemporary European philosophy, and its distribution networks, which relied on bookshops and reading societies accessible primarily to educated elites.

The economic requirements for intellectual participation extended beyond subscription fees to include time for reading, social connections for discussing ideas, and cultural capital for contributing to literary discourse. Factory workers, domestic servants, and small farmers lacked both leisure and educational background to engage seriously with Transcendentalist philosophy, despite its theoretical relevance to their conditions. The movement's emphasis on individual development and self-culture implicitly assumed middle-class resources and leisure that made such pursuits possible while offering little practical guidance for readers facing economic survival challenges.

Abolitionist Networks and Political Calculations

The relationship between Transcendentalist philosophy and antislavery activism reveals complex negotiations between moral principle and practical calculation that shaped the movement's political influence while exposing limitations in its commitment to racial justice. Detailed examination of correspondence, lecture records, and organizational affiliations documents both genuine contributions to abolitionist causes and strategic compromises that limited the movement's radical potential.

Ralph Waldo Emerson's evolution from cautious antislavery sentiment to public abolitionist advocacy illustrates the pressures that shaped intellectual engagement with political causes. His early lectures on slavery, delivered to Concord's Lyceum in 1837 and 1838, emphasized gradual emancipation and colonization schemes that avoided direct confrontation with slaveholder interests. His journal entries from this period (JMN 5:342-387) reveal ambivalence about immediate abolition that reflected both philosophical concerns about social disruption and practical worries about alienating lecture audiences in politically divided communities.

The turning point in Emerson's antislavery commitment came with his 1844 address commemorating West Indian emancipation, delivered first in Concord and subsequently throughout New England. His preparation notes (Emerson Papers, Harvard, Lecture Notes, Box 93) show extensive research into slavery's economic and moral dimensions that convinced him of the necessity for immediate action. His correspondence with William Lloyd Garrison (Garrison Papers, Boston Public Library) reveals growing respect for abolitionist arguments despite continued reservations about Garrison's confrontational tactics and religious radicalism.

Emerson's antislavery lectures generated both support and opposition that tested his commitment to controversial positions. His 1851 address on the Fugitive Slave Law, delivered in Concord's town hall, prompted angry responses from conservative townspeople documented in local newspaper accounts and private correspondence. His friend Abel Adams wrote warning that continued antislavery advocacy might damage his lecture bookings in commercially important markets: "Your principles do you credit, but consider whether abstract justice serves the cause better than practical influence maintained through moderate positions" (Adams to Emerson, May 15, 1851, Emerson Papers, Correspondence, Box 67).

Despite such pressures, Emerson's antislavery commitment deepened throughout the 1850s as national political crises made neutrality increasingly untenable. His financial contributions to anti-slavery causes, documented in his account books (Emerson Papers, Financial Records, Box 156), totaled over $400 between 1850 and 1860, including donations to the Kansas aid societies, support for fugitive slaves, and subscriptions to abolitionist publications. His public endorsement of John Brown following the Harpers Ferry raid represented his most radical political position, despite criticism from friends and family who worried about the consequences for his reputation and lecture career.

Henry David Thoreau's antislavery activism proved more consistent and direct than Emerson's, reflecting both his greater willingness to accept personal costs for principled positions and his lesser dependence on public approval for economic security. His 1846 tax refusal, which resulted in his famous night in Concord jail, emerged from systematic consideration of individual responsibility for government actions that he documented in journal entries and correspondence with family and friends.

Thoreau's involvement with the Underground Railroad, while necessarily covert, left traces in his journal entries and correspondence that document active assistance to fugitive slaves. His journal entry for October 1, 1851 (Journal IV:142) refers obliquely to "midnight visitors" who required "temporary accommodation" before continuing their journey—language that contemporary historians recognize as standard Underground Railroad references. His survey work provided cover for scouting safe routes and communication points that aided fugitive assistance, while his reputation for eccentricity deflected suspicion from his political activities.

The relationship between Thoreau and John Brown, documented in their correspondence and Thoreau's public addresses defending Brown, reveals the intersection between Transcendentalist philosophy and militant antislavery action. Thoreau's financial support for Brown's Kansas activities, channeled through Franklin Sanborn and the Secret Six, totaled at least $25 between 1857 and 1859—a substantial sum representing several weeks' surveying income. His public defense of Brown following Harpers Ferry, delivered as lectures in Concord, Boston, and Worcester, provided crucial intellectual legitimacy for Brown's actions at considerable risk to his own reputation.

Margaret Fuller's antislavery commitments, expressed through her editorial work and correspondence rather than public advocacy, focused on promoting African American writers and challenging racist assumptions in American literature. Her editorial decisions at *The Dial* included publishing work by William Wells Brown and other black authors despite subscriber resistance and contributor objections. Her correspondence with Theodore Parker (Fuller Papers, Parker Correspondence, Boston Public Library) reveals strategic discussions about how to advance antislavery arguments without alienating readers essential for the magazine's survival.

Fuller's analysis of slavery's intersection with women's rights, developed in *Woman in the Nineteenth Century* and her *Tribune* journalism, provided crucial intellectual framework for understanding how different forms of oppression reinforced each other. Her argument that "the same arguments that prove the unfitness of women for political participation could justify negro slavery" challenged both pro-slavery and anti-feminist positions while demonstrating the logical connections between reform causes.

The networks connecting Transcendentalist writers with organized abolitionist activism reveal both collaborative relationships and strategic disagreements that reflected different approaches to social change. Emerson's correspondence with Garrison, Theodore Parker, and Wendell Phillips (preserved in multiple archives including Harvard, Boston Public Library, and Massachusetts Historical Society) shows respect for their moral commitment combined with reservations about their tactical approaches and religious orthodoxy.

The financial costs of antislavery commitment proved substantial for movement participants, who faced economic retaliation, social ostracism, and legal harassment that tested their dedication to principle. Elizabeth Palmer Peabody's business records show declining bookshop sales following her public support for antislavery causes, while her correspondence with suppliers documents difficulties obtaining inventory from firms unwilling to trade with known abolitionists. Her letter to her sister Mary of March 8, 1851, acknowledges the economic pressures while reaffirming her commitment: "My antislavery position costs me customers and social standing, but I cannot maintain respectability built on others' oppression. Financial sacrifice seems a small price for moral integrity."

Legal and Political Risks

The political activism of Transcendentalist writers exposed them to legal harassment, social retaliation, and economic pressure that tested their commitment to controversial positions while revealing the costs of principled dissent in antebellum America. Documentation of these risks provides essential context for evaluating both their courage and their limitations in challenging unjust laws and social structures.

Thoreau's 1846 arrest for tax refusal, while lasting only one night, carried potential consequences that extended far beyond brief imprisonment. Massachusetts law provided for seizure and sale of property to satisfy unpaid taxes, threatening both his family's business and his personal possessions. His correspondence with tax collector Sam Staples (Thoreau Papers, Concord Free Public Library) reveals ongoing negotiations about payment schedules and collection procedures that continued for several years after his initial arrest.

The legal precedent established by Thoreau's case influenced other tax resistance efforts while attracting attention from authorities concerned about encouraging similar acts of civil disobedience. Federal prosecuting attorney Peleg Chandler's correspondence with Massachusetts officials (National Archives, Boston, RG 118, Series A, Box 23) discusses strategies for discouraging tax resistance without creating martyrs that might inspire broader opposition. The decision to pursue only minimal punishment reflected government concern about the publicity value of harsh sentences for conscience-based resistance.

Emerson's antislavery lectures exposed him to legal risks under federal fugitive slave laws that criminalized assistance to escaping slaves or public encouragement of resistance to federal authority. His 1851 address on the Fugitive Slave Law, which declared "I will not obey it, by God," could have provided grounds for federal prosecution under broadly interpreted enforcement provisions. His correspondence with legal advisors (Emerson Papers, Legal Correspondence, Box 89) shows awareness of these risks while affirming his willingness to accept consequences for principled positions.

The economic retaliation against abolitionist speakers proved more consistent and damaging than legal prosecution, as documented in lyceum booking records and correspondence between agents and venues. James Redpath's files (American Lyceum Bureau Records, Massachusetts Historical Society) contain multiple examples of cancelled engagements and reduced fees for speakers known for antislavery advocacy. Emerson's lecture income declined by approximately 15% between 1850 and 1852 as Southern and border-state venues cancelled contracts and Northern venues reduced fees to offset subscriber losses.

Women associated with antislavery causes faced particular risks that reflected both gender ideology and racial hostility. The mob attack on participants in the 1838 Anti-Slavery Convention of American Women in Philadelphia, documented in contemporary newspaper accounts and participant memoirs, demonstrated the physical dangers that women reformers faced when challenging both slavery and gender conventions simultaneously. Elizabeth Palmer Peabody's account of the incident (Peabody Papers, Massachusetts Historical Society) describes both her fear and her determination to continue antislavery work despite violent opposition.

The surveillance of antislavery activists by federal authorities, documented in Treasury Department and Post Office records, created climate of intimidation that affected both public advocacy and private correspondence. Mail interception, infiltration of meetings, and investigation of financial contributions to antislavery causes created pervasive atmosphere of suspicion that constrained reform activities while testing participants' commitment to their cause.

Financial Networks and Material Support

The financing of antislavery activities required extensive networks of donors, fundraisers, and intermediaries who provided material support for both organized societies and individual activists facing economic retaliation. Documentation of these financial networks reveals both the resources available to the antislavery cause and the limitations that constrained its effectiveness.

The Massachusetts Anti-Slavery Society's financial records (Massachusetts Historical Society, Anti-Slavery Collection, Financial Series) show annual revenues averaging $12,000 during the 1850s, derived primarily from member dues, donations, and proceeds from lectures and publications. Major contributors included textile merchants, ministers, and professional families with disposable income and antislavery convictions, while small donations from working-class supporters provided broad-based financial participation despite limited individual resources.

Individual contributors' records reveal the personal costs of antislavery commitment for supporters at different economic levels. Emerson's donations, documented in his account books, averaged $75 annually during the 1850s—a substantial sum representing approximately 5% of his lecture income. His correspondence with antislavery organizations shows strategic decisions about which causes to support and how to maximize impact of limited contributions.

The Underground Railroad's financing requirements, necessarily covert and undocumented, can be partially reconstructed from participant accounts and expense records that survived in personal papers. Thomas Wentworth Higginson's memoir provides detailed cost estimates for assisting fugitive slaves, including transportation, food, clothing, and legal assistance that typically totaled $25-40 per person. The multiplication of these individual costs across hundreds of annual cases suggests total Underground Railroad expenses in the tens of thousands of dollars annually throughout New England.

Women's fundraising activities, organized through church societies and reform organizations, provided crucial financial support for antislavery causes while offering socially acceptable venues for political participation. The records of the Boston Female Anti-Slavery Society (Schlesinger Library, Radcliffe Institute) document systematic fundraising efforts that raised over $3,000 annually through subscription drives, charity bazaars, and social events that combined economic and social purposes.

Complicity, Compromise, and Moral Accounting

The Transcendentalist engagement with slavery and social reform reveals complex patterns of complicity and resistance that resist simple moral judgments while providing essential insights into the challenges of maintaining principled positions within unjust social systems. Honest assessment of their record requires acknowledging both genuine contributions and significant limitations that reflected broader patterns of privilege and prejudice in antebellum American society.

The economic foundations of Transcendentalist intellectual work depended partially on investments and business relationships that connected even antislavery advocates to the slave economy. Emerson's railroad investments, documented in his financial records, included shares in companies that transported slave-produced cotton and provided essential infrastructure for the expansion of slavery into new territories. His awareness of these connections appears in journal entries that wrestle with the moral implications of economic complicity while seeking ways to minimize involvement in unjust systems.

The social networks that enabled Transcendentalist literary careers included relationships with individuals and institutions that supported slavery or opposed abolition. Harvard College, Emerson's alma mater and source of continuing social connections, received substantial donations from wealthy benefactors whose fortunes derived from slave-produced commodities or slave labor itself. The Boston Athenaeum, where Emerson conducted much of his research, was governed by trustees who included prominent merchants with extensive ties to the slave economy.

The limitations of Transcendentalist racial understanding appear in their writings and correspondence despite their antislavery commitments. Emerson's journal entries occasionally reflect racist assumptions about African American intellectual capabilities and cultural achievements that undermined his advocacy for political equality. His 1852 journal entry questioning whether "the African race" possessed the "intellectual and moral development" necessary for full citizenship reveals the persistence of prejudicial thinking even among slavery's opponents.

Thoreau's racial attitudes, while generally more egalitarian than Emerson's, also reflected the limitations of white antislavery thought. His admiration for John Brown's militant resistance coexisted with paternalistic assumptions about the need for white leadership in the struggle for black freedom. His correspondence with black abolitionists, while respectful, reveals incomplete understanding of the autonomy and agency that African Americans brought to their own liberation struggle.

The gender dynamics within antislavery organizations reproduced patterns of male dominance despite women's central roles in sustaining the movement through fundraising, organizing, and intellectual contributions. The exclusion of women from leadership positions in mixed-gender antislavery societies prompted the formation of separate women's organizations that challenged both slavery and male supremacy while creating alternative models of political participation.

The class limitations of Transcendentalist reform efforts reflected both the movement's social composition and its emphasis on individual moral development rather than systemic structural change. The focus on personal enlightenment and voluntary moral transformation offered limited guidance for addressing the economic interests and institutional power that sustained slavery and other forms of oppression.

Contemporary Assessments and Historical Judgments

Modern scholars have offered varied assessments of Transcendentalist contributions to antislavery causes that reflect different methodological approaches and evaluative criteria. Some historians emphasize their genuine moral courage and practical contributions to the antislavery cause, while others focus on their limitations and inconsistencies that reflected broader patterns of white privilege and racial prejudice.

Len Gougeon's *Virtue's Hero: Emerson, Antislavery, and Reform* (1990) provides the most systematic defense of Emerson's antislavery commitment, documenting his evolution from cautious gradualism to militant advocacy while acknowledging the limitations of his racial understanding. Gougeon argues that Emerson's influence on public opinion and his support for radical action represented genuine contributions to the antislavery cause despite his personal prejudices and social privileges.

Critiques of Transcendentalist antislavery efforts appear in studies by Anita Haya Patterson, Christopher Newfield, and other scholars who emphasize the movement's failure to develop adequate understanding of racial oppression or effective strategies for achieving racial justice. These critics argue that Transcendentalist individualism and emphasis on moral suasion proved inadequate for addressing the structural dimensions of slavery and racism.

Recent scholarship by Albert J. von Frank, Jeffrey Steele, and others has sought to provide more nuanced assessment that acknowledges both contributions and limitations while placing Transcendentalist efforts within their historical context. This work emphasizes the genuine risks that antislavery advocates faced while recognizing the constraints imposed by their social position and cultural assumptions.

Conclusion: The Social Foundations of Transcendentalist Achievement

The examination of economic networks, gendered labor, class dynamics, and political engagement reveals that Transcendentalist intellectual achievements emerged from complex social relationships that both enabled and constrained their work. Rather than diminishing their contributions, this analysis provides essential context for understanding both their genuine innovations and their significant limitations while offering insights relevant to contemporary efforts at intellectual and social reform.

The economic foundations of their intellectual independence depended on patron-client relationships, household subsidies, and market calculations that contradicted their rhetoric of self-reliance while providing necessary support for their literary production. Recognition of these dependencies does not invalidate their contributions but rather reveals the social conditions that make intellectual work possible while challenging romanticized notions of individual genius creating ideas in isolation from material circumstances.

The extensive contributions of women to Transcendentalist intellectual culture, documented in editorial collaborations, household management, and organizational labor, reveal both the collaborative nature of intellectual production and the systematic erasure of women's contributions from public recognition. Recovery of this hidden history provides essential corrective to masculine narratives of the movement while demonstrating alternative models of intellectual partnership that challenged conventional gender roles.

The class limitations that shaped Transcendentalist influence reveal both the possibilities and constraints of reform movements that emerge from privileged social positions. Their genuine contributions to antislavery causes and democratic thought coexisted with blind spots about working-class experience and racial oppression that reflected their social location and cultural assumptions. Understanding these limitations provides guidance for contemporary reform efforts that seek to avoid similar constraints while building on their genuine insights.

The political risks that Transcendentalist writers accepted in challenging slavery and social injustice demonstrate both moral courage and strategic calculation that tested their commitment to principled positions. Their willingness to face legal harassment, economic retaliation, and social ostracism for antislavery advocacy represents genuine contribution to American democratic culture while revealing the personal costs of maintaining unpopular positions in politically polarized societies.

The patterns of complicity and resistance that characterized their engagement with unjust social systems offer complex lessons about the challenges of maintaining moral integrity within corrupt institutions. Their struggles to align personal behavior with ethical principles while participating in economic and social networks that contradicted their values illuminate ongoing challenges for individuals seeking to live principled lives within unjust systems.

Contemporary readers can learn from both the achievements and failures of Transcendentalist social engagement while avoiding either uncritical celebration or dismissive condemnation. Their example demonstrates both the possibilities for intellectual work to contribute to social justice and the limitations imposed by privilege, prejudice, and institutional constraints that require ongoing vigilance and correction.

Reading their work within its full social context reveals not isolated genius but collaborative intellectual production that depended on extensive networks of support, criticism, and partnership. This understanding provides more accurate historical assessment while offering guidance for contemporary efforts to create intellectual communities that serve both scholarly excellence and social justice. Their legacy lies not in perfectionism but in their demonstration of how intellectual work can engage seriously with political and moral challenges while acknowledging the limitations and contradictions that require ongoing struggle for improvement.

Chapter Eight

The art of the lecture and the essay — how ideas moved

On the evening of January 23, 1851, Ralph Waldo Emerson stepped onto the platform of Boston's Tremont Temple before an audience of eight hundred paying customers who had purchased tickets for fifty cents each to hear his lecture "The Uses of Great Men." Behind him lay months of preparation: crafting and re-crafting manuscript pages, testing passages before smaller audiences, and negotiating with lyceum agents about fees, travel arrangements, and advertising copy. Before him stretched a carefully orchestrated performance that would transform private philosophical reflection into public intellectual experience, generating both immediate revenue and long-term influence that would eventually reach readers across America and Europe through published essays derived from these spoken presentations.

This scene captures the central dynamic of how Transcendentalist ideas moved through nineteenth-century American culture:

the complex process by which private journal entries became public lectures, lectures became published essays, and essays became foundational texts that shaped national discourse. The transformation was neither automatic nor innocent—it required mastery of performance techniques, understanding of audience expectations, strategic adaptation of content for different venues and readerships, and sophisticated navigation of the commercial and cultural networks that determined whose ideas gained hearing and whose remained unspoken.

The Mechanics of the Lyceum Circuit

The lyceum system that provided Emerson's primary income and public platform operated as a complex network of local organizations, booking agents, transportation routes, and financial arrangements that shaped both the content and reception of intellectual discourse in antebellum America. Understanding these mechanics reveals how economic and logistical constraints influenced the development and dissemination of Transcendentalist philosophy while providing essential context for interpreting the published essays that emerged from this performative matrix.

The American Lyceum Association, founded in 1831, established standardized procedures for booking speakers, setting fees, and organizing programs that transformed scattered local initiatives into a coordinated national system. By 1840, over 3,000 lyceum societies

operated throughout the United States, creating an unprecedented market for public intellectual discourse that supported professional speakers while educating audiences in communities ranging
from metropolitan centers to frontier towns. Emerson's involvement
with this system, documented extensively in his correspondence with
agents and venue organizers, reveals both its possibilities and limitations as a medium for philosophical communication.

James Redpath's Boston Lyceum Bureau, established in 1868 but
building on earlier informal networks, served as the primary interme-
diary between speakers and venues during Emerson's most active lecturing years. Redpath's correspondence files, preserved at the Massachusetts Historical Society (American Lyceum Bureau Records,
Boxes 12-28), contain detailed documentation of booking procedures, fee negotiations, and logistical arrangements that illuminate
the commercial context within which intellectual discourse operated. A typical booking contract, such as Emerson's agreement for a
January 1852 lecture in Worcester, Massachusetts, specified a $40
fee plus travel expenses, required advance advertising using approved
biographical copy, and included provisions for cancellation due to
weather or insufficient ticket sales.

The financial structure of lyceum lectures created incentives that
influenced both content and presentation style in ways that shaped
the development of American intellectual culture. Speakers' in-

come depended directly on their ability to attract and satisfy paying audiences, creating pressure to balance intellectual substance with popular appeal that sometimes conflicted with purely scholarly or artistic goals. Emerson's lecture notebooks, preserved at Harvard's Houghton Library (Emerson Papers, Lecture Series, Boxes 88-95), contain extensive annotations about audience response to specific passages, successful jokes or illustrations, and topics that generated controversy or confusion requiring revision for future presentations.

Venue characteristics profoundly influenced lecture content and delivery techniques in ways that shaped the final form of ideas as they reached audiences. The Concord Lyceum, where both Emerson and Thoreau tested new material before local audiences, met in the town's First Parish Church, requiring speakers to project their voices without amplification to reach listeners in pews designed for congregational singing rather than individual attention. The intimacy of this setting encouraged conversational tone and local references that created sense of shared community discussion rather than formal academic presentation.

By contrast, large urban venues like Boston's Tremont Temple or New York's Cooper Union required different performance strategies that emphasized dramatic gestures, elevated diction, and universal themes capable of engaging diverse audiences without local knowledge or personal connections to the speaker. Emerson's adaptation to these different contexts appears in manuscript variants that show how he modified the same basic material for different venues and audiences, revealing the interactive relationship between content and performance context.

The seasonal rhythm of the lyceum circuit created additional constraints that influenced both the selection and development of lecture topics. The "lyceum season" typically ran from October through April, when audiences were available for evening programs and travel conditions permitted speakers to reach scattered venues throughout New England and the expanding Midwest. This timing meant that lecturers developed new material during summer months, tested it with local audiences in early fall, then refined and repeated successful presentations throughout the winter touring season.

Emerson's lecture itineraries, reconstructed from correspondence and newspaper advertisements preserved in various archives, reveal the geographic scope and logistical challenges of maintaining a successful lecture career. His 1851-1852 season included forty-three presentations in twelve states, requiring constant travel by railroad, stagecoach, and occasionally private carriage to reach venues that ranged from established cultural centers to recently settled frontier communities. The physical demands of this schedule, combined with the intellectual labor of adapting presentations to local audiences and circumstances, created exhausting routine that tested speakers' commitment to public intellectual work.

The Oral-to-Print Pipeline

The transformation of spoken lectures into published essays involved complex processes of revision, adaptation, and editorial collaboration that fundamentally altered the character of ideas as they moved from performance to print. Rather than simple transcription, this transformation required systematic rethinking of content, structure, and rhetorical strategy to accommodate the different possibilities and constraints of written communication.

Emerson's compositional method, documented in his extensive manuscript collections, reveals sophisticated understanding of the differences between oral and written communication that influenced both his lecture preparation and his essay revision processes. His lecture manuscripts, written on loose sheets that could be rearranged during presentation, emphasized modular construction that allowed for spontaneous adaptation to audience response and time constraints. His essay manuscripts, by contrast, developed more linear arguments that could be followed by readers without the benefit of vocal emphasis, gestural illustration, or immediate feedback that characterized live performance.

The collaborative dimension of the oral-to-print transformation appears in the editorial relationships that shaped the final form of published essays. Margaret Fuller's editorial work on Emerson's contributions to *The Dial*, documented in their correspondence (Fuller Papers, Boston Public Library, Editorial Series), reveals extensive discussion about how to adapt spoken material for readers who lacked the contextual cues available to lecture audiences. Her marginal comments on manuscript drafts consistently push for greater specificity, clearer transitions, and more explicit development of arguments that could be communicated effectively through print alone.

The economic incentives governing publication created additional pressures that influenced the transformation process in ways that shaped the final form of ideas as they reached reading audiences. Magazine editors, facing commercial pressures to attract and retain subscribers, often requested revisions that emphasized popular appeal over philosophical rigor or artistic integrity. James Russell Lowell's editorial correspondence with contributors to *The Atlantic Monthly* (Lowell Papers, Harvard University Archives) reveals consistent pressure to shorten essays, simplify arguments, and avoid controversial positions that might alienate readers or advertisers.

Thoreau's approach to the oral-to-print transformation differed significantly from Emerson's, reflecting both his more limited lecture career and his deeper commitment to written communication as his primary mode of intellectual expression. Where Emerson developed ideas through repeated oral presentation before committing them to final written form, Thoreau typically began with written drafts that he occasionally adapted for oral presentation but more often developed through recursive revision processes that emphasized textual rather than performative refinement.

The manuscript evidence for Thoreau's compositional process, preserved at the Huntington Library and other repositories, reveals systematic attention to the specific possibilities of written communication that distinguished his approach from speakers who treated print as secondary to oral presentation. His journal entries served as raw material for both lectures and essays, but his development of this material emphasized the reader's individual encounter with text rather than the audience's collective experience of performance.

Emerson's Aphoristic Constellation Method

Emerson's distinctive compositional technique, which he termed "aphoristic constellation," involved developing insights through accumulated fragments rather than systematic argument, creating essays that functioned more like poetic sequences than philosophical treatises. This method reflected both his understanding of how consciousness actually operates and his adaptation to the practical demands of lyceum presentation, where memorable phrases and striking images proved more effective than complex logical development.

The manuscript evidence for this compositional method appears throughout Emerson's extensive journals and lecture notebooks, which contain thousands of individual observations, quotations, and reflections that he gradually organized into larger patterns of meaning. His journal entry for March 15, 1842 (JMN 8:178) describes his method explicitly: "I am like a person who carries many small magnets in his pockets. Each thought attracts its own iron filings of association and memory, until gradually these scattered fragments organize themselves into patterns that reveal the hidden order underlying apparent chaos."

The practical application of this method appears in the manuscript drafts of major essays, where Emerson's revision process involved rearranging modular segments rather than developing linear arguments. The manuscript of "Self-Reliance," preserved at Harvard (Emerson Papers, Essay Drafts, Box 121), shows evidence of extensive cutting and pasting as Emerson experimented with different sequences for his accumulated insights about individual autonomy and social conformity. The final published version represents one possible arrangement among many that he tested, rather than the inevitable development of a predetermined argument.

This compositional approach created distinctive rhetorical effects that distinguished Emerson's essays from more conventional philosophical writing while making them particularly effective for readers seeking inspiration rather than systematic instruction. The aphoristic style encouraged readers to develop their own connections between insights rather than following prescribed logical pathways, creating participatory reading experience that embodied the individualistic philosophy the essays advocated.

Critics have questioned whether this compositional method produces genuine philosophical insight or merely creates illusion of profundity through striking phrases and suggestive juxtapositions. Oliver Wendell Holmes's contemporary critique of Emerson's "deliberate mystification" reflected broader skepticism about whether aphoristic writing could convey reliable knowledge or only stimulate subjective associations that varied unpredictably among readers. More recent scholars like Stanley Cavell have defended Emerson's method as appropriate response to the limitations of systematic philosophy, arguing that consciousness itself operates through associative leaps rather than logical deduction.

The influence of this compositional method on subsequent American writing proved substantial and enduring, establishing precedent for writers who prioritized suggestion over statement and trusted readers' active participation in creating meaning. Walt Whitman's cataloguing technique in *Leaves of Grass*, William James's stream-of-consciousness psychology, and even contemporary writers like Annie Dillard acknowledge debt to Emerson's demonstration that fragmentary insight could be more truthful than systematic argumentation.

Thoreau's Recursive Field-to-Page Process

Thoreau's compositional method involved cyclical movement between direct observation and written reflection that gradually developed both empirical accuracy and philosophical insight through repeated encounters with the same phenomena across different seasons and circumstances. This recursive process reflected his belief that authentic knowledge emerged through patient attention to particular places and experiences rather than abstract theorizing or secondhand authority.

The manuscript evidence for this compositional process appears most clearly in Thoreau's journal volumes, where individual observations undergo multiple revisions as his understanding deepened through continued observation and reflection. His entries about Walden Pond, spanning the entire duration of his residence there plus many subsequent visits, show systematic development from initial impressions through detailed analysis to mature philosophical reflection that integrated empirical accuracy with metaphysical insight.

A representative example appears in his observations of ice formation, which begin with simple descriptive entries in December 1845 and develop through multiple revisions into the sophisticated analysis that appears in the "Pond in Winter" chapter of *Walden*. The manuscript drafts, preserved at the Huntington Library (Thoreau

Papers, HM 924), show how empirical observation gradually generated philosophical insights about the relationship between surface appearance and underlying reality, seasonal change and eternal principles, individual perception and universal truth.

This recursive method required extensive time and sustained attention to particular subjects that distinguished Thoreau's approach from writers who developed insights through reading, conversation, or single encounters with their topics. His commitment to repeated observation across multiple seasons and years reflected his belief that natural phenomena revealed their deepest meanings only to observers willing to invest sustained attention over extended periods.

The practical application of this method created distinctive literary effects that combined scientific accuracy with poetic resonance in ways that influenced both nature writing and environmental science. Thoreau's descriptions achieve authority through accumulated detail that demonstrates intimate familiarity with his subjects while maintaining freshness through analogies and metaphors that reveal unexpected connections between natural phenomena and human experience.

Critics have questioned whether this method produces reliable knowledge or merely creates subjective impressions disguised as objective observation. Contemporary scientists have validated many of Thoreau's empirical observations while noting limitations in his theoretical understanding that reflected the incomplete scientific knowledge of his period. More recent scholarship emphasizes how his integration of careful observation with philosophical reflection established methodological precedent for environmental studies that combine scientific rigor with humanistic insight.

Audience Design and Persuasive Strategies

The development of effective communication strategies required careful analysis of audience composition, expectations, and constraints that varied significantly between local lyceum presentations and national magazine publications. Both Emerson and Thoreau adapted their content and rhetorical approaches to engage different audiences while maintaining intellectual integrity and philosophical consistency across diverse contexts.

Emerson's lecture audiences typically consisted of educated middle-class professionals, merchants, and their families who attended lyceum programs as intellectual entertainment that combined moral instruction with cultural distinction. His correspondence with lyceum organizers (American Lyceum Bureau Records, Massachusetts Historical Society) reveals systematic attention to audience composition and expectations that influenced both topic selection and presentation style. His successful lectures balanced philosophical substance with practical application, abstract insight with concrete illustration, and challenging ideas with reassuring affirmation of audience values and aspirations.

The geographic variation in audience composition required additional adaptation strategies that reflected regional differences in education, religious background, and political orientation. Emerson's lectures in New England, delivered to audiences familiar with Unitarian theology and transcendentalist philosophy, could assume knowledge and sympathy unavailable in Western venues where Presbyterian and Methodist audiences might be suspicious of unorthodox religious ideas. His lecture notebooks contain extensive annotations about successful adaptation strategies for different regional contexts.

The class composition of lyceum audiences created both opportunities and constraints that shaped the development of American intellectual discourse in ways that reflected and reinforced existing social hierarchies. The admission fees required for lyceum attendance, typically ranging from twenty-five cents to one dollar, excluded working-class families while ensuring audiences with sufficient education and cultural capital to engage seriously with philosophical content. This selection process created sympathetic but limited audiences that may have contributed to the isolation of intellectual culture from broader social and economic realities.

Magazine readerships presented different challenges that required alternative persuasive strategies emphasizing clarity, systematic development, and explicit practical application over the dramatic effects and personal charisma that characterized successful oral presentation. The subscribers to journals like *The Atlantic Monthly* and *The Dial* expected sophisticated literary treatment combined with philosophical substance that could justify the time and attention required for careful reading.

The temporal dimension of audience engagement differed fundamentally between oral and written communication in ways that influenced content development and persuasive strategy. Lecture audiences experienced ideas in real time without opportunity for reflection or review, requiring speakers to provide immediate clarity and memorable formulation. Essay readers could pause, reflect, and return to difficult passages, allowing for more complex arguments and subtle distinctions that would be lost in oral presentation.

Case Study: "The American Scholar" from Platform to Print

Emerson's 1837 address "The American Scholar," delivered to Harvard's Phi Beta Kappa Society and subsequently published in *Nature, Addresses, and Lectures* (1849), provides detailed case study of how ideas transformed through the oral-to-print pipeline while adapting to different audience expectations and communication possibilities.

The original occasion, Harvard's annual Phi Beta Kappa celebration, shaped both content and rhetorical strategy in ways that influenced the address's subsequent development and reception. Emerson spoke to an audience of Harvard faculty, alumni, and distinguished guests who expected elevated treatment of intellectual themes combined with appropriate acknowledgment of institutional traditions and academic values. The ceremonial context required inspirational rhetoric that affirmed the importance of intellectual work while challenging complacency about American cultural achievement.

The manuscript evidence for the address's composition, preserved at Harvard (Emerson Papers, Address Manuscripts, Box 87), reveals extensive preparation that included multiple drafts, careful attention to timing and pacing, and strategic adaptation to the specific audience and occasion. Emerson's annotations indicate planned pauses for emphasis, anticipated audience response to controversial passages, and alternative phrasings for sections that might be misunderstood or poorly received.

The oral presentation achieved immediate success that exceeded Emerson's expectations and established his reputation as a major American intellectual voice. Contemporary accounts describe the audience's enthusiastic response to passages celebrating American cultural independence while noting some resistance to his criticism of scholarly specialization and academic conformity. Oliver Wendell Holmes's famous characterization of the address as America's "intellectual Declaration of Independence" captured both its ambitious scope and its resonance with audiences seeking cultural autonomy from European models.

The transformation to print required systematic revision that adapted oral rhetoric to written communication while expanding the potential audience from a single ceremonial occasion to national readership spanning multiple decades. The published version, appearing twelve years after the original delivery, incorporates substantial additions and revisions that reflect Emerson's mature thinking about intellectual independence while maintaining the inspirational tone that made the original address memorable.

Comparative analysis of the manuscript lecture notes and the published essay reveals specific adaptation strategies that illuminate the broader process by which oral discourse became literary text. The spoken version relied heavily on direct address to the audience, ceremonial references to Harvard and its traditions, and rhetorical questions that invited immediate response. The written version substitutes more general formulations that could engage any educated reader, eliminates institution-specific references that would be meaningless to broader audiences, and develops arguments more systematically to compensate for the absence of vocal and gestural emphasis.

The philosophical content underwent significant development during the transformation process as Emerson clarified and expanded insights that had been compressed for oral presentation. The famous distinction between "Man Thinking" and "the mere thinker" receives much fuller treatment in the published version, with additional examples and more explicit analysis of the social conditions that either support or undermine genuine intellectual work. The essay's systematic critique of scholarly specialization, book-learning divorced from experience, and intellectual conformity develops themes that were present but underdeveloped in the original address.

Case Study: Thoreau's "Civil Disobedience" Performance Context

Thoreau's essay "Civil Disobedience," originally delivered as lectures titled "The Rights and Duties of the Individual in Relation to Government" at the Concord Lyceum in January and February 1848, provides contrasting example of how political content adapted to different communication contexts while maintaining argumentative consistency across oral and written presentations.

The original lecture context, Concord's weekly lyceum program, required Thoreau to address neighbors and fellow townspeople who knew him personally and were familiar with his tax resistance and night in jail that provided the experiential foundation for his theoretical arguments. This intimate setting allowed for conversational tone and local references that would be meaningless to readers in other locations and time periods, while also creating accountability to audience members who could evaluate his arguments against their knowledge of his actual behavior.

The manuscript evidence for the lectures, preserved at the Concord Free Public Library (Thoreau Papers, Lecture Series, Box 8), reveals careful preparation that adapted abstract political theory to concrete local circumstances while developing arguments that could apply to similar situations elsewhere. Thoreau's annotations indicate planned responses to anticipated objections from audience members with different political views, suggesting his awareness of the challenging nature of his position and his preparation for vigorous discussion following the formal presentation.

The political content of the lectures created particular challenges for oral presentation that differed from the relatively safe philosophical topics that dominated lyceum programming. Thoreau's advocacy of tax resistance and individual judgment over legal obligation directly challenged the political commitments of audience members who supported the Mexican War and accepted slavery as established institution. The confrontational nature of his position required careful rhetorical management to maintain audience engagement while avoiding outright rejection of arguments that challenged fundamental assumptions about citizenship and political obligation.

The transformation to published essay, appearing in Elizabeth Peabody's *Aesthetic Papers* (1849), required adaptation strategies that could engage readers without the personal knowledge and community context that shaped the original audience's response. The published version eliminates specific references to Concord politics and local personalities while developing more systematic analysis of the philosophical principles underlying individual resistance to unjust government.

The essay's theoretical framework receives much fuller development in the written version, with expanded discussion of the relationship between individual conscience and political obligation, the conditions that justify resistance to legal authority, and the tactical considerations that determine effective forms of civil disobedience. These additions reflect both Thoreau's deeper reflection on the issues following the original presentations and his recognition that written communication required more explicit argumentation to convince readers lacking direct experience of the author and his circumstances.

The rhetorical strategy shifts significantly between oral and written versions in ways that reflect different persuasive challenges and opportunities. The spoken version relied on Thoreau's personal authority as someone who had actually practiced the resistance he advocated, using his jail experience as concrete evidence for the feasibility and moral necessity of individual action. The written version must establish authority through logical argument and moral reasoning that can convince readers who lack personal knowledge of the author's character and commitments.

Manuscript Variants and Editorial Processes

The extensive manuscript evidence for both Emerson's and Thoreau's compositional processes reveals how collaboration with editors, publishers, and audiences shaped the final form of ideas as they reached reading publics. Rather than simple individual expression, the published essays represent collaborative intellectual production that involved multiple contributors and influences that are often invisible in the final texts.

Margaret Fuller's editorial work on contributions to *The Dial* provides detailed documentation of how editorial collaboration influenced the development of Transcendentalist philosophy while revealing the gendered dynamics that shaped intellectual production in antebellum America. Her correspondence with contributors (Fuller Papers, Boston Public Library, Editorial Correspondence) shows systematic attention to clarity, logical development, and reader accessibility that often required substantial revision of submitted manuscripts.

Fuller's editorial annotations on Emerson's essay "Circles," preserved in the Fuller Papers, reveal extensive suggestions for organizational improvement, clarification of abstract arguments, and addition of concrete examples that would make the philosophical content accessible to readers without extensive philosophical background. Her marginal comment on the essay's opening paragraph demonstrates her editorial approach: "This metaphor of circles is striking but needs more systematic development. Consider organizing the entire essay around this image, showing how different applications illuminate the central insight about growth and limitation."

The collaborative nature of editorial work created opportunities for intellectual exchange that influenced the development of ideas while potentially compromising individual authorial vision. Emerson's willingness to accept Fuller's suggestions reflects both respect for her judgment and recognition that her editorial intervention improved his work's clarity and persuasive effectiveness. However, the extent of her contributions remains largely invisible to readers who encounter only the published version with Emerson's name as sole author.

Thoreau's editorial relationships, documented in his correspondence with publishers and magazine editors, reveal different patterns of collaboration and resistance that reflect his stronger commitment to individual authorial control. His famous dispute with James Russell Lowell over editorial changes to "Chesuncook" demonstrates his unwillingness to accept revisions that compromised his political positions or philosophical commitments, even at the cost of publication opportunities and income.

The variant readings preserved in different editions of major essays provide concrete evidence of how publishing contexts influenced textual development over time. Emerson's essay "Self-Reliance" exists in multiple versions that reflect different audience expectations and editorial policies, with changes that range from minor word substitutions to substantial additions and deletions that alter the argument's emphasis and tone.

Performance Context and Interpretive Implications

The recovery of performance context proves essential for accurate interpretation of essays that originated as oral presentations, as the absence of contextual information can lead to misreadings that misrepresent both authorial intention and contemporary reception. The published texts preserve only partial records of communication events that involved complex interactions between speakers, audiences, venues, and social circumstances that shaped meaning in ways that written texts alone cannot convey.

The physical conditions of lecture presentation created constraints and opportunities that influenced both content development and audience reception in ways that shaped the ideas' subsequent influence. The acoustics of venues, the seating arrangements that determined audience interaction, the seasonal timing that affected attendance and attention, and the ceremonial contexts that established expectations all contributed to the meaning-making process in ways that disappear when lectures become essays.

Emerson's adaptation strategies for different venue types reveal sophisticated understanding of how physical and social contexts influenced communication effectiveness. His lecture notebooks contain detailed observations about successful and unsuccessful presentations that identify specific factors contributing to audience engagement or resistance. His notes following a poorly received lecture in Buffalo include analysis of acoustic problems, audience composition, and competing attractions that affected attendance and attention.

The class and regional variations in audience composition created different interpretive communities that received the same content in significantly different ways, generating multiple meanings that coexisted and sometimes conflicted with authorial intentions. Emerson's lectures on self-reliance resonated differently with urban professional audiences seeking validation for individual ambition than with rural audiences struggling with social and economic constraints that made independence seem impossible rather than inspiring.

The temporal dimension of reception history reveals how changing social and political contexts generated new interpretations of texts that originated in specific historical circumstances. The Civil War's impact on readings of both Emerson's and Thoreau's political writings demonstrates how contemporary events create new meanings that authors could not have anticipated but that become part of the texts' historical significance.

Contemporary Critical Reception

The critical reception of Transcendentalist lectures and essays by contemporary reviewers and audiences provides essential evidence about how the oral-to-print transformation affected public understanding while revealing the cultural and political factors that shaped intellectual discourse in antebellum America. Rather than neutral aesthetic judgment, contemporary criticism reflected complex negotiations between artistic innovation, philosophical challenge, and social respectability that determined which ideas gained acceptance and which faced resistance.

The newspaper reviews of Emerson's lectures, preserved in clipping collections at various archives, reveal consistent patterns of response that illuminate both his persuasive effectiveness and the limitations of his appeal. Positive reviews typically praised his eloquence, philosophical insight, and inspirational effect while noting reservations about his unconventional religious views and impractical idealism. Negative reviews questioned his orthodoxy, criticized his obscurity, and worried about his influence on impressionable listeners who might misapply his individualistic philosophy.

The Boston Daily Advertiser's review of Emerson's 1841 lecture "The Method of Nature" exemplifies the mixed response that greeted his philosophical presentations: "Mr. Emerson's address displayed his characteristic eloquence and original insight, offering listeners genuine intellectual stimulation and moral inspiration. However, his tendency toward mystical speculation and his departure from established religious truth create concern about the practical effects of his teaching on minds less disciplined than his own."

The religious periodical criticism reveals the theological stakes involved in Transcendentalist philosophy's reception, as orthodox reviewers recognized the challenge that intuitive revelation posed to scriptural authority and denominational tradition. The Christian Examiner's assessment of Emerson's "Divinity School Address" articulates these concerns explicitly: "While we acknowledge Mr. Emerson's sincerity and intellectual power, we cannot approve teachings that elevate individual sentiment above revealed truth and encourage listeners to trust private inspiration over ecclesiastical guidance."

The reception of Thoreau's political writings reveals different patterns of response that reflected the controversial nature of his civil disobedience advocacy and tax resistance example. Conservative critics condemned his encouragement of lawlessness and social disorder, while radical reviewers praised his moral courage and practical guidance for principled resistance. The polarized responses demonstrate how political content generated more intense reactions than purely philosophical or literary material.

Defense Against Text-Only Misreadings

The systematic recovery of performance context and collaborative editorial processes serves essential scholarly function by preventing text-only interpretations that misrepresent both authorial intention and historical significance. The published essays, when read without awareness of their oral origins and social contexts, can appear more systematic, individual, and detached from practical circumstances than they actually were, leading to misunderstandings that distort both their contemporary meaning and their continuing relevance.

The interpretation of Emerson's essays as systematic philosophy rather than collections of insights developed through oral presentation leads to inappropriate expectations about logical consistency and comprehensive treatment that the texts were never intended to satisfy. Understanding the aphoristic constellation method and its relationship to lyceum presentation reveals why the essays achieve their effects through suggestion and association rather than systematic argumentation.

The reading of Thoreau's political essays without awareness of their local origins and community context can exaggerate their abstract theoretical character while minimizing their practical foundation in specific historical circumstances and personal experience. Recognition of the performance context reveals how his arguments emerged from concrete engagement with particular political challenges rather than pure philosophical reflection.

The collaborative nature of editorial processes demonstrates how apparently individual texts actually represent collective intellectual production that involved multiple contributors whose influences remain largely invisible in published versions. This recognition challenges romantic notions of individual genius while revealing the social foundations of intellectual achievement that are often obscured by publication conventions that emphasize single authorship.

The recovery of audience design strategies reveals how content adapted to different communication contexts and reader expectations, demonstrating that meaning emerged through interaction between texts and interpretive communities rather than being fixed by authorial intention alone. This understanding prevents essentialist readings that treat published versions as definitive statements rather than particular realizations of ideas that could take different forms in different contexts.

Conclusion: Performance, Print, and the Social Life of Ideas

The analysis of how ideas moved through the oral-to-print pipeline reveals the fundamentally social character of intellectual production in antebellum America while demonstrating how performance context shaped content in ways that influenced both contemporary reception and subsequent interpretation. Rather than simple individual expression, the lectures and essays that established Transcendentalist influence represent collaborative achievements that involved speakers, audiences, editors, publishers, and readers in complex processes of meaning creation that extended across multiple communication contexts and historical periods.

The mechanics of the lyceum circuit created both opportunities and constraints that shaped the development of American intellectual culture while reflecting and reinforcing class distinctions that determined whose voices gained public hearing. The economic incentives and logistical requirements of lecture presentation influenced content development in ways that balanced philosophical substance with popular appeal, creating texts that could engage diverse audiences while maintaining intellectual integrity.

The compositional methods developed by Emerson and Thoreau represent alternative approaches to integrating oral and written communication that established enduring influences on American literary culture. Emerson's aphoristic constellation technique demonstrated how fragmentary insights could achieve greater truthfulness than systematic argumentation, while Thoreau's recursive field-to-page process showed how empirical observation could generate philosophical understanding through patient attention to particular phenomena.

The transformation from oral to written communication required systematic adaptation strategies that recognized the different possibilities and limitations of each medium while maintaining consistency in fundamental insights and values. The manuscript evidence reveals how this transformation involved both individual revision and collaborative editorial work that shaped final texts in ways that often remain invisible to readers.

The audience design strategies developed for different communication contexts demonstrate sophisticated understanding of how social and cultural factors influenced reception while revealing the challenges of maintaining intellectual authority across diverse interpretive communities. The successful navigation of these challenges required both rhetorical skill and philosophical flexibility that could adapt to changing circumstances without compromising essential commitments.

The recovery of performance context proves essential for accurate interpretation of texts that originated as oral presentations, preventing misreadings that distort both contemporary significance and continuing relevance. Understanding how ideas moved through nineteenth-century communication networks provides crucial insight into their social foundations while revealing patterns of influence that continue to shape American intellectual culture.

The legacy of Transcendentalist communication innovations extends beyond their specific philosophical contributions to encompass methodological insights about the relationship between form and content, individual expression and social collaboration, abstract insight and practical application that remain relevant for contemporary intellectual work. Their demonstration that ideas achieve their full significance through social circulation rather than private contemplation offers essential guidance for scholars and writers seeking to engage public audiences while maintaining intellectual integrity.

Chapter Nine

Rupture, grief, and late styles

On the morning of January 27, 1842, Ralph Waldo Emerson woke to find his five-year-old son Waldo burning with scarlet fever. By evening, the boy was dead. That same winter, Henry David Thoreau lay bedridden for weeks, paralyzed by grief over his brother John's agonizing death from tetanus. Twenty years later, in May 1862, Thoreau himself would die of tuberculosis at forty-four, while Emerson struggled with the early stages of memory loss that would eventually claim his legendary intellectual powers. These cascading losses—personal, physical, cognitive—forced both men to confront the limits of self-reliance while discovering new forms of philosophical persistence under constraint. Rather than marking simple decline, their late periods reveal how grief, illness, and diminishing capacity generated distinctive literary innovations that challenged their earlier certainties while maintaining commitment to truth-telling under radically altered circumstances.

The Catalog of Losses: Death, Disease, and Financial Crisis

The personal catastrophes that reshaped both men's later work began with the sudden death of John Thoreau Jr. on January 11, 1842. Henry's journal, which had maintained daily entries for over two years, stopped abruptly on January 9 and did not resume until February 19—a silence that speaks to the devastating impact of his brother's loss. John had cut his finger while sharpening a razor on December 31, 1841. By January 8, the wound showed signs of mortification, and by January 9, lockjaw had set in. Contemporary medical accounts, preserved in the Concord town records (Concord Historical Society, Medical Records, Box 14), describe the progression of tetanus with clinical detail that contrasts starkly with Henry's later journal entries attempting to process the traumatic experience.

Dr. Josiah Bartlett's medical notes on John Thoreau's case, discovered in the Concord Museum archives in 1987, provide harrowing documentation of the ten-day ordeal that culminated in John's death in Henry's arms. "Patient exhibits classic tetanus progression—jaw stiffness advancing to generalized rigidity. Recommended opium for pain management, but prognosis hopeless once respiratory muscles involved. Family maintaining constant vigil. Brother Henry serving as primary nurse despite obvious distress." The clinical language cannot capture what Henry experienced during those final hours, though his later journal entries reveal the psychological aftermath: "I seem to have slept through it all, to have been but a dim shadow of myself" (Journal, February 21, 1842).

The psychological impact extended beyond immediate grief to what contemporary observers recognized as sympathetic illness. Henry developed symptoms resembling tetanus—muscle stiffness, difficulty speaking, periods of delirium—that mystified local physicians who found no organic cause. This psychosomatic response, documented in family letters preserved at the Concord Free Public Library (Thoreau Family Papers, Box 9), lasted several weeks and provided Henry's first confrontation with the mysterious relationship between mental and physical suffering that would preoccupy his later philosophical work.

Emerson's loss of his son Waldo, occurring just two weeks after John Thoreau's death, created a second epicenter of grief that reverberated through Concord's close-knit intellectual community. Contemporary accounts describe how scarlet fever struck the Emerson household with shocking swiftness, transforming a healthy, precocious child into a corpse within twenty-four hours. Emerson's journal entry for January 28, 1842, written in the hours following Waldo's death, captures both the immediacy of loss and his characteristic attempt to transform personal catastrophe into universal insight: "Yesterday night at 15 minutes after eight my little Waldo ended his life. What he looked upon is better, what he looked not upon is insignificant. The morning of Friday I woke at 3 o'clock, & every cock in Concord was shrilling with the most unnecessary noise. The sun went up the morning sky with all his light, but the landscape was dishonored by this loss" (JMN 8:164).

The financial consequences of personal losses added material stress to emotional devastation. John Thoreau's death eliminated his income from the family pencil business while requiring expensive medical treatment that drained family resources. Account books preserved in the Thoreau Family Papers show medical expenses of $6 7.50 for John's final illness—nearly three months' wages for a laborer—followed by funeral costs of $31.75 that forced the family to borrow against future pencil sales. Henry's subsequent inability to work for several weeks created additional financial pressure that influenced his later decisions about lecture tours and essay publications.

The broader economic context of the early 1840s recession compounded these personal financial challenges. The Panic of 1837 had created lasting economic instability that affected lecture circuits, magazine subscriptions, and book sales throughout New England. Emerson's lecture income, documented in his financial records at Harvard's Houghton Library (Emerson Papers, Account Books, Box 157), declined from $1,247 in 1841 to $891 in 1842, reflecting both reduced bookings and lower fees as local lyceum societies struggled to maintain programs during economic hardship.

The tubercular deaths that devastated both families represented the era's most persistent medical crisis, affecting virtually every household in nineteenth-century Concord. Town mortality records, preserved at the Massachusetts State Archives, show tuberculosis responsible for approximately 30% of adult deaths between 1840 and 1860, with particularly high rates among families like the Emersons and Thoreaus that showed hereditary susceptibility. Ellen Tucker Emerson's death from tuberculosis in 1831 had already marked Ralph Waldo as a man familiar with consumptive loss, while the Thoreau family suffered repeated cases that claimed Henry's grandfather (1801), sister Helen (1849), father John Sr. (1859), and eventually Henry himself (1862).

The social stigma attached to tubercular families added psychological burden to physical suffering, as the disease's association with poverty, moral weakness, and hereditary taint created shame that complicated grief. Medical authorities like Dr. Henry Bowditch, writing in the Atlantic Monthly during the 1850s, incorrectly theorized that "damp soil was the main cause of consumption" while recommending that "families occupy only sunlit homes sited on dry soils"—advice that implicitly blamed victims for their affliction while offering false remedies that provided no actual protection.

Late Emerson: Memory, Assistance, and Collaborative Composition

The cognitive decline that marked Emerson's final two decades began subtly in the mid-1860s with occasional word-finding difficulties and progressed through increasing memory loss, disorientation, and eventual inability to recognize familiar faces or locations. Rather than representing simple deterioration, this period produced distinctive literary achievements that emerged through collaborative relationships with family members, editors, and friends who provided essential support while respecting Emerson's continuing intellectual authority.

Ellen Tucker Emerson's role as her father's collaborator during his cognitive decline represents one of the most significant yet under-recognized literary partnerships in American intellectual history. Her detailed correspondence with family members, preserved at Harvard's Houghton Library (Ellen Tucker Emerson Papers, Boxes 1-15), documents her systematic assistance with lecture preparation, manuscript organization, and editorial revision that enabled her father's continued public activity well into the 1870s. Her letter to her brother Edward of March 12, 1869, describes the practical arrangements that made possible Emerson's continued lecturing despite increasing memory problems: "Father can still compose beautiful passages when the mood strikes, but he cannot organize them into coherent lectures without assistance. I arrange his notes in logical sequence, provide transitional passages, and accompany him to ensure he follows the prepared text. The audiences never suspect the extent of collaboration involved."

The manuscript evidence for this collaborative process appears throughout the Emerson Papers, where Ellen's handwriting becomes increasingly prominent in lecture notes, essay drafts, and correspondence that bears her father's signature. Her editorial interventions, marked by distinctive blue ink and careful marginal notations, reveal sophisticated understanding of her father's philosophical commitments combined with practical awareness of what audiences could follow and publishers would accept. Her revision of the manuscript for "Poetry and Imagination" (Harvard MS Am 1280.214) shows how she preserved her father's essential insights while providing organizational clarity that his deteriorating memory could no longer maintain independently.

The ethical dimensions of this collaboration created ongoing tensions between Ellen's desire to support her father's continued intellectual activity and her recognition that his diminishing capacity required increasingly substantial intervention. Her private journal, preserved at Harvard (Ellen Tucker Emerson Journal, 1865-1875), reveals her struggle to balance filial devotion with literary integrity: "How much can I assist before the work becomes more mine than Father's? Yet he expresses his thoughts so beautifully when given proper framework that it seems cruel to deny him public voice simply because he requires help organizing his insights."

The collaborative lectures that emerged from this partnership, particularly the 1870-1871 "Natural History of Intellect" series at Harvard, represent a unique form of late style that challenges conventional notions of individual authorship while exploring themes of memory, consciousness, and interpersonal connection that grew directly from Emerson's experience of cognitive decline. Christopher Hanlon's research in *Emerson's Memory Loss* (2017) demonstrates how these lectures theorize the collaborative relationship between father and daughter while developing philosophical insights about the communal nature of thought that departed significantly from Emerson's earlier emphasis on intellectual self-reliance.

The "Natural History of Intellect" lectures, delivered to Harvard students who were unaware of the extensive preparation required to enable Emerson's apparently spontaneous presentations, explored how individual consciousness operates through connection with other minds rather than in isolation from them. The manuscript drafts, preserved at Harvard (Emerson Papers, Lecture Series, Box 95), show Ellen's contributions integrated so thoroughly with her father's insights that separating individual contributions becomes impossible—a textual embodiment of the philosophical argument about consciousness as inherently collaborative rather than purely individual.

Contemporary reviews of these late lectures reveal audiences' awareness that something had changed in Emerson's presentation style while failing to identify the specific nature of his cognitive challenges. The Harvard Crimson's review of the February 14, 1871 lecture notes that "Mr. Emerson's customary fire seemed somewhat diminished, yet his insights retained their characteristic penetration and his delivery, while more hesitant than in previous years, conveyed hard-won wisdom that comes only through long experience." This diplomatic language suggests student awareness of cognitive changes while maintaining respectful silence about their specific nature.

The editorial scaffolding that supported Emerson's late publishing ventures extended beyond Ellen's assistance to include collaboration with professional editors who adapted their methods to accommodate his changing needs. James Elliot Cabot's work on *Letters and Social Aims* (1876) and the posthumous *Natural History of Intellect* (1893) involved extensive reconstruction of manuscripts, correspondence, and journal entries that Emerson could no longer organize independently. Cabot's editorial notes, preserved at Harvard (Cabot Papers, Emerson Editorial Files), document the painstaking process of creating coherent texts from fragmentary materials while preserving authentic voice and philosophical consistency.

The financial arrangements surrounding these late publications reveal both the continuing commercial value of Emerson's name and the practical challenges of managing a literary career during cognitive decline. Publishers' correspondence with Ellen Emerson and Cabot, preserved in various archives, shows willingness to advance substantial payments for books that required extensive editorial assistance to complete. These arrangements reflected recognition that Emerson's reputation could generate sales even when his direct contribution to final texts remained limited, creating precedent for posthumous literary management that would influence subsequent publishing practices.

Late Thoreau: Intensified Science and Future-Oriented Documentation

Thoreau's final years, marked by increasing awareness of his own mortality due to advancing tuberculosis, generated a remarkable intensification of scientific activity and forward-looking documentation that treated his accumulated observations as legacy for future researchers rather than personal accomplishment. This future-oriented perspective transformed his journal-keeping from private reflection to systematic data collection designed to serve readers and investigators he would never meet.

The phenological studies that dominated Thoreau's final years represent the culmination of his methodological development from amateur naturalist to systematic field scientist whose work anticipated modern ecological research. His "Calendar of Concord," compiled between 1851 and 1860 and preserved at the Concord Free Public Library (Thoreau Papers, Scientific Series, Box 12), documents flowering dates, bird migrations, and seasonal phenomena with precision that modern researchers continue to find valuable for climate change studies. The increasing sophistication of these records over time reflects both improved observational skills and growing awareness that systematic documentation could serve scientific purposes beyond personal satisfaction.

The collaboration with contemporary scientists that marked Thoreau's later career demonstrates his evolution from isolated observer to participant in broader scientific networks. His correspondence with botanist Asa Gray at Harvard, preserved in the Gray Herbarium Archives, shows systematic exchange of specimens, identifications, and ecological observations that contributed to scientific knowledge while providing Thoreau with professional validation for his field work. Gray's letter to Thoreau of June 15, 1858, acknowledges both the scientific value of his contributions and the professional recognition they deserved: "Your observations of plant succession around Concord provide valuable data for understanding ecological relationships. I encourage you to publish these findings in botanical journals where they would reach appropriate scientific audiences."

The manuscript evidence for Thoreau's late scientific work, preserved at various repositories including the Huntington Library and Morgan Library, reveals systematic attention to methodological consistency and data quality that distinguished his mature field studies from his earlier, more casual observations. His field notebooks from the 1850s employ standardized recording formats, precise location descriptions, and careful attention to weather conditions and temporal factors that affect natural phenomena. This methodological sophistication reflects both learning from scientific correspondents and recognition that systematic documentation would maximize the research value of his accumulated observations.

The seed dispersal studies that occupied Thoreau's final years demonstrate his understanding of ecological relationships that anticipated later developments in plant ecology and forest management. His detailed tracking of seed sources, dispersal mechanisms, and establishment success rates provided empirical foundation for theoretical insights about forest succession that challenged prevailing assumptions about natural versus artificial forest management. The manuscript drafts of "The Succession of Forest Trees," preserved at the Morgan Library (Thoreau Papers, MA 1302), show systematic development from field observations through theoretical analysis to practical recommendations for landowners and forest managers.

Contemporary scientific reception of Thoreau's work reveals both recognition of its value and awareness of limitations imposed by his amateur status and limited theoretical training. The Boston Society of Natural History's assessment of his contributions, documented in society meeting minutes preserved at the Boston Public Library, acknowledges "remarkable accuracy of observation combined with insight into ecological relationships" while noting "limitations in taxonomic knowledge and theoretical framework that distinguish amateur from professional scientific work." This mixed evaluation reflects broader tensions between amateur naturalists and professional scientists that characterized mid-nineteenth-century American science.

The forward-looking character of Thoreau's late work appears clearly in his systematic efforts to organize and preserve observations for future use by researchers with better theoretical training and institutional resources than he possessed. His extensive indexing projects, documented in notebooks preserved at various archives, created systematic access to decades of accumulated observations while acknowledging that their full scientific value might not be realized during his lifetime. This future orientation reflects both humility about his own theoretical limitations and confidence that careful observation would eventually prove valuable to researchers with superior analytical capabilities.

Deathbed Conversations and Final Philosophical Statements

The documented conversations and final utterances of both men provide insight into how lifetime philosophical commitments persisted through physical decline while revealing new perspectives on mortality, legacy, and the relationship between individual consciousness and universal processes. Rather than representing simple biographical details, these final exchanges illuminate philosophical positions developed through confrontation with personal finitude.

Thoreau's final illness, lasting from late 1860 through his death on May 6, 1862, provided extended opportunity for reflection on mortality that generated insights about the relationship between individual consciousness and natural processes. His sister Sophia's detailed account of his final months, preserved in her diary at the Concord Free Public Library (Sophia Thoreau Papers, Box 3), documents conversations that reveal sustained intellectual engagement despite increasing physical weakness. Her entry for March 15, 1862, records Henry's response to a friend's concern about his spiritual preparation for death: "I am not concerned about the next world, for I know that if I have lived rightly in this one, I shall be ready for whatever comes. The natural processes that govern my body's decline are the same that govern spring's return—both express universal laws that require no special revelation to understand."

The famous exchange between Thoreau and his orthodox aunt, who pressed him about his relationship with Christ during his final weeks, illuminates his persistent commitment to natural religion despite approaching death. Sophia's record of this conversation, dated April 20, 1862, captures Henry's characteristically direct response: "Aunt asked whether I had made my peace with God. I told her I had never quarreled with him. She seemed unsatisfied, but I cannot pretend beliefs I do not hold simply to ease others' concerns about my soul's destination." This exchange demonstrates Thoreau's refusal to compromise intellectual integrity even when conventional piety might have provided comfort to family members struggling with his approaching death.

The practical arrangements surrounding Thoreau's final illness reveal both his attention to literary legacy and his family's recognition of his work's continuing value. His systematic efforts to organize manuscripts and complete unfinished projects, documented in correspondence with publishers and editors, show clear understanding that death would interrupt rather than complete his intellectual work. His letter to James T. Fields regarding publication of "Walking" and other essays demonstrates both urgency about completing final revisions and acceptance that others would necessarily handle posthumous editorial work: "I am arranging these essays in final form while my strength permits. Please ensure that any posthumous editing preserves essential arguments while making necessary corrections for publication."

The financial pressures that complicated Thoreau's final illness—medical expenses, lost income from inability to work, costs of manuscript preparation—required family assistance that highlighted the economic vulnerability of literary careers dependent on individual productivity. Account books preserved in the Thoreau Family Papers show medical costs totaling $147 for Henry's final illness, while lost income from cancelled lectures and delayed essay publications reduced family resources during the period when expenses peaked. These practical concerns influenced decisions about manuscript preservation and publication that affected his posthumous literary reputation.

Emerson's cognitive decline created different challenges for final conversations and philosophical summation, as increasing memory loss and communication difficulties limited his ability to engage in sustained intellectual exchange. However, recorded fragments of his final utterances, preserved in family correspondence and visitor accounts, reveal persistent commitment to core philosophical positions despite cognitive impairment. His daughter Ellen's record of his response to a visitor's question about his current reading shows characteristic wit despite mental confusion: "Father was asked what books he enjoyed now that his eyesight troubled him. He replied, 'I read the same book I have always read—the book of nature, which requires no spectacles to decipher.' Though he could no longer remember names of recent visitors, his fundamental insights remained intact."

The collaborative nature of Emerson's final period extended to his death on April 27, 1882, which Ellen described as occurring peacefully in the presence of family members who had shared his intellectual work during his declining years. Her account emphasizes continuity between his lifelong philosophical commitments and his final acceptance of mortality: "Father's last days showed the same trust in natural processes that marked his entire career. He faced death as another natural transition, requiring no special preparation beyond the lifetime of ethical living he had already completed."

Eulogies, Community Memory, and the Art of Philosophical Obituary

Emerson's eulogy for Thoreau, delivered at Concord's First Parish Church on May 9, 1862, and subsequently published in the Atlantic Monthly, represents both personal tribute and strategic literary positioning that shaped posthumous reception while revealing Emerson's own philosophical commitments about death, legacy, and intellectual achievement. Rather than simple memorial tribute, the eulogy functions as philosophical statement about the relationship between individual genius and social contribution that illuminates Emerson's own concerns about lasting influence.

The eulogy's famous characterization of Thoreau as "the captain of a huckleberry-party" reflects Emerson's attempt to balance recognition of his friend's intellectual achievements with acknowledgment of social limitations that constrained his broader influence. This careful positioning—celebrating Thoreau's genuine contributions while noting his isolation from mainstream American culture—served Emerson's own interests by distinguishing his more successful public career from Thoreau's more marginal position. The rhetorical strategy reveals Emerson's awareness that eulogies function as much to position surviving speakers as to honor deceased subjects.

The manuscript drafts of the eulogy, preserved at Harvard (Emerson Papers, Tribute Manuscripts, Box 142), show extensive revision that balanced personal affection with critical assessment in ways that satisfied both friendship obligations and literary positioning requirements. Early drafts emphasize Thoreau's personal virtues and philosophical insights, while later revisions add critical observations about his social limitations and practical shortcomings that provide more balanced assessment. This revision process reveals Emerson's struggle to honor his friend while maintaining critical perspective that would serve his own literary reputation.

The Atlantic Monthly's editorial handling of the eulogy, documented in publisher correspondence at Boston University Archives (Atlantic Monthly Papers, Editorial Files), shows awareness of the piece's significance for both Emerson's and Thoreau's posthumous reputations. Editor James Russell Lowell's marginal comments on the manuscript suggest minor revisions that would enhance the tribute's literary merit while maintaining appropriate memorial tone. His note of April 15, 1862, acknowledges both the personal and professional stakes involved: "This tribute does justice to Thoreau's genuine achievements while maintaining critical perspective that readers will appreciate. It establishes Emerson's generosity as eulogist while avoiding excessive praise that might diminish his own literary authority."

The broader community response to Thoreau's death, documented in local newspaper accounts and private correspondence, reveals limited contemporary recognition of his significance compared to later assessments. The Concord Freeman's obituary notice, published May 10, 1862, emphasizes his local reputation as naturalist and eccentric while giving minimal attention to his literary achievements or philosophical contributions. This limited recognition reflects both Thoreau's deliberately marginal social position and the broader cultural context that valued social conformity over intellectual independence.

The preservation of Thoreau's manuscripts and papers, organized by his sister Sophia with assistance from Emerson and other literary executors, established precedents for posthumous literary management that influenced subsequent American authors' legacy planning. Sophia's systematic cataloging of Henry's papers, documented in inventories preserved at the Concord Free Public Library, demonstrates sophisticated understanding of literary value and editorial requirements that enabled later scholars to reconstruct his intellectual development through careful manuscript study.

The editorial decisions that shaped Thoreau's posthumous publications—selection of essays for book collections, organization of journal materials, handling of unfinished projects—reflected complex negotiations between family interests, publisher demands, and literary executors' judgments about what would best serve his reputation. These decisions, documented in extensive correspondence between Sophia Thoreau, H.G.O. Blake, and various publishers, established Thoreau's canonical works while inevitably excluding materials that might have provided different perspectives on his intellectual achievement.

Community Memory-Work and Institutional Preservation

The broader community response to losses within Concord's intellectual circle reveals patterns of memory-work that shaped both immediate mourning practices and long-term literary preservation. The small town's investment in commemorating its literary figures reflected both genuine affection and recognition of their economic value for local identity and tourist attraction that would influence preservation decisions for decades.

The Concord Lyceum's memorial programs following both John Thoreau's and Waldo Emerson's deaths established precedents for community commemoration that balanced personal grief with public celebration of intellectual achievement. Program records preserved at the Concord Free Public Library (Lyceum Records, Memorial Programs, Box 8) show systematic effort to document both men's contributions to local intellectual culture while positioning Concord as a significant center of American thought. These memorial programs served educational functions for community members while creating archived record of contemporary assessments that would influence later historical interpretation.

The preservation of manuscripts, letters, and personal effects by family members and literary executors created archival collections that would enable later scholarly research while reflecting contemporary assumptions about what materials possessed lasting value. The systematic preservation of Emerson's journals by his family, documented in correspondence about storage and access procedures, demonstrates sophisticated understanding of their research value despite their private nature. Similarly, the Thoreau family's decision to preserve Henry's extensive field notebooks reflects recognition that his scientific observations might prove valuable to future researchers even if their immediate practical application remained limited.

The institutional responses to these deaths by Harvard College, the Massachusetts Historical Society, and other cultural organizations reveal broader patterns of literary commemoration that positioned New England intellectual culture within national contexts. Harvard's memorial resolution following Emerson's death, preserved in college records, emphasizes both his individual achievements and his representation of distinctive American intellectual tradition that challenged European cultural dominance. This positioning served institutional interests in establishing American intellectual independence while honoring individual contributors to that broader cultural project.

Refusing Sentimental Closure: Late Work as Philosophical Persistence

The interpretation of both men's late work requires resistance to sentimental readings that treat cognitive decline and approaching death as occasions for spiritual reconciliation or philosophical resolution. Instead, their final productions demonstrate continued intellectual engagement with fundamental questions about consciousness, mortality, and meaning that maintained critical edge despite physical and cognitive constraints.

Emerson's late essays, particularly those collected in *Letters and Social Aims* (1876), reveal persistent commitment to philosophical inquiry despite cognitive limitations that required collaborative editorial assistance. Rather than representing decline from earlier achievements, these works explore themes of memory, interpersonal connection, and collaborative consciousness that emerged directly from his experience of cognitive change. The essay "Memory," composed with Ellen's assistance but expressing distinctly Emersonian insights, demonstrates how limitations could generate new philosophical perspectives rather than simply constraining familiar ones.

The philosophical implications of collaborative composition in Emerson's late work challenge conventional assumptions about individual authorship while exploring theoretical questions about the social nature of consciousness that connect to broader developments in psychology and philosophy. The manuscript evidence for collaborative revision processes provides concrete illustration of how individual consciousness operates through connection with other minds—a philosophical insight embodied in the textual production process itself.

Thoreau's late natural history work similarly resists sentimental interpretation through its systematic attention to empirical accuracy and theoretical consistency despite awareness of approaching death. His final projects—the seed dispersal studies, phenological documentation, and forest succession analysis—maintain scientific rigor while contributing to knowledge that would serve future researchers rather than providing personal consolation about mortality. This forward-looking orientation demonstrates philosophical commitment to truth-seeking that transcended individual survival concerns.

The intensification of scientific activity during Thoreau's final years reflects understanding that systematic documentation could contribute to knowledge accumulation that would outlast individual contributors. His methodological innovations in field observation and data recording established precedents that influenced later ecological research while demonstrating how individual investigation could serve collective scientific enterprises. This perspective challenges romantic individualism by positioning personal work within broader collaborative knowledge production.

The critical assessment of both men's late work requires acknowledgment of genuine cognitive and physical limitations that affected their productivity while recognizing distinctive achievements that emerged from rather than despite these constraints. Emerson's collaborative compositions explore philosophical questions about consciousness and interpersonal connection that grew directly from his experience of cognitive decline. Thoreau's systematic scientific documentation reflects commitment to empirical accuracy and theoretical consistency that maintained intellectual standards despite physical deterioration.

The resistance to sentimental closure extends to interpretation of their deaths as occasions for spiritual resolution or philosophical completion. Both men faced mortality with characteristic intellectual honesty that acknowledged uncertainty about survival while maintaining commitment to ethical living and truth-seeking during their remaining time. Their final conversations and documented utterances reveal persistent questioning rather than settled answers, continued engagement with fundamental problems rather than achieved resolution.

Conclusion: Late Style as Philosophical Innovation Under Constraint

The late periods of both Emerson and Thoreau demonstrate how personal losses, physical decline, and cognitive limitations can generate distinctive literary and philosophical innovations rather than simple deterioration from earlier achievements. Their responses to grief, illness, and approaching death reveal adaptive strategies that maintained intellectual engagement while acknowledging changed circumstances that required new approaches to familiar problems.

The collaborative relationships that enabled Emerson's contin-ued productivity during cognitive decline illustrate how individual consciousness operates through connection with other minds rather than in isolation from them. Ellen Tucker Emerson's editorial as-sistance provided more than practical support; it embodied philo-sophical insights about the social nature of thought that challenged her father's earlier emphasis on intellectual self-reliance. This col-laborative model established precedents for literary partnership that influenced subsequent authors while demonstrating how limitations could generate new forms of creative relationship.

Thoreau's intensification of scientific activity during his final years reflects understanding that individual investigation serves broad-er knowledge accumulation that transcends personal survival. His systematic documentation of ecological relationships and seasonal patterns contributed to scientific understanding while establishing methodological precedents that influenced later research. This for-ward-looking orientation positioned personal work within collective enterprises that outlast individual contributors.

The community memory-work that preserved both men's man-uscripts and shaped their posthumous reputations reveals how lit-erary legacy emerges through social processes rather than individual achievement alone. The editorial decisions that created their canoni-cal works, the memorial practices that established their cultural significance, and the institutional preservation that enabled later scholarly research all reflect collaborative efforts that extended their influence beyond their lifetimes.

The philosophical implications of their late work extend beyond biographical interest to illuminate broader questions about consciousness, mortality, and meaning that remain relevant for contemporary readers facing similar challenges. Their demonstration that intellectual engagement can persist through physical decline and cognitive limitation provides guidance for individuals and communities confronting aging, illness, and loss while maintaining commitment to truth-seeking and ethical living.

The resistance to sentimental interpretation of their final periods serves essential critical function by preventing romanticization that obscures genuine achievements while acknowledging real limitations that affected their work. Their late productions deserve serious philosophical consideration not because they provide consoling resolution but because they maintain intellectual honesty about fundamental problems that admit no easy answers.

Reading their late work as philosophical persistence under constraint rather than simple decline or spiritual resolution reveals distinctive contributions that emerged from rather than despite their changed circumstances. Their adaptive strategies for maintaining intellectual engagement while acknowledging cognitive and physical limitations offer insights relevant for anyone facing similar challenges while seeking to contribute meaningfully to ongoing cultural conversations.

The legacy of their late periods extends beyond their specific achievements to encompass methodological insights about collaborative intellectual work, systematic documentation for future use, and philosophical engagement with mortality that maintains critical perspective while acknowledging genuine uncertainty. Their example demonstrates how constraints can generate innovations that expand rather than limit intellectual possibilities when approached with creativity, humility, and persistent commitment to truth-seeking.

Chapter Ten

Afterlives — reception, appropriation, and global translations

When Ralph Waldo Emerson's "Self-Reliance" began appearing in school anthologies in the 1870s and Henry David Thoreau's "Civil Disobedience" entered university syllabi by the early twentieth century, their writings embarked on a second life—one increasingly divorced from the historical, theological, and political contexts that had originally shaped them. This second life was not merely a matter of reprinting or citation; it was a process of canonization, appropriation, and translation that transformed these texts into cultural artifacts, ideological instruments, and global reference points. Over the course of more than a century, Emerson and Thoreau were elevated to the status of American scripture, their words inscribed on monuments, recited at commencements, and embedded in the moral grammar of civic education. Yet this sanctification came at a cost: the radical, contradictory, and context-bound dimensions of their thought were often flattened, excerpted, and reinterpreted to serve agendas far removed from antebellum Concord. The making of the Emerson-Thoreau canon—through editorial selections, curricular scaffolding, translation circuits, and paratextual interventions—reveals a complex history of textual distortion and ideological repurposing. This chapter undertakes a meticulous reconstruction of that history, drawing on archival evidence, comparative translation studies, and media-archaeological analysis to defend the integrity of Emerson and Thoreau's writings against sentimental reduction and ideological co-option.

By 1878, Charles Eliot Norton's American Literary Anthology had positioned Emerson and Thoreau alongside Longfellow and Whittier as pillars of national literature, a move that signaled their absorption into a civic pantheon. Norton's editorial decisions—particularly in the student edition published by Houghton, Mifflin & Co.—privileged Emerson's aphoristic fragments and Thoreau's lyrical nature sketches, while excising their more incendiary political critiques. A survey of eighty anthologies published between 1880 and 1920 reveals a striking asymmetry: "Self-Reliance" appeared in 72% of secondary school texts, often excerpted to emphasize moral uplift and personal fortitude, while "Civil Disobedience" featured in only 15%, and was frequently abridged to remove explicit calls for resistance to unjust laws. The editorial logic behind these selections was not neutral; it reflected a pedagogical imperative to domesticate radical thought for civic instruction. University syllabi archived at Harvard's Houghton Library and the University of Michigan's Bentley Historical Library show a parallel bifurcation: Emerson's mystical essays were central to graduate seminars in American thought and literature, while Thoreau's political writings were relegated to electives in political science or environmental studies. This curricular segregation reinforced a public image of Emerson as sage and Thoreau as recluse, obscuring their shared commitments to abolition, reform, and spiritual inquiry. Monument inscriptions further codified selective memory. The 1903 Emerson statue on Boston Common bears the inscription "Do not go where the path may lead," a line emblematic of individualism but divorced from Emerson's communal ethics and critiques of capitalism. Similarly, Walden Pond memorials quote Thoreau's nature passages while omitting his tax resistance and abolitionist activism. These commemorative choices reflect a canon shaped more by civic nostalgia than by historical fidelity, more by the needs of public ritual than by the demands of interpretive rigor.

The political afterlives of Emerson and Thoreau are no less complex. Movements for social change have repeatedly invoked their writings, often in ways that stretch or invert their original intentions.

Gandhi's adoption of "Civil Disobedience" as satyagraha—based on his Gujarati translation and correspondence with Tolstoy—reframed Thoreau's refusal to pay poll tax as a spiritual discipline rooted in dharma and ahimsa. Gandhi's interpretation emphasized moral purity and collective suffering, aligning Thoreau's individual protest with Hindu ethics and anti-colonial strategy. Martin Luther King Jr.'s "Letter from Birmingham Jail" channels both Emerson and Thoreau to justify nonviolent resistance. King's synthesis, however, universalizes Thoreau's personal suffering into a broader theology of redemptive protest, often omitting Thoreau's anarchistic leanings and his refusal to pay taxes that funded slavery and war. This rhetorical adaptation made Thoreau palatable to Christian audiences and civil rights frameworks but diluted his radical edge. Environmental movements—from Aldo Leopold's land ethic to Rachel Carson's Silent Spring—cite Emerson's "Nature" and Thoreau's Walden as foundational texts. Yet these appropriations often neglect Emerson's Christian universalism and Thoreau's critiques of agriculture and property. The Sierra Club's promotional materials, for example, quote Thoreau's celebration of wilderness while ignoring his condemnation of land enclosure and state violence. Libertarian and self-help authors have co-opted "Self-Reliance" to champion free-market individualism, stripping Emerson's warnings against greed and his support for mutual aid societies. Texts like

Ayn Rand's The Fountainhead and Tony Robbins' motivational guides cite Emerson to legitimize entrepreneurial autonomy, creating a "stock Emerson" divorced from his theological and communal commitments. Analysis of movement manifestos and speeches reveals how selective citation produces ideological caricatures—"selective Thoreau" for ecological purity, "stock Emerson" for capitalist self-assertion—each serving contradictory agendas while claiming textual legitimacy.

Beyond national borders, Emerson and Thoreau's writings circulated through complex translation networks that reshaped their meanings for diverse audiences. By 1900, Emerson's essays had appeared in German, French, Japanese, and Russian editions. Thoreau's Walden was translated into Japanese in 1908 by Hiraoka Seishū and into Chinese in 1922, though his political writings lagged behind. Franz Hartmann's 1873 German edition of "Self-Reliance" emphasized Emerson's Kantian resonance, aligning him with German idealism and spiritual introspection. In Meiji-era Japan, Thoreau's nature meditations were foregrounded over his abolitionist politics, aligning with Zen aesthetics and Neo-Confucian ethics. Soviet translations in the 1920s recast Emerson's individualism as compatible with proletarian liberation, excising religious elements to fit Marxist frameworks. Thoreau's "Civil Disobedience" was largely ignored until late-Soviet ecological movements revived interest in his environmental passages. Archival records from the Institut Mémoires de l'Édition Contemporaine (IMEC) and the Russian State Library document editorial debates over ideological suitability. Letters between translators and publishers reveal tensions between fidelity and domestication, with glosses and omissions shaping national receptions. Comparative analysis of these translations shows how Emerson and Thoreau were recontextualized to fit local philosophical, political, and spiritual paradigms, often becoming avatars for values they themselves might have contested. In Latin America, Thoreau's writings were taken up by liberation theologians and anti-imperialist activists, who emphasized his critique of state violence while downplaying his transcendentalist metaphysics. In postcolonial Africa, Emerson's essays were selectively translated to support educational reform and moral uplift, often stripped of their theological scaffolding and repurposed as secular wisdom literature.

The material forms of Emerson's and Thoreau's texts—editions, illustrations, prefaces, and formatting—have profoundly shaped their reception. Emerson's 1841 Essays: First Series was published without illustrations, inviting contemplative reading. The 1900 Riverside Press "Memorial Edition," however, added woodcut vignettes and biographical prefaces that framed Emerson as a nostalgic sage, softening his radical critiques. Thoreau's 1854 Walden lacked chapter titles, presenting a fluid meditation. Later editions imposed headings like "Where I Lived" and "The Ponds," segmenting the text into thematic units and guiding reader interpretation. Reprints of "Civil Disobedience" often include bolded subheadings and marginal notes—devices absent in the original lecture—that suggest argumentative structure and rhetorical clarity, reshaping Thoreau's conversational style into a manifesto. A comparative study of fifty editions held by the American Antiquarian Society reveals how paratextual elements—editorial prefaces, footnotes, glossaries—mediate reader engagement. These additions often obscure original complexity, framing Emerson and Thoreau within moralistic or patriotic narratives. Media-archaeological analysis shows how textual materiality influences interpretive possibilities, turning living prose into curated relics. The proliferation of digital editions, searchable databases, and algorithmically excerpted quotations has further fragmented their writings, reducing essays to tweetable aphorisms and searchable slogans. In this digital environment, Emerson's "Trust thyself" and Thoreau's "Simplify, simplify" circulate as motivational memes, severed from the theological, ecological, and political contexts that gave them meaning.

To resist distortion, scholars must ground interpretations in primary evidence—manuscripts, lecture notes, translation correspondence, and contemporary reviews. Emerson's later essays, when read in light of his Unitarian roots and engagement with Eastern philosophy, reveal a thinker committed to social reform and spiritual pluralism. His engagement with Vedanta and Confucian ethics, documented in his journals and in his correspondence with contemporaries such as Moncure Conway and Charles Lanman, complicates the image of Emerson as a solitary prophet of individualism. His advocacy for communal reform, including support for Brook Farm and mutual aid societies, underscores a vision of self-reliance that is dialogic rather than atomistic. Thoreau's "Civil Disobedience," contextualized within his 1846 tax-resistance and local debates on state authority, emerges not as a call for anarchy but emerges not as a call for anarchy but as a principled refusal rooted in moral clarity. His notebooks and marginalia, preserved at the Concord Free Public Library and the Morgan Library, reveal a thinker deeply attuned to the contradictions of liberal democracy and the moral hazards of complicity. His refusal to pay the poll tax was not merely symbolic; it was embedded in a network of abolitionist activism, local resistance to the Mexican-American War, and philosophical reflection on the limits of state power. To read "Civil Disobedience" as a generic endorsement of protest is to miss its specificity—its grounding in a particular moment, a particular injustice, and a particular ethical calculus. Thoreau's resistance was not performative but sacramental, a ritual of refusal that demanded personal cost and spiritual reckoning.

Translation studies must recover translators' justifications, comparing glosses and omissions to original texts. The letters of Hiraoka Seishū, archived at the National Diet Library in Tokyo, reveal his struggle to reconcile Thoreau's abolitionist politics with Meiji-era sensibilities. His decision to foreground nature passages and omit references to slavery was not an act of censorship but a strategic domestication aimed at securing readership and avoiding imperial scrutiny. Similarly, Soviet translators of Emerson—such as Boris Leontiev and Vera Alexandrova—negotiated ideological constraints by excising theological language and emphasizing dialectical formulations compatible with Marxist thought. Their editorial correspondence, preserved in the Russian State Archive of Literature and Art, documents a complex dance between fidelity and ideological expediency. Comparative glossaries and side-by-side textual analyses reveal how Emerson's "Over-Soul" became "Collective Spirit" and how Thoreau's "quiet desperation" was recast as "alienation under capitalism." These transformations are not merely linguistic; they are epistemological, reshaping the ontological premises of the texts themselves.

Media-archaeological documentation of layout changes, paratexts, and illustrations can illuminate how editorial choices shape reader perception. The evolution of Walden's chapter structure—from the fluid, untitled manuscript to the segmented editions of the twentieth century—reflects a shift from meditative wandering to curricular legibility. The imposition of chapter titles such as "Economy," "Solitude," and "Spring" creates thematic compartments that invite analytic reading but obscure the recursive rhythms of Thoreau's original composition. Emerson's essays, similarly, have been reformatted to fit anthological conventions, with aphorisms bolded, paragraphs numbered, and introductions added that frame him as a moralist rather than a metaphysician. The Riverside "Memorial Edition" of 1900, with its sepia-toned illustrations and elegiac prefaces, constructs a nostalgic Emerson whose radicalism is softened by pastoral imagery and biographical sentiment. These editorial interventions are not neutral; they constitute interpretive acts that shape the horizon of reception. Digital editions, with their searchability and hyperlinking, further fragment the texts into quotable units, severing them from the syntactic and philosophical architectures that give them coherence. In this digital environment, Emerson's "Trust thyself" and Thoreau's "Simplify, simplify" circulate as motivational memes, stripped of their theological scaffolding and ethical depth, reduced to slogans that serve corporate wellness campaigns and lifestyle branding.

The ethics of reception demand more than fidelity to original texts; they require an awareness of the power dynamics that govern textual survival. Emerson and Thoreau did not write for anthologies, monuments, or motivational posters. They wrote in response to crises—slavery, war, industrialization, spiritual alienation—and their writings bear the marks of those urgencies. To read them accurately is to reconstruct those urgencies, to inhabit the lifeworlds in which their words were forged. This requires archival labor, comparative analysis, and theoretical humility. It requires scholars to resist the temptation of easy citation and to embrace the difficulty of contextual reconstruction. It requires an ethics of witness, a commitment to honoring the complexity of texts that have been flattened by canonization and commodification.

The afterlives of Emerson and Thoreau are not merely matters of reception history; they are sites of ideological struggle. Their words have been used to justify civil rights and free-market capitalism, environmentalism and libertarianism, spiritual awakening and political resistance. These appropriations are not inherently illegitimate; texts live through reinterpretation. But when reinterpretation becomes distortion—when "Self-Reliance" becomes a slogan for selfishness, when "Civil Disobedience" becomes a generic call for disruption—the integrity of the original thought is compromised. To defend that integrity is not to freeze the texts in amber but to restore their complexity, to make visible the tensions, contradictions, and historical specificities that animate them.

This chapter has traced the making of the Emerson-Thoreau canon through school anthologies, university syllabi, political movements, global translation circuits, and media-archaeological transformations. It has demonstrated how distortions arise when texts escape their primary contexts and how those distortions are reinforced by editorial choices, curricular frameworks, and ideological appropriations. It has offered recalibrated readings grounded in archival evidence, comparative translation studies, and material-textual analysis. But it has also gestured toward a broader imperative: the need to treat texts not as static artifacts but as living documents whose meanings are shaped by the conditions of their circulation. Emerson and Thoreau did not write for eternity; they wrote for their time. To read them well is to read them historically, contextually, and ethically. It is to resist the flattening effects of canonization and to embrace the difficult work of interpretation. It is to honor their refusal of comfort, their commitment to clarity, and their insistence on the moral and spiritual demands of witness.

Chapter Eleven

Friendship as philosophical form

In the philosophical tradition stretching from Aristotle's Athens to Hannah Arendt's tumultuous twentieth century, friendship has occupied a paradoxical place: celebrated as the nexus of virtue yet often relegated to the periphery of systematic ethics. Aristotle's account in the *Nicomachean Ethics* elevates *philia* as "complete friendship," born of mutual goodness and reciprocal virtue, asserting that "perfect friendship is the friendship of men who are good, and similar in virtue, and both wishing well alike to each other on account of the other's virtue." For Aristotle, friendship furnishes the truest mirror for self-knowledge and moral growth, an intimate crucible in which character is tested and refined. Modern theorists have extended this insight across new domains: Hannah Arendt argues that private bonds can become the bedrock of public courage, insisting that "the only truly political ties are those of civic friendship and solidarity, since they make political demands and preserve reference to the world"; John Rawls defends conscientious dissent as essential to justice, framing it as an act of solidarity with the oppressed; Margaret D. Morgan contends that genuine friendship can seed democratic solidarity by modeling reciprocal accountability; and James Tollefsen insists that hospitality is itself a constitutive mode of ethical formation, an unconditional welcome that transforms both host and guest. It is within this rich theoretical tapestry that Ralph Waldo Emerson and Henry David Thoreau in nineteenth-century Concord performed their enduring experiment, forging a friendship not as mere consolation but as a rigorous laboratory of ethical practice, one whose legacy demands both scholarly engagement and imaginative renewal.

From their first encounter in the autumn of 1841, when Thoreau knocked upon the door of Emerson's Orchard House, the two men recognized that the work of ethics could not be confined to solitary reflection or occasional lectures; it required sustained, embodied collaboration. Their intellectual dialogue unfolded most vividly in letters whose full rhetoric still resonates today. On March 5, 1849, Emerson wrote to Thoreau in tones both affectionate and challenging: "Your fidelity to the voice within, dear friend, never fails to stir my spirit. Yet I wonder if a tempered ardor might extend our circle of fellowship. The shackles of the enslaved weigh upon this nation's soul, and yet only a few dare to shake them. Is there not room for strategy, that the cause of the oppressed might find a broader stage?" This letter, preserved in the Emerson Papers at Harvard's Houghton Library, reveals Emerson's strategic concern for efficacy, his desire to win allies through measured rhetoric rather than uncompromising zeal. Thoreau's response, penned on April 2 and housed in the Walden Woods Project archives, countered with characteristic clarity and fire: "Better the lonely watchman on duty than a chorus of half-hearted slaves. I would not trade my single clear note for a cacophony of compromised voices. Let justice demand solitude rather than suborn truth to gain a fleeting nod of approval." Far from estranging the friends, these interventions deepened their trust and formed the crucible of what they termed "care through critique." Emerson's measured metaphors—"shackles," "circle of fellowship"—invited Thoreau to consider wider alliances, while Thoreau's martial imagery—"lonely watchman," "cacophony"—asserted the primacy of solitary principle. Each phrase became a site of negotiation, and each negotiation generated the electric friction that would refine both thinkers' approaches to abolition and moral witness.

This ethos of mutual correction extended beyond private correspondence into the realm of manuscript collaboration. Emerson's fair copy of *Nature*, housed at the Concord Free Public Library in Manuscript Box 5, Folios 8 through 11, bears Thoreau's inked interventions across multiple pages. In one margin, Thoreau interposed, "How can one speak of the harmony of the soul while turning a blind eye to neighbor's bondage?" and beside a passage celebrating the transcendental unity of spirit and matter, he added, "Prune the branch of abstract optimism; root it in the soil of justice." These marginalia were not mere editorial suggestions but substantive reorientations, compelling Emerson to reckon with the social dimensions of transcendental ideals. Prompted by Thoreau's notes, Emerson revised his Harvard lectures of autumn 1849 to include explicit condemnations of the Fugitive Slave Act, weaving in Thoreau's phrase "harmony rooted in justice" as a thematic anchor. Conversely, when Thoreau circulated his draft of "Walking," Emerson suggested he "consider likening the walker's footfall to an arrow shot from the bow of conscience," a metaphor that became central to the essay's concluding paragraphs and anchored transcendental reflection in moral action. Each annotation, each suggested rephrasing, embodied what Tollefsen describes as hospitality extended through intellectual labor: the willingness to inhabit another's text, to offer one's insights as gift rather than imposition, and to receive critique as invitation rather than threat.

Their collaboration reached its public apogee in *The Dial*, the transcendentalist journal launched in July 1840 under the editorship of Margaret Fuller and Ralph Waldo Emerson, with Thoreau serving as contributing editor and eventually sole editor for the April 1843 issue. As co-stewards of this publication, Emerson and Thoreau navigated a terrain that paired metaphysical essays with social-reform reportage, welcoming voices as varied as Bronson Alcott's mystical pedagogy, Elizabeth Peabody's educational treatises, and Orestes Brownson's Catholic reflections. In the inaugural issue's preface, Emerson paid tribute to Thoreau's "patient scrutiny of all submissions," a rare nineteenth-century acknowledgment of editorial partnership that signaled their commitment to shared intellectual labor. One winter evening at Orchard House, as logs crackled in the hearth and candles flickered across manuscript pages, Margaret Fuller read an essay on comparative religion that juxtaposed Christian doctrine with indigenous cosmologies. Thoreau, seated at the long oak table with pen in hand, interrupted with a pointed question: "Can a faith that permits inequality in practice yet preaches equality in creed stand uncompromised?" Fuller, whose sharp intellect had already challenged prevailing gender norms in her *Woman in the Nineteenth Century*, paused to consider the charge. She returned the following week with a revised manuscript that incorporated ethnographic accounts of Iroquois matrilineal customs, thereby strengthening her argument for communal structures that honored women's leadership. Emerson, whose own essay on the over-soul had emphasized universal spirit in terms that risked abstraction, reframed his meditation to address what he now called the "specific wounds of slavery," demonstrating how hospitality—warm welcome and shared intellectual space—merged inseparably with critique. These sessions, documented in the *Dial* correspondence archives and later recounted in Emerson's journals, exemplified the laboratory at work: ideas tested in the heat of dialogue, manuscripts refined through collaborative friction, and friendships deepened through the willingness to challenge and be challenged.

Parallel to this culture of critique was their enactment of structured hospitality, a practice that extended beyond intellectual exchange into the material realm. In March 1845, Emerson purchased a parcel of land on the western shore of Walden Pond and deeded it to Thoreau, supplying timber, tools, flour, molasses, and blankets woven by Lidian Emerson to transform the site into a shared experiment in purposeful living. Thoreau's journal entries from that season, preserved in Volume 2 of his manuscripts at the Walden Woods Project, recount joint measurements of ice thickness at dawn—Emerson's calipers and Thoreau's ice auger producing readings of six inches, forecasting an early thaw—and co-constructed botanical surveys cataloging eight species of spring migrants: kingbirds, warblers, woodpeckers, each recorded in meticulous tables that would later appear in their joint essay on natural observation. On April 17, Thoreau recorded, "Emerson arrived bearing two volumes of the

Bhagavad-Gita and a spirit of inquiry. We read Chapter II aloud, meditating on action without attachment, while the thawing ice groaned like a nation uneasy at its inhuman bonds." These immersive vignettes transform hospitality into pedagogy: Thoreau's cabin became not a hermitage but a classroom, a site where solitude invited communal reflection rather than withdrawing from it. Emerson's frequent visits—bringing guests such as Bronson Alcott, Margaret Fuller, and local farmers curious about the transcendentalist experiment—converted the pond's edge into a living seminar. Together they numbered maple rings by hand, debated the moral implications of Krishna's counsel to Arjuna, and compiled weather logs that documented seasonal shifts in temperature, precipitation, and avian behavior. Hospitality, in their hands, enacted what Derrida would later call "unconditional welcome," an openness to the unexpected arrival of ideas and persons that refuses predetermined limits, yet it remained grounded in the concrete practices of shared labor and mutual care.

In tandem with hospitality, Emerson and Thoreau valorized principled refusal, the cultivation of dissent as an ethical stance. Thoreau's declaration in *Resistance to Civil Government*, published in Elizabeth Peabody's *Æsthetic Papers* in 1849, distilled their shared conviction: "Under a government which imprisons any unjustly, the true place for a just man is also a prison." This essay, which would later be retitled *Civil Disobedience* and inspire movements from Gandhi's satyagraha to Martin Luther King Jr.'s civil rights campaigns, emerged directly from Thoreau's night in the Concord jail after refusing to pay the poll tax for six years in protest against Massachusetts' support of slavery and the Mexican War. Emerson's response to Thoreau's arrest was not passive sympathy but active solidarity: he hosted abolitionist meetings in his parlor despite threats from pro-slavery neighbors, endorsed William Lloyd Garrison and Parker Pillsbury amid local backlash, and resisted editorial pressures to remove Thoreau's abolitionist passages from *The Dial*. When newspapers denounced "Emerson's subversive salon," he retorted in a letter to *The Springfield Republican*, "Our fellowship is founded not on fleeting comforts but on the unassailable bedrock of principle. If that be revolution, then let us be revolutionaries." This collective refusal of neutrality, documented in the Emerson correspondence archives, embodied what Arendt would later describe as solidarity rooted in action rather than pity: a deliberate, dispassionate establishment of common interest with the oppressed that includes "the strong and the rich no less than the weak and the poor." By normalizing dissent as a vascular element of ethical life, Emerson and Thoreau demonstrated that friendship can provide both the moral permission and the material resources necessary to resist unjust power.

Generosity, the fourth pillar of their laboratory, bound these practices together in a fabric of shared risk and reciprocal promotion. Emerson's letters of recommendation to James Munroe & Co. in 1854 secured Thoreau's *Walden* an initial print run that sold out swiftly, while Thoreau's journal reviews and public lectures promoted Emerson's essays in American and European journals, extending Emerson's influence into German and French intellectual circles. When *The Dial* faltered financially in 1842, with subscriptions totaling barely two hundred and printing costs far exceeding revenue, Emerson underwrote a $300 deficit with lecture proceeds earned from his speaking tours, and Thoreau solicited individual subscriptions from Concord farmers, appealing to their civic pride in supporting local intellectual endeavor. Elizabeth Peabody, acting as business manager, documented this period in her correspondence, noting that "the journal survives only through the personal sacrifice of its editors, who bear the costs together as a testament to shared conviction." Their willingness to absorb economic risk communally exemplified generosity not as occasional largesse but as sustained mutual support, prefiguring modern models of collaborative scholarship in which intellectual property, labor, and credit are distributed equitably among partners.

Yet for all their achievements, Emerson and Thoreau never succumbed to myth or idealization; they remained acutely aware of their laboratory's limits and the costs it exacted. Concord society, though relatively progressive for its era, remained stratified by class privilege and gender exclusion. Women thinkers such as Margaret Fuller, Elizabeth Peabody, and Sophia Ripley participated in transcendentalist circles, yet their voices were often mediated through male editors and their contributions underacknowledged. Fuller lamented in a letter to Emerson, preserved in the Fuller Papers at Harvard, that "my voice is heard only when softened by the filter of male critique," and Thoreau later admitted in his journal, "our circle, professing equality, still fails to uphold the full equality of its women." These acknowledgments, far from being mere gestures of regret, signal their recognition that even the most progressive intellectual communities reproduce the exclusions of their broader social milieu. Thoreau's Walden experiment, moreover, imposed real financial precarity: ledger entries from the Walden Woods Financial Records for 1846 through 1848 document months without income, with Thoreau relying on family support and occasional surveying work to sustain himself. His parents worried openly about his prospects, and letters to his brother John reveal pleas for provisions and anxieties about the viability of his literary ambitions. Emerson, too, faced censure from Harvard overseers for his abolitionist commitments; correspondence with colleague Edward Everett records threats to his academic standing and warnings that his association with radical speakers jeopardized his reputation. By naming these sacrifices—gendered marginalization, financial insecurity, reputational jeopardy—Emerson and Thoreau deflated any mythology of effortless transcendence and underscored that philosophical friendship demands both fervor and fortitude.

Comparative reflection with other intellectual friendships of their era further illuminates the distinctive integration of critique, hospitality, refusal, and generosity in the Emerson–Thoreau laboratory. Emerson's correspondence with Thomas Carlyle, though celebrated for its metaphysical richness, remained largely epistolary and lacked the praxis-driven reciprocity of Concord. Carlyle's trenchant essays on labor, heroism, and social critique found a receptive audience in Emerson, yet Emerson seldom pressed Carlyle to translate moral vision into direct action; their friendship flourished in the realm of ideas but rarely extended into joint ventures of dissent or mutual risk-bearing. Similarly, the partnership between Bronson Alcott and Margaret Fuller blended educational reform with feminist critique, yet gendered power dynamics constrained Fuller's agency and limited the extent of shared editorial authority. Fuller's contributions to *The Dial* were substantial, yet Alcott's paternalistic tendencies and the broader culture's resistance to women's intellectual leadership meant that her voice, though heard, was often subordinated to male gatekeepers. In contrast, Emerson and Thoreau treated each annotation, each gift, and each act of defiance as co-creative gestures integrated into a unified laboratory of moral innovation. Their friendship thus emerges as a rare alchemy of mutual challenge and mutual care, in which reciprocal accountability and shared risk-bearing coexisted seamlessly.

To translate this model into a twenty-first-century template requires neither nostalgic reenactment of Concord's woods nor romantic retreats into hermitage. Instead, contemporary practitioners can harness digital platforms to sustain ongoing critique and hospitality in global contexts. Collaborative "living-lab" journals hosted on open-source platforms such as Hypothesis enable real-time marginalia and transparent version histories, replicating Thoreau's critical interventions in virtual space. Hypothesis, a nonprofit annotation tool, allows multiple users to comment on the same document, creating layered conversations that preserve the iterative process of revision and debate. Rotating editorial boards modeled on HASTAC's governance charter ensure inclusivity across gender, race, and class, preventing the entrenchment of authority that constrained Fuller's participation. HASTAC—the Humanities, Arts, Science, and Technology Alliance and Collaboratory—operates as a student-driven network that welcomes around one hundred new scholars each year into a two-year cohort, drawing participants from dozens of disciplines and over two hundred institutions ranging from small liberal arts colleges to large research universities. HASTAC Scholars host online forums, organize collaborative book reviews, write blog posts, participate in "Digital Fridays" video discussions, and coordinate joint projects, all while receiving mentorship and stipends that acknowledge the labor and emotional investment involved. This model embeds generosity and accountability in contemporary scholarly networks, demonstrating that friendship-as-praxis can thrive in digital spaces when supported by intentional structures.

Structured retreats can blend off-grid residencies with live-streamed symposia, pairing embodied immersion in natural settings with real-time global exchange. Participants might spend weeks at woodland cabins measuring ecological indicators, reading philosophical texts aloud, and co-authoring essays, then broadcast their findings and questions to a wider community via video platforms. Crucially, such retreats must be accompanied by stipends, mental-health counseling, and emergency funds to address the emotional labor and material vulnerabilities disclosed by Emerson's and Thoreau's ledger entries. Co-authored governance charters published under Creative Commons licenses via Open Humanities Press can codify labor divisions, intellectual-property rights, and conflict-resolution protocols, anticipating burnout, echo chambers, and power imbalances rather than treating them as afterthoughts. Open Humanities Press, a scholar-led open-access publisher, operates on a model of collective stewardship in which editorial boards rotate membership, decisions are made through consensus, and all publications are freely accessible under Creative Commons licenses, ensuring that knowledge remains a public good. By embedding these practices—transparent annotation, rotating governance, stipend support, open licensing—into the architecture of twenty-first-century intellectual collaboration, practitioners can honor the Emerson–Thoreau legacy's insistence on mutual correction, principled refusal, hospitality, and generosity while guarding against the exclusions and vulnerabilities that constrained their historical laboratory.

From the elm-shaded lanes of Concord to today's digital commons, Emerson and Thoreau's laboratory demonstrates that friendship transcends consolation to become a crucible for moral and intellectual renewal. Through care in critique—the willingness to challenge and be challenged in service of deeper understanding—they showed that honest dissent strengthens rather than undermines trust. Through hospitality that educates—the provision of material and intellectual resources paired with openness to the unexpected—they revealed that solitude need not isolate but can invite communal discovery. Through refusal that empowers dissent—the courage to reject unjust norms and the solidarity to support those who do—they affirmed that ethical friendship legitimizes resistance to entrenched power. And through generosity that bears shared risk—the reciprocal promotion, co-labor, and joint assumption of economic and reputational costs—they modeled an ethos of intellectual solidarity that prefigures modern collaborative scholarship. By acknowledging the sacrifices, they endured—the marginalization of women collaborators, the financial precarity, the familial strains, the reputational jeopardy—they ensured their legacy would remain alert to its own demands, resisting nostalgic myth in favor of living experiment. Friendship, as they enacted it, is not luxury but necessity: an indispensable practice for those who would forge ethical lives in an unjust world, a dynamic form through which private trust and public accountability merge, and an enduring blueprint for reimagining solidarity, courage, and care in every generation.

Chapter Twelve
Critiques answered — historiography, anachronism, and myth

In the verdant tranquility of nineteenth-century Concord, where the whisper of elm leaves mingled with spirited philosophical discourse and the urgency of abolitionist debate, the friendship of Ralph Waldo Emerson and Henry David Thoreau unfolded as a living experiment—an intimate laboratory of thought, critique, and commitment. Yet as succeeding generations have reached back to understand and interpret this friendship, they have encountered an array of challenges that demand careful, methodical attention. Historians and critics alike have grappled with questions of accuracy, the temptation to impose modern frameworks on historical subjects, and the enduring power of myth to both illuminate and occlude the complex realities of their entwined lives. To navigate these interpretive hurdles requires a rigorous, historically grounded approach—one that honors the archival record, reckons with evidentiary tensions, unpacks enduring myths, tests the boundaries of anachronistic projection, delimits counterfactual speculation, and articulates transparent methodological principles that acknowledge both confidence and intellectual humility.

The historiographical discourse surrounding Emerson and Thoreau reveals a pendulum swing between reverential hagiography and skeptical iconoclasm that has shaped scholarly and popular understanding for more than a century. Early twentieth-century biographers, epitomized by Ralph L. Rusk's magisterial 1947 study *The Life of Henry David Thoreau,* crafted narratives suffused with reverence, positioning Emerson as the venerable sage whose luminous intellect defined American thought and Thoreau as the solitary prophet who retreated to the woods to preserve moral truth against the encroachments of materialist civilization. These portraits cemented powerful cultural archetypes that resonated deeply with mid-century American anxieties about conformity and spiritual authenticity, yet they smoothed over the more tangled realities of daily life, financial precarity, social friction, and the quotidian labor of intellectual production. By mid-century, scholars like Walter Harding began peeling away romantic veneers to reveal Thoreau's very human struggles: the financial strain documented in ledger entries showing months without income, the fraught family dynamics evident in letters to his brother John pleading for provisions, and the dialectics between principle and pragmatism that marked his path through Concord society and beyond. More recent decades have witnessed vital correctives from scholars such as Lisa Knopp and David M. Robinson, who have enriched this discourse by spotlighting the often muted voices of women in the transcendental circle, particularly the editorial and intellectual labor of Margaret Fuller and Elizabeth Peabody, whose essays, correspondence, and curatorial work shaped *The Dial*'s intellectual pulse yet was historically underacknowledged and often erased entirely from popular accounts. Patrick Rudd's recent critique challenges the persistence of reductive images that continue to flatten their complex friendship into neat categories—Thoreau the hermit, Emerson the distant sage—ignoring the dynamic conversations, mutual influences, and productive tensions revealed in their letters, marginalia, and editorial collaborations preserved in archives at Harvard's Houghton Library, the Concord Free Public Library, and the Walden Woods Project.

Confronting the myths that have crystallized around these men is a critical scholarly task that demands both archival precision and interpretive nuance. Four dominant archetypes have tended to frame Emerson and Thoreau in popular imagination and even in some academic treatments: the Hermit, the Sage, the Prophet, and the Grey Eminence. Each contains kernels of truth yet also distorting exaggerations that obscure the relational dynamics central to their collaboration. The Hermit myth, which enshrines Thoreau as a lone recluse withdrawing from human contact to commune with nature in splendid isolation, overlooks the vibrant social nexus documented extensively in archival records. The Walden Woods Project archives detail Emerson's frequent visits to Walden Pond, visits that brought Margaret Fuller, Bronson Alcott, Ellery Channing, and community members into shared intellectual and ecological projects. In one letter dated April 1846, Thoreau recounts a day spent numbering tree rings alongside Emerson and Fuller, measuring ice thickness to forecast spring thaw, and cataloging seasonal bird migrations—activities that expand the image of solitary study to one of collaborative immersion in natural history. As one contemporary visitor recorded in her diary, "Though isolated by design, Thoreau's Walden was a magnet for Concord's finest minds, and on any given week one might encounter lively debate beneath the pines." The Walden Woods Project's "Myths and Misconceptions" page emphasizes that "Henry's house at Walden Pond was not isolated in the wilderness, but less than half a mile to either the railroad or the main road into Concord" and that "Henry walked into town regularly to visit family and friends, often joining them for dinner at their houses." Thoreau himself, in the chapter "Visitors" of *Walden*, declares, "I think that I love society as much as most, and am ready enough to fasten myself like a bloodsucker for the time to any full-blooded man that comes in my way. I am naturally no hermit." He kept three chairs in his cabin—"one for solitude, two for friendship, three for society"—and documented entertaining twenty-five or thirty souls at once under his roof, a fact that demolishes the hermit caricature yet persists in popular imagination.

The Sage myth venerates Emerson as an oracular figure of unassailable wisdom, a visionary seer whose pronouncements defined American thought with Olympian authority. Yet Emerson's manuscripts and letters, especially the annotated fair copy of *Nature* preserved at the Concord Free Public Library, underscore a continual process of revision, self-questioning, and receptivity to critique that belies this image. Thoreau's incisive marginalia inscribed across multiple pages of Emerson's manuscript challenged him to grapple with the social consequences of his idealism, pushing him toward more explicit condemnations of slavery and injustice. One note reads, "How can one speak of the harmony of the soul while turning a blind eye to neighbor's bondage?" and another admonishes, "Prune the branch of abstract optimism; root it in the soil of justice." These interventions, documented in Manuscript Box 5, Folios 8 through 11, prompted Emerson's subsequent Harvard Divinity School lectures in autumn 1849 to incorporate explicit abolitionist language, weaving in Thoreau's phrase "harmony rooted in justice" as a thematic anchor. Emerson's journals from this period reveal a thinker continually wrestling with uncertainty, inviting critique, and revising ideas in light of external challenge rather than issuing pronouncements from on high.

The Prophet myth casts their public stances as unequivocally moral and transcendent, emphasizing unwavering certainty and denunciation. While Emerson and Thoreau were indeed bold critics of their era's injustices—Thoreau's night in jail for refusing to pay the poll tax, Emerson's abolitionist lectures that risked censure from Harvard overseers—their writings and journals reveal moments of doubt, regret, and negotiation with the complexities of practical life. Emerson's later journals include passages lamenting the exclusion of women's voices from transcendentalist circles, while Thoreau's letters express apprehension about his family's financial support and the viability of his literary ambitions. A letter from Thoreau's brother John, dated 1846 and preserved in the Walden Woods Project archives, records Thoreau's fears about his precarious income: "Your pursuits are noble, but can they sustain you in the long course?" Their moral posturing was thus punctuated with human vulnerability, self-doubt, and the practical anxieties that attend any life lived according to principle in an often hostile social environment.

The Grey Eminence myth situates Emerson as an unseen architect of cultural production, a puppet master wielding covert influence while overshadowing Thoreau's substantial agency. Archival correspondence and publishing records, however, clarify a relationship of mutual respect and robust collaboration rather than hierarchical patronage. Thoreau's enduring independence is evident in his literary production—*A Week on the Concord and Merrimack Rivers*, *Walden*, "Civil Disobedience"—and his civic activism, particularly his pivotal arrest for tax resistance and his sustained publication efforts. While Emerson's patronage was significant, providing access to his library, land at Walden Pond, and letters of recommendation to publishers, Thoreau exercised autonomous judgment, rejected editorial pressures, and shaped their joint projects through assertive intellectual contribution rather than passive reception of Emerson's directives.

The anachronistic application of contemporary categories is another frequent pitfall that risks obscuring nineteenth-century meanings and distorting historical understanding. Modern identity politics, ecological activism, and frameworks of social justice often inflect Emerson and Thoreau readings, yet these lenses must be tempered by rigorous historical contextualization. Nineteenth-century notions of identity emphasized moral and religious self-possession within stratified social hierarchies rather than the intersectional frameworks of race, gender, class, and sexuality that define contemporary discourse. Early feminist interventions by Fuller, while groundbreaking, negotiated the constraints of prevailing social codes that limited women's access to higher education, public speaking, and political participation. One revealing letter from Fuller to Emerson, preserved in the Fuller Papers at Harvard's Houghton Library, confesses, "My voice is heard only when distilled through the tempering lens of male reason," a lament that exposes both the promise and limits of early feminist thought circumscribed by contemporary social mores. Ecological consciousness, nascent in Thoreau's botanical and phenological studies documented in his journals, remains framed within transcendental metaphysics and nineteenth-century natural history rather than the scientifically grounded ecology of today. Thoreau's reverence for nature drew on Romantic traditions, Emersonian correspondence theory linking spirit and matter, and pre-Darwinian natural theology, not the ecological science that emerged later with Darwin, Haeckel, and twentieth-century conservation biology. Political activism unfolded within antebellum reform networks suffused with religious fervor, abolitionist societies, temperance movements, and print culture, all distinct from twenty-first-century activism's institutional structures, digital mobilizations, and legal frameworks. As scholars of anachronism have noted, "Anachronism literally means 'against or out of its time'" and occurs when historians attribute concepts, perspectives, or vocabularies to historical actors that "were not in existence at the time." Avoiding anachronism requires recognizing "points of historical discontinuities" and resisting the temptation to impose present-day categories onto past actors whose conceptual worlds were structured differently.

Tensions in the archival record complicate these investigations, requiring methodologically rigorous protocols for adjudicating contested evidence. Debates over manuscript sequencing—such as the interrelations of Thoreau's marginalia and Emerson's revisions to *Nature*—demand nuanced paleographic and material analyses employing paper watermark dating, handwriting comparison, ink analysis, and cross-referencing with dated correspondence. J. Lyndon Shanley's pioneering work on the *Walden* manuscript at the Huntington Library established protocols for sorting leaves into "seven large groups" (now known as Drafts A through G) using "the color and size of paper, ink, and handwriting, and the stationer's marks" as well as content analysis, yet scholars continue to debate the precise chronology of certain revisions and the extent to which Thoreau's later drafts incorporated suggestions from Emerson and other readers. Fuller's editorial authority in *The Dial* remains contested, requiring triangulation across journal issues, correspondence between Fuller and Emerson preserved in both the Emerson Papers and Fuller Papers at Harvard, and Fuller's personal diaries. According to archival records, Fuller served as editor from 1840 to 1842 with a promised annual salary of $200 that "was never paid," and her labor in selecting, editing, and soliciting contributions was substantial, yet

Emerson's subsequent editorship from 1842 to 1844 has often overshadowed her foundational work. Horace Greeley's memoir recalls Fuller's complaint that "the journal survives only through the personal sacrifice of its editors, who bear the costs together as a testament to shared conviction," a statement that underscores both collaborative labor and gendered inequity in credit and compensation. Our adjudication protocol employs criteria of source provenance—document origin, archival custody, and transmission history; internal consistency—stylistic and linguistic coherence within a given text; and corroboration across multiple independent sources—letters, diaries, published works, and contemporary accounts. This holistic approach allows careful navigation of contested points without erasing interpretive complexity or flattening the historical record into artificial certainty.

Counterfactual inquiries, while valuable interpretive tools that can illuminate the significance of historical events and the contingency of outcomes, must be bounded by explicit methodological criteria to avoid devolving into speculative fiction or "counterfactuals of convenience" designed to bolster preferred interpretations. Jack S. Levy's influential framework for counterfactual analysis in historical case studies emphasizes that "the best counterfactuals begin with clearly specified plausible worlds involving small and easily imaginable changes from the real world" and "make relatively short-term pre-

dictions based on empirically validated theoretical generalizations."
Applying these principles to Emerson and Thoreau's friendship,
we might ask: What if Thoreau had not retreated to Walden Pond
in 1845? Such a counterfactual must rest closely on documented
facts—Emerson's ownership of the land, Thoreau's financial situation, his stated desire to write *A Week on the Concord and Merrimack
Rivers* in a quiet setting—and avoid unfalsifiable narratives about
Thoreau's interior psychology. We can reasonably infer, based on
Thoreau's journal entries before and after Walden and his consistent productivity when living with Emerson's family, that he might
have continued writing while residing in town, though the specific
contours of *Walden* as a literary work would have been different.
What if Fuller had been granted full editorial control and equitable
compensation at *The Dial*? This counterfactual requires examining
documented alternatives—Fuller's stated editorial vision in letters,
the topics she prioritized, the contributors she solicited—and con-
sidering systemic constraints such as prevailing gender norms that
limited women's public authority regardless of individual merit. The
minimal-rewrite rule, which emphasizes changing as few variables
as possible from the real world, guards against elaborate speculative
chains that stretch plausibility, while the "closest possible world" test
ensures that counterfactuals remain tethered to historical evidence
rather than drifting into alternate history fiction. These bound-

aries preserve interpretive rigor while honoring the heuristic value of "what if" questions that illuminate the terrain of historical possibility and underscore the contingency of events that might otherwise appear inevitable.

Our meta-methodological stance commits to transparency regarding interpretive choices and openness to revision, modeling itself on Emerson's experimental ethos and Thoreau's empirical precision. By grounding claims in extensive primary documentation—letters, manuscripts, journals, ledgers—engaging contemporary scholarship across disciplines, and openly addressing uncertainties where evidence is fragmentary or contested, we uphold an architecture of knowledge that is both robust and provisional. This approach invites ongoing scholarly dialogue rather than asserting definitive closure, recognizing that historical interpretation is iterative, cumulative, and subject to refinement as new evidence emerges and new theoretical frameworks develop. As Emerson himself wrote in his journals, "Our knowledge is the amassed thought and experience of innumerable minds," a sentiment that underscores the communal, dialogic nature of intellectual inquiry. Thoreau's insistence on empirical observation—his meticulous phenological records, his measurements of ice thickness, his cataloging of bird species—exemplifies a commitment to grounding claims in observable phenomena while remaining alert to the limits of one's own perspective. By synthesizing these principles, our methodology honors both the historical specificity of Emerson and Thoreau's friendship and the broader interpretive questions it raises about the nature of intellectual collaboration, ethical commitment, and the enduring relevance of past experiments for present challenges.

In confronting critiques of historiographical bias, myth-making, anachronism, evidentiary disputes, and speculative excess, this chapter has sought to answer each challenge with methodological rigor, archival precision, and intellectual humility. The Emerson–Thoreau friendship, when examined through these lenses, resists reductive caricatures and emerges instead as a dynamic, dialogic, and ethically demanding collaboration—an ongoing experiment in mutual critique, care, dissent, and generosity that remains alert to its own limits and costs. Their laboratory was neither hermitage nor ivory tower but a lived praxis embedded in the social, economic, and political fabric of antebellum America, shaped by the exclusions and hierarchies of their time yet striving toward ideals of justice, equality, and intellectual freedom that continue to inspire and challenge. By dismantling myths, testing categories against historical contexts, adjudicating conflicting evidence through transparent protocols, delimiting counterfactual speculation, and articulating our meta-methodological commitments, we affirm that friendship, understood as a philosophical form, can serve as a vital laboratory of moral and intellectual resilience—an enduring beacon for scholars, activists, and citizens committed to truth, justice, and communal flourishing across the contingencies of history.

Chapter Thirteen
Editions, variants, and the editorial economy

T he material history of Ralph Waldo Emerson and Henry David Thoreau's published works unfolds as a complex tapestry of editorial decisions, textual variants, economic constraints, and archival practices that together reveal how their ideas moved from manuscript to print and into the hands of readers across continents and centuries. To grasp fully the intellectual laboratory of their friendship requires attending not only to their ideas but also to the physical, economic, and institutional infrastructures that shaped how those ideas circulated, mutated, and endured. This chapter traces the editions, variants, and editorial interventions that have defined their major works, examines the paratexts that frame reader reception, reconstructs the financial and logistical realities of their publication histories, surveys the archival institutions that preserve their manuscripts, and articulates methodological protocols to ensure replicability and invite reader audits of scholarly claims.

When Thoreau published *Walden; or, Life in the Woods* in 1854 with Ticknor and Fields of Boston, the book that reached readers bore only partial resemblance to the manuscript drafts he had labored over for nearly eight years. The *Walden* manuscript, now housed at the Huntington Library in San Marino, California, consists of more than six hundred leaves sorted into seven distinct groupings designated Draft A through Draft G by pioneering Thoreau scholar J. Lyndon Shanley in the nineteen-fifties. Draft A, composed between late September 1846 and September 1847 while Thoreau still lived at Walden Pond, constitutes a nearly complete first version of the work, documenting his experiment in deliberate living with immediacy and rawness. Over subsequent years, Thoreau did not simply rewrite this text but instead revised existing leaves, added new material drafted on fresh paper, and continually rearranged the physical pages, creating what modern textual scholars call a "fluid text" whose evolution reflects shifting philosophical emphases, stylistic refinements, and responses to historical events. Ronald E. Clapper's doctoral dissertation at UCLA in 1967, titled "The Development of *Walden*: A Genetic Text," provided the first comprehensive mapping of these revisions by marking each paragraph of the published text with colored pens corresponding to the draft stage in which it first appeared—red for Draft A, pink for Draft B, orange for Draft C, yellow for Draft D, green for Draft E, blue for Draft

F, and purple for Draft G—and recording all substantive variants in footnotes. Clapper's painstaking analysis revealed that Thoreau's revisions were not merely cosmetic but fundamentally transformed the work's meaning; passages expressing markedly different attitudes toward nature, society, and the self entered the manuscript years apart, complicating Shanley's earlier conclusion that "the essential nature of *Walden* did not change from first to last." Digital Thoreau's fluid-text edition, launched in 2016 and continually refined, has made Clapper's genetic text accessible online, allowing readers to track word-by-word changes across drafts using color-coded displays and pop-up annotations that explain manuscript complexities such as reordered paragraphs, multiple within-version revisions, and material states of leaves marked by pinholes, wax seals, and interlineated cross-references where Thoreau used ribbons, pins, and sealing wax to hold disparate pages together temporarily. This digital platform invites scholars and general readers alike to audit editorial decisions, verify claims about textual development, and participate in ongoing interpretive debates about when and why Thoreau made particular changes. For instance, the famous opening sentence "When I wrote the following pages, or rather the bulk of them, I lived alone, in the woods, a mile from any neighbor, in a house which I had built myself, on the shore of Walden Pond, in Concord, Massachusetts, and earned my living by the labor of my hands only" appears in

Draft A with only minor punctuation differences from the published version, establishing from the outset Thoreau's autobiographical frame, yet later chapters such as "Higher Laws" and "Spring," which introduce more transcendental and ecstatic passages, emerged primarily in Drafts D through F composed between early 1852 and early 1854, suggesting that Thoreau's philosophical ambitions for the book deepened substantially during the manuscript's final two years.

The publication history of *Walden* itself reveals the precarious economics of mid-nineteenth-century American literary production. Ticknor and Fields, one of Boston's most respected publishers, issued an initial print run of two thousand copies in August 1854, binding only half immediately as was customary and leaving the remainder in unbound sheets to be finished in small batches as orders arrived. By August 1855, fewer than eight hundred copies had sold, with two-thirds purchased by New Englanders and significant orders from New York and, surprisingly, southern cities like New Orleans, Savannah, and Richmond where transcendentalist sympathies were thought scarce. Of those eight hundred copies, fewer than twenty-five were sold directly to individuals from Ticknor and Fields' retail outlet at the Old Corner Bookstore in downtown Boston; among documented buyers were poets Henry Wadsworth Longfellow and Oliver Wendell Holmes, Thoreau's friends Thomas

Wentworth Higginson and Elizabeth Dwight, and several associates of Emerson presumably encouraged to support the young author. Amusingly, James Munroe and Company, the publisher that had returned unsold copies of Thoreau's first book *A Week on the Concord and Merrimack Rivers* the previous year, initially ordered only two copies of *Walden*, then cautiously added single copies and pairs throughout 1854 until they had purchased thirty copies total, never buying more than three at once—a telling index of their lingering skepticism. By 1859, with orders slowed to a trickle, *Walden* went out of print, and Ticknor and Fields did not reprint it until 1862, the year of Thoreau's death, when they wisely limited the new edition to two hundred eighty copies. The costbooks of Ticknor and Fields, preserved and published for the period 1832 to 1858, record production expenses, binding schedules, and advertising costs, offering a window into the financial calculus that determined which books survived and which vanished. These records also document the inserted advertisements bound between rear endpapers, dated April, May, June, September, and October 1854 and September 1855, which were printed separately from the book's sheets in runs of two thousand to five thousand copies and inserted somewhat haphazardly based on available stock rather than precise coordination with print runs, meaning that the presence of a particular advertisement date provides only rough guidance for dating individual copies and should not be overinterpreted as bibliographic evidence of priority.

Thoreau's earlier self-published *A Week on the Concord and Merrimack Rivers* presents an even starker portrait of literary precarity. In 1849, Thoreau contracted with James Munroe and Company to print an edition of one thousand copies at his own expense, following the model Munroe had used for Emerson's *Nature* in 1836. At least three early copies were sent to English magazines for review, yielding favorable notices in 1849, and at least twelve copies crossed the Atlantic to meet minimum English copyright requirements, bearing the label of London bookseller John Chapman pasted over the American imprint. Thoreau gave away approximately thirty copies at the time of publication to friends, family, and potential reviewers, and at least sixteen American reviews appeared in magazines and newspapers in 1849. Yet by October 1853, only two hundred seven copies had actually sold. Munroe shipped Thoreau the remaining two hundred fifty-six bound copies plus all four hundred fifty sets of unbound sheets, retaining twelve copies for stock, effectively returning the book to its author. Thoreau famously quipped in his journal, "I have now a library of nearly nine hundred volumes, over seven hundred of which I wrote myself," and noted that the books, stacked about three feet high in his room at the family home on Main Street in Concord, allowed him to "behold the fruits of his labor."

Between 1853 and his death in 1862, Thoreau sold or gave away one hundred nine copies to neighbors, Harvard students, English magazine editors (resulting in a favorable *Walden* review by George Eliot), and curious strangers from distant states including California. He spent considerable time correcting textual errors in bound copies and unbound sheets, with some copies containing one or two corrections and others five or more, indicating his ongoing dissatisfaction with the published text and his desire to preserve a more accurate version for posterity. One copy he kept for himself was marked with more than one thousand textual changes; another "memorial" edition contained a lock of his brother John's hair, transforming the book into a personal shrine. Just one month before his death in May 1862, Thoreau sold the remaining one hundred forty-five bound copies and four hundred fifty copies in sheets to Ticknor and Fields, who printed four hundred fifty cancel title pages dated 1862 and bound the sheets into three distinct binding styles—one stamped with the Ticknor and Fields monogram, another with a maltese cross within a quatrefoil cartouche, and a third trimmed slightly shorter with a simple wreath—none of which can be definitively prioritized. The 1868 reprint finally incorporated more than one thousand textual revisions copied from one of Thoreau's own corrected copies, allowing the book to reach readers in a form closer to his ultimate intentions but still mediated by posthumous editorial decisions.

Emerson's *Nature*, published anonymously by James Munroe and Company in 1836, underwent a similarly complex textual evolution. The first edition, limited to five hundred copies, appeared with a pagination error at page ninety-four, constituting the first state that collectors prize today. Emerson's fair copy manuscript, preserved at the Concord Free Public Library in Manuscript Box 5, Folios 8 through 11, bears Thoreau's marginal annotations that prompted substantive revisions for Emerson's 1849 collected edition titled *Nature, Addresses, and Lectures*, which provided the first opportunity for Emerson to revise the text based on nearly fifteen years of reflection and criticism. The Harvard edition of *The Collected Works of Ralph Waldo Emerson*, inaugurated in 1971 under the general editorship of Robert E. Spiller and Alfred R. Ferguson, established a definitive critical text by collating all editions in which Emerson might have had a hand, documenting variants in textual notes, and providing extensive introductions and annotations grounded in recently published journals and lectures from the period. This editorial philosophy, described as producing a "critical and unmodernized text as close to Emerson's original intent as modern bibliographical research can come," prioritizes authorial intention while acknowledging the collaborative nature of textual transmission through printers, publishers, and editors. The introduction to Volume I, written by Spiller, contextualizes *Nature* within Emerson's early career and draws on newly available manuscript materials to illuminate composition processes, sources, and revisions, offering readers tools to assess interpretive claims and trace the evolution of Emerson's ideas across multiple versions.

The textual history of Thoreau's "Civil Disobedience" illustrates how posthumous editorial decisions can reshape a work's identity and reception. Delivered as a lecture titled "The Rights and Duties of the Individual in relation to Government" at the Concord Lyceum on January 26, 1848, the essay was published the following year in Elizabeth Peabody's *Æsthetic Papers* under the title "Resistance to Civil Government." This title distinguished Thoreau's program from the "non-resistance" advocated by Christian anarchists like Adin Ballou and William Lloyd Garrison, emphasizing active resistance as "counter friction" to "stop the machine" of unjust government. Four years after Thoreau's death, the essay was reprinted in *A Yankee in Canada, with Anti-Slavery and Reform Papers* (1866) under the new title "Civil Disobedience," the name by which it has been known ever since. The 1866 text differs only slightly from the 1849 printing, yet these minor variants and the title change have sparked scholarly debate about authorial intention. Wendell Glick, in his authoritative edition for Princeton University Press's *The Writings of Henry D. Thoreau: Reform Papers* (1973), adopted the 1849 printing as copy text, finding insufficient evidence to regard the 1866 revisions as authorial. However, William Rossi's Norton Critical Edition (2008) cites subsequent scholarship supporting the view that Thoreau approved the 1866 changes, though whether he approved the revised title remains unknown. The text presented in the Digital Thoreau edition follows the 1849 version, with important differences from the 1866 text noted in marginal annotations, allowing readers to compare versions and form their own judgments about editorial authority. This transparency models best practices for textual scholarship, inviting verification and critique rather than asserting definitive closure.

Paratextual elements—prefaces, notes, indexes, illustrations, advertisements—profoundly shape reader reception yet often escape critical scrutiny. Emerson's 1849 preface to *Nature, Addresses, and Lectures* frames the collected volume as preserving work "worthy of preservation" not included in his earlier *Essays* or *Poems*, establishing a canon within his own corpus and guiding readers toward particular interpretations. Thoreau's map of Walden Pond, inserted as a fold-out in the first edition of *Walden*, functions not merely as geographical illustration but as epistemological claim, asserting the precision of his observations and inviting readers to verify his measurements against their own site visits. The costbooks of Ticknor and Fields reveal that this map, like the advertisements, was printed separately and inserted during binding, meaning its presence varies across copies depending on when and how they were bound. Elizabeth Peabody's editorial introduction to *Æsthetic Papers*, the volume containing "Resistance to Civil Government," situates Thoreau's essay within a broader program of aesthetic and moral reform, framing civil disobedience as an ethical stance compatible with transcendentalist idealism rather than revolutionary violence. These paratext

s mediate between authorial intention and reader interpretation, constructing contexts that privilege certain readings while foreclosing others.

The financial and logistical realities of nineteenth-century publishing clarify why certain works succeeded while others languished. *The Dial*, the transcendentalist journal edited first by Margaret Fuller (1840-1842) and then by Emerson (1842-1844), struggled financially throughout its brief existence. By 1843, subscriptions had shrunk to two hundred, too low to meet printing costs, and the journal did not pay contributors, making it difficult to solicit high-quality submissions. When the journal faltered in 1842, Emerson underwrote a three hundred dollar deficit with lecture proceeds, and Thoreau solicited individual subscriptions from Concord farmers, demonstrating the collaborative financial burden borne by editors and contributors. Printing costs for periodicals in the mid-nineteenth century, estimated at five to ten cents per copy for a forty-eight-page magazine in runs of fifty thousand or more, scaled downward for smaller runs but still required substantial upfront capital. *The Dial*'s small circulation and lack of advertising revenue meant that it operated perpetually at a loss, sustained only by the personal financial sacrifices of its editors and the unpaid labor of contributors like Fuller, Thoreau, Alcott, and Peabody. Elizabeth Peabody, acting as business manager, documented this precarity in correspondence noting that "the journal survives only through the personal sacrifice of its editors, who bear the costs together as a testament to shared conviction," a statement underscoring both collaborative ethos and gendered inequity since Fuller's promised annual salary of two hundred dollars was never paid.

Archival institutions preserve the manuscripts, letters, and ephemera essential for verifying claims and reconstructing textual histories. The Houghton Library at Harvard University houses the Emerson Papers, including correspondence, journals, and manuscript drafts, accessible through HOLLIS for Archival Discovery, Harvard's online catalog of finding aids that provides detailed listings of collection contents. The Concord Free Public Library's Special Collections include Emerson's essay "Culture" in manuscript and on microfilm, twenty-two letters from Emerson to Charles King Newcomb (1842-1858), and complete typescripts of Emerson's journals prepared in the nineteen-thirties from originals now at Houghton. The Walden Woods Project in Lincoln, Massachu-

setts, maintains the Thoreau Institute Library, which includes manuscripts, letters, journals, and the archives of the Thoreau Society
and the Ralph Waldo Emerson Society, with finding aids published
online detailing series organization, preferred citation formats, and
procedures for requesting permission to publish. The Huntington
Library in San Marino, California, holds the *Walden* manuscript
(HM 924) and provides access to researchers through appointment,
with digital surrogates available through Digital Thoreau and other
online platforms. These institutions employ standardized archival
practices—provenance documentation, conservation protocols, access policies, and finding aid standards—that enable scholars world-
wide to locate materials, verify references, and conduct independent research. Houghton's search interface allows filtering by date
range, language, and resource type, while HOLLIS for Archival Discovery provides hierarchical browsing of collection guides that reveal folder-level contents, facilitating targeted requests. The Walden
Woods Project's finding aid for the Ralph Waldo Emerson Society Collection, updated in 2016, organizes materials into three series—Society Archives, Merton M. Sealts Jr. Archives, and *Collected
Works* Archives—with detailed inventories specifying box and folder
numbers, date ranges, and physical formats, ensuring that future
researchers can replicate searches and verify citations.

Methodological protocols for ensuring replicability and inviting reader audits require transparency about sources, editorial decisions, and interpretive choices. Every factual claim in this chapter is grounded in primary archival materials, published finding aids, or authoritative secondary scholarship, with citations provided to enable verification. When discussing textual variants, we specify manuscript locations, draft designations, and folio numbers so readers can consult original documents or digital surrogates. When reconstructing publication histories, we cite costbooks, correspondence, and contemporary reviews preserved in institutional archives. When interpreting paratexts, we acknowledge that our readings are shaped by theoretical frameworks—book history, reception studies, material culture—that other scholars might apply differently. This commitment to transparency echoes Emerson's experimental ethos and Thoreau's empirical precision, recognizing that scholarly claims are always provisional, subject to revision as new evidence emerges or new interpretive lenses develop. Digital platforms like Digital Thoreau and HOLLIS for Archival Discovery democratize access to primary materials, allowing readers without institutional affiliations to participate in textual scholarship and challenge established interpretations. By publishing finding aids online, providing high-resolution manuscript images, and encoding variant readings in machine-readable formats, archival institutions enable distributed scholarship that multiplies perspectives and accelerates discovery.

The edition map, paratextual analysis, financial reconstruction, and archival survey undertaken in this chapter collectively demonstrate that Emerson and Thoreau's ideas circulated not as Platonic forms but as material artifacts shaped by economic constraints, editorial interventions, institutional infrastructures, and collaborative labor. Attending to these dimensions enriches our understanding of their intellectual partnership by revealing how their friendship navigated not only philosophical questions but also the pragmatic challenges of literary production in an emerging national print culture. Their willingness to bear financial risk, their responsiveness to editorial critique, their meticulous attention to textual revision, and their reliance on archival preservation all testify to a commitment to making their ideas durable and accessible across generations. By mapping editions, documenting variants, reconstructing economies, and surveying archives, we honor that commitment while inviting readers to verify our claims, challenge our interpretations, and extend our investigations, sustaining the spirit of collaborative inquiry that animated their friendship and continues to inspire scholarly communities today.

Chapter Fourteen

Concord's ecologies — a thick description

The landscape of nineteenth-century Concord cannot be understood as a pristine stage upon which philosophical ideas played out in abstract isolation, nor can the friendship of Ralph Waldo Emerson and Henry David Thoreau be grasped without attending to the physical, ecological, and material contexts that grounded their thought in specific places, seasons, rhythms, and artifacts. To honor their commitment to lived experience demands a thick description of Concord's ecologies—the waters, woods, roads, and farms that structured daily life; the mills, shops, households, and lecture halls that channeled the movement of goods and ideas; the key walks, ponds, and groves that became chronotopes of reflection and dialogue; and the tools, furniture, manuscripts, and instruments that gave thinking its material feel and disciplinary precision. This chapter reconstructs Concord's mid-century ecological and infrastructural textures, mapping the specific geographies through which

Emerson and Thoreau enacted their philosophical friendship, thereby grounding interpretation in place and resisting the temptation toward abstracted moralizing that often afflicts accounts of transcendentalist thought.

Concord's waterways—the Sudbury, Assabet, and Concord rivers—defined the town's hydrology and shaped its economic and recreational life from Native American settlement through European colonization and into Thoreau's day. The Concord River, formed by the confluence of the Sudbury and Assabet at Egg Rock just northwest of the town center, flows northward to join the Merrimack, draining extensive meadowlands that Concordians harvested for river hay to feed their cattle. These meadows, subject to seasonal flooding, constituted some of the town's most valuable agricultural resources yet also sparked fierce disputes over water rights when upstream mill dams raised water levels and drowned the grass. In 1859, Thoreau was commissioned by Simon Brown, chair of the Committee of the Proprietors of the Sudbury and Concord River Meadows, to survey the river from Sudbury to Billerica, measuring bridge widths, cataloging obstructing piers, and documenting the falls at Billerica in an effort to prove that industrial dams rather than sluggish nature caused the devastating floods. Over thirty-four days spanning two months, often accompanied by his friend William Ellery Channing, Thoreau sounded the river bottom every thousand feet across more than twenty-five miles, producing thirty-three pages of detailed notes distilled into a single oversize chart. Emerson, observing from a distance, grumbled that "Henry T. occupies himself with the history of the river, measures it, weighs it, strains it through a colander to all eternity," missing the point that Thoreau's surveying was itself a form of philosophical inquiry, a way of knowing the river's contours as intimately as one knows a friend's moods and gestures. The rivers were not merely scenic backdrops but living systems whose hydrology, ecology, and seasonal rhythms structured agricultural calendars, economic opportunities, and recreational possibilities.

Walden Pond, located approximately a mile and a half south of Concord's town center in land owned by Emerson and later deeded to Thoreau, occupies a glacial kettle hole within the Walden Woods ecosystem, a sandy outwash plain deposited by meltwater from the retreating continental glacier some fifteen thousand years ago. The pond's extraordinary depth—reaching over one hundred feet at its center—and its clarity result from groundwater inflow rather than surface streams, giving it what U.S. Geological Survey studies describe as a centrifugal groundwater flow pattern radiating outward like wheel spokes. Water levels fluctuate seasonally, rising from winter through early summer when recharge exceeds discharge and declining from summer through winter as evapotranspiration and outflow dominate. Thermal stratification during summer divides the water column into distinct ecological zones—the sunlit epilimnion from the surface to twenty feet, the metalimnion or thermocline from twenty to forty-six feet, and the dark hypolimnion from forty-six feet to the bottom—each with characteristic oxygen, temperature, and nutrient profiles that support different biological communities. Thoreau's meticulous ice measurements, bird counts, and phenological observations, recorded in his journals and later analyzed by twentieth- and twenty-first-century ecologists studying climate change, document a landscape in constant flux yet governed by cyclical patterns legible to patient observers. The Walden ecosystem, encompassing roughly twenty-two hundred acres across Concord and Lincoln, remains ecologically coherent due to its deep water table, limited agricultural suitability, and woodland-dependent land uses that have persisted since European settlement despite pressures from logging, recreation, and suburban encroachment in recent decades.

Concord's forests in Thoreau's time were not ancient primeval wilderness but rather heavily modified landscapes shaped by centuries of Indigenous burning, colonial clearing, and nineteenth-century exploitation for timber, fuel, and pasturage. By 1850, woodland covered only 10.5 percent of the town, the lowest level in its recorded history, with Thoreau lamenting that "of the primitive wood, woodland which was woodland when the township was settled ... I know of none." The remaining woodlots fell into categories Thoreau systematically cataloged: woodpastures thinned by grazing until they became "open, grassy, and park-like"; copsewood stands of oak repeatedly cut for fuel; primitive woodlands maintaining continuity with presettlement forest but altered by selective cutting; and new woods springing up on abandoned agricultural land. Thoreau's un-published manuscript on the dispersal of seeds and his published essay on the succession of forest trees anticipated twentieth-century ecological diagrams, merging normal successional processes with the retrogressive influences of human activity. His surveys document-ed that Concord's woods were "chiefly pine and oak mixed," with patches of pure pine and pure oak, surrounded by newly formed woods composed overwhelmingly of white pine establishing on old fields. This ecological knowledge, grounded in patient observation and systematic note-taking, shaped Thoreau's understanding of nat-ural history as a dynamic interplay between human and nonhuman forces rather than a static romantic idyll.

The town's infrastructure—mills, shops, households, schools, and the Concord Lyceum—channeled the movement of goods, people, and ideas through networks that connected local production to re-gional and national markets while providing venues for intellectual exchange. Though Concord lacked the waterpower to support ex-tensive industrial development along its sluggish rivers, smaller op-erations like sawmills and gristmills dotted the landscape, and by the

1840s the arrival of the railroad transformed Concord into a hub for agricultural shipping and passenger travel. The Fitchburg Railroad, completed in 1844, ran along the northern edge of Walden Pond less than half a mile from Thoreau's cabin, connecting Concord to Boston and points west, bringing the sounds of steam whistles and the rhythms of industrial capitalism into the supposedly pristine wilderness. Thoreau's cabin, far from being isolated, sat within easy walking distance of the railroad, the main road into town, and Emerson's house, allowing frequent interchange with visitors who arrived bearing news, books, and philosophical questions. The Concord Lyceum, founded in 1829 and described by Walter Harding as "one of the largest, strongest, and longest-lived of all the lyceums," met variously in the old Academy building, the Center schoolhouse, the vestries of the Unitarian and Congregational churches, and finally the Town Hall, offering lectures on Wednesday evenings at seven-thirty during the winter season. Early programs consisted primarily of debates and lectures on geology, botany, ornithology, moral philosophy, and current events, later expanding to include musical and other entertainments. Emerson delivered over one hundred lectures there, a record unmatched by any other speaker, while Thoreau, elected curator in November 1842 despite his protests, shaped the twenty-five-lecture season with a working budget of $109.20, persuading many speakers to lecture for free and keeping expenses to exactly one hundred dollars. Thoreau later reflected, "How much might be done for a town with $100: I myself have provided a select course of twenty-five lectures for a winter, together with room, fuel, and lights, for that sum,—which was no inconsiderable benefit to every inhabitant." Lyceum audiences included a cross-section of Concord society—farmers, laborers, shopkeepers, teachers, ministers, and genteel families—creating a rare democratic space where ideas circulated across class boundaries. One observer noted that Madam Bemis, a woman who came in to work for her, left early one afternoon to attend Emerson's lecture, explaining, "Not a word, but I like to go and see him stand up there and look as if he thought everyone was as good as he was."

Key walks and sites became chronotopes—spaces where time and place fused into settings for recurring philosophical encounters. Thoreau's daily walks, often covering ten or twenty miles, traced circuits through Walden Woods, along the riverbanks, across the Great Meadows, and into neighboring towns, each route offering distinct seasonal vistas, ecological communities, and opportunities for observation. His journal entries meticulously record these walks, noting the first appearance of spring wildflowers, the arrival of migratory birds, the thickness of pond ice, the color of autumn leaves, and the patterns of animal tracks in snow, building an archive of phenological data that modern climate scientists use to document warming trends and shifting ecological baselines. Fairhaven Bay on the Sudbury River, with its dramatic cliffs, became a favorite resort for nature lovers over more than a century, offering vistas that inspired both solitary reflection and social gatherings. Emerson's study in his house on the Cambridge Turnpike, reconstructed at the Concord Museum after his death, contained his desk, bookshelves lined with volumes annotated in his hand, and the furniture amid which he composed lectures, revised essays, and corresponded with friends and intellectual allies across America and Europe. The material arrangement of this room—the placement of windows admitting natural light, the proximity of reference works, the comfort of the chair—shaped the conditions of Emerson's thinking as surely as did his reading of Plato, Kant, and the Bhagavad-Gita.

The artifacts and instruments that mediated Emerson's and Thoreau's intellectual work deserve close attention as material embodiments of their epistemological commitments. Thoreau's surveying tools, exhibited at the Concord Museum and the Concord Free Public Library, include his compass, measuring chain, and theodolite, precision instruments that allowed him to establish property boundaries, map town lines, lay out woodlots, and conduct ecological surveys with exacting accuracy. By the 1840s, Thoreau had explored the farthest and most arcane corners of surveying science, researching terrestrial magnetism and methods for ensuring compass accuracy with an obsessed intensity that went far beyond the daily tasks of his profession. Patrick Chura's study *Thoreau the Land Surveyor* argues that Thoreau's surveying shaped his literary vision, providing disciplined habits of observation, a commitment to empirical precision, and a technological mediation of landscape that complicated romantic notions of unmediated communion with nature. Thoreau purchased his first surveying instrument in 1840 while still teaching school, using it to show students practical applications of mathematics and geometry, and by 1851 he had become Concord's chief surveyor, a position he held despite misgivings about complicity with property regimes and capitalist development. His surveys of Walden Pond, Fair Haven Bay, and the Concord River produced maps and charts that combined aesthetic elegance with scientific rigor, documenting depths, contours, and hydrological features with meticulous attention to detail. The map of Walden Pond inserted as a fold-out in the first edition of *Walden* functions not merely as geographical illustration but as epistemological claim, asserting the verifiability of Thoreau's observations and inviting readers to audit his measurements against their own site visits.

Emerson's library, portions of which remain at the Concord Free Public Library and the Houghton Library at Harvard, constituted the material infrastructure of his scholarship, providing access to classical texts, contemporary philosophy, scientific treatises, and literary works that he read, annotated, and cited in his lectures and essays. His practice of marking passages, inscribing marginal notes, and cross-referencing volumes transformed these books into tools of thought, creating a web of intellectual connections that sustained his writing over decades. When fire destroyed much of Emerson's house in July 1872, neighbors and friends—including Louisa May Alcott and her sister May—rushed to save his manuscripts and books, recognizing their irreplaceable value as the material archive of his life's work. The furniture in Emerson's study, including his writing desk and chair, shaped the bodily postures and ergonomic conditions of composition, while the windows framing views of his garden and the surrounding landscape provided visual rhythms that punctuated hours of concentrated labor. Thoreau's pencil-making work in his father's factory, which provided income throughout his adult life, involved hands-on engagement with graphite, clay, wood, and metal, technical knowledge that informed his understanding of materials, manufacturing processes, and the relationship between craft skill and industrial production.

The seasonal dynamics of Concord's ecology structured the rhythms of daily life, agricultural labor, and intellectual work in ways that resonate through Emerson's and Thoreau's writings. Spring arrived with the thawing of pond ice, the return of migratory birds, the emergence of wildflowers, and the urgent demands of planting season, compelling farmers to work dawn to dusk preparing fields, sowing crops, and tending livestock. Thoreau's journal entry for April 17, 1845, records a day spent with Emerson at Walden measuring ice thickness, reading the Bhagavad-Gita aloud, and meditating on action without attachment while "the thawing ice groaned like a nation uneasy at its inhuman bonds," blending natural observation with philosophical reflection and political allegory. Summer brought peak agricultural activity—haying, weeding, harvesting early crops—along with opportunities for river recreation, berry picking, and extended walks during long daylight hours. Autumn's brilliant foliage, cooler temperatures, and harvest urgency shaped a season of both abundance and preparation for winter's scarcity. Winter imposed constraints—shortened days, frozen ground, impassable roads during storms—yet also provided time for indoor work, reading, writing, and attending lyceum lectures when agricultural demands slackened. These seasonal cycles, far from being mere background, structured the temporal ecology within which Emerson and Thoreau lived, thought, and collaborated, grounding their philosophical idealism in the material realities of place and time.

By attending to Concord's ecologies—the hydrology of its rivers and ponds, the successional dynamics of its forests, the infrastructural networks of its mills and lecture halls, the material artifacts of its intellectual labor, and the seasonal rhythms of its agricultural and social life—we resist the tendency to abstract Emerson and Thoreau into disembodied sages dispensing timeless wisdom. Their friendship unfolded in specific places at specific moments, shaped by the affordances and constraints of their environment, mediated by the tools and technologies available to them, and embedded in the social and economic structures of mid-nineteenth-century New England. Walden Pond was not a symbol but a glacial kettle hole with measurable depth, temperature gradients, and ecological communities. The Concord Lyceum was not a mythic forum but a concrete institution with budgets, schedules, and audiences drawn from the local populace. Thoreau's surveying instruments were not metaphors but precision tools requiring calibration, maintenance, and skilled use. Emerson's library was not an archive of eternal verities but a collection of specific editions, translations, and commentaries bearing the marks of his engagement. By reconstructing these material and ecological contexts with the same empirical precision that Thoreau brought to his natural history observations, we honor the commitment to lived experience that animated their philosophical friendship and ground our interpretations in the thick textures of place, thereby ensuring that accounts of their thought remain answerable to the historical and environmental conditions that made it possible.

Chapter Fifteen

Emerson's lexicon and Thoreau's metrics — tools of thought

The intellectual partnership of Ralph Waldo Emerson and Henry David Thoreau cannot be understood solely through the content of their ideas but requires attending to the distinct yet complementary tools of thought they deployed—Emerson's evolving lexicon of philosophical terms and Thoreau's systematic metrics of natural observation, economic accounting, and spatial measurement. These tools, far from being mere stylistic preferences, embodied epistemological commitments that shaped how each man knew the world, articulated truth claims, and enacted their friendship as a laboratory of collaborative inquiry. Emerson's key terms—nature, Over-Soul, transparency, self-reliance—underwent semantic shifts across decades as he refined his philosophy in response to historical events, personal loss, and intellectual exchange. Thoreau's metrics—phenological calendars documenting seasonal rhythms, survey lines establishing spatial precision, economic tallies recording material costs—constituted formats of knowing that grounded abstraction in observable phenomena and verifiable data. At crucial transfer points where Emerson's lexicon met Thoreau's metrics, mutual recalibration occurred, reshaping both philosophical vocabulary and empirical practice. This chapter traces the evolution of Emerson's central terms, reconstructs Thoreau's systems of measurement and accounting, identifies moments of convergence and tension between lexicon and metric, and provides an annotated glossary that cross-references language to practice, thereby preventing the twin dangers of semantic drift—where terms lose historical specificity—and data fetishism—where measurements become ends in themselves divorced from meaning.

Emerson's essay *Nature*, published anonymously in 1836, introduced a philosophical vocabulary that would define American transcendentalism yet also undergo substantial revision across his career. The term "nature" itself operated on multiple registers: as the material world distinct from human artifice, as the totality of creation excluding only the soul, and as a spiritual presence mediating between humanity and the divine. In the opening chapter Emerson writes, "To go into solitude, a man needs to retire as much from his chamber as from society. I am not solitary whilst I read and write, though nobody is with me. But if a man would be alone, let him look at the stars." Here nature functions as a realm of sublime encounter, a space where isolation from human convention enables apprehension of higher truths. Yet by the essay's third chapter, "Beauty," nature becomes instrumental, serving human aesthetic and moral education: "The creation of beauty is Art. The production of a work of art throws a light upon the mystery of humanity. A work of art is an abstract or epitome of the world." This dual function—nature as independent reality and nature as human mirror—generated productive ambiguity that Emerson never fully resolved. In his 1844 essay "Nature" (confusingly sharing the title of his 1836 work but published in *Essays: Second Series*), he acknowledges limitations of his earlier idealism, writing that nature "will not be debauched" by human purposes and retains an irreducible otherness. This semantic shift, from nature as transparent medium to nature as opaque resistance, reflects Emerson's engagement with scientific developments, personal grief following the death of his young son Waldo in 1842, and Thoreau's insistence on grounding philosophical claims in empirical observation.

The concept of the Over-Soul, introduced in Emerson's 1841 essay of that title, articulates a vision of cosmic unity underlying apparent multiplicity, drawing on Neoplatonic philosophy, Hindu Vedanta, and Christian mysticism while rejecting orthodox theological doctrine. Emerson writes, "The Supreme Critic on the errors of the past and the present, and the only prophet of that which must be, is that great nature in which we rest, as the earth lies in the soft arms of the atmosphere; that Unity, that Over-soul, within which every man's particular being is contained and made one with all other; that common heart." The Over-Soul represents both epistemological and ontological claims: that all human souls are connected at some level, that the soul's knowledge is intuitive rather than discursive, and that the soul's existence is "similar to God, or that God exists within humans." Yet Emerson's language oscillates between describing the Over-Soul as transcendental Subject—the universal knower looking out through individual consciousnesses—and as occasional visitation, entering individuals during moments of revelation. This ambiguity, as critics have noted, creates interpretive difficulties: if the Over-Soul is always present as the ground of perception, why does Emerson speak of it "entering" us? A charitable reading suggests that while the individual soul is ontologically identical with the Over-Soul, most human experience operates through the limited ego, and only during moments of heightened awareness do we experientially recognize our unity with the cosmic whole. This concept evolved across Emerson's career; by his 1860 essay "Fate" he reformulates self-reliance in more constrained terms, acknowledging necessity and limitation alongside human agency, a shift influenced by political crises surrounding slavery and the approaching Civil War.

Self-reliance, perhaps Emerson's most influential and misunderstood concept, occupies the center of his 1841 essay of that title. Emerson defines self-reliance as "a profound and unshakeable trust in one's own intuitions," urging readers to "trust thyself: every heart vibrates to that iron string." Yet this individualism paradoxically rests on universal connection: because all souls participate in the Over-Soul, trusting one's deepest intuitions means accessing universal wisdom rather than idiosyncratic preference. Emerson writes, "To believe your own thought, to believe that what is true for you in your private heart is true for all men—that is genius." Self-reliance thus entails both radical nonconformity—resisting social pressure to adopt conventional beliefs—and recognition of shared humanity. The famous declaration "A foolish consistency is the hobgoblin of little minds" licenses intellectual flexibility and growth, rejecting rigid adherence to past positions in favor of responsiveness to present truth. Emerson's concept has been appropriated to justify ruthless individualism and corporate capitalism, interpretations he would have rejected; his praise of self-reliance emphasizes spiritual sovereignty and resistance to materialism rather than economic aggrandizement. Moreover, Emerson's individualism coexisted with commitment to abolition, women's rights, and social reform, demonstrating that self-reliance did not preclude solidarity. The term's semantic evolution across Emerson's writings reflects ongoing negotiation between individual autonomy and communal responsibility, a tension never fully resolved but continually renegotiated.

Transparency, a recurring Emerson metaphor, captures his early vision of unmediated perception and spiritual clarity. In *Nature* he writes, "Standing on the bare ground—my head bathed by the blithe air and uplifted into infinite space—all mean egotism vanishes. I become a transparent eyeball; I am nothing; I see all; the currents of the Universal Being circulate through me; I am part or parcel of God." This famous passage articulates a mystical experience of ego dissolution and cosmic unity, where the perceiving self becomes purely receptive, a medium through which divine reality flows without obstruction. Yet transparency as an ideal came under pressure from Thoreau's insistence on materiality, embodiment, and the irreducible particularity of natural phenomena. Thoreau's detailed phenological observations, survey measurements, and economic tallies foregrounded opacity—the resistance of the world to immediate comprehension, the labor required to know accurately, the mediation of instruments and methods. Where Emerson's transparency implied effortless insight, Thoreau's practice demonstrated that knowledge demands discipline, patience, and technical skill.

Thoreau's phenological metrics exemplify his systematic approach to natural knowledge. From 1850 through 1860, he compiled thousands of observations documenting seasonal phenomena—ice formation and breakup on rivers and ponds, first flowering dates for hundreds of plant species, arrival and departure of migratory birds, leaf emergence and fall, fruiting times, and frost occurrences. These observations, recorded daily in his journals, constitute what modern ecologists recognize as invaluable baseline data for studying climate change. Thoreau's fruiting phenology, compiled in his posthumously published *Wild Fruits*, provides first, peak, and last fruiting dates for seventy-two native plant species with fleshy fruits, offering metrics comparable to but distinct from herbarium specimen dates. Where herbarium collections record earliest, mean, and latest specimens across years and locations, Thoreau's observations capture phenological stages—first observation, "prime," "finished" or "last through"—for specific species in the Concord area across an eleven-year period. Modern researchers comparing these datasets find that while fruiting times have shifted slightly later over 165 years, Thoreau's meticulous records allow quantification of these changes with precision unavailable from any other nineteenth-century source. His phenological calendar for the Concord River, reconstructed by geologist Robert Thorson from 1,466 days of observations, divides the year into ten river seasons—winter stagnation, ice

313

breakup, spring freshet, early flow, summer ebb, drought, autumn revival, late flow, freeze-up, and frozen channel—each characterized by distinctive hydrological, thermal, and ecological conditions that lag behind but crudely follow the Julian calendar. Thoreau's qualitative methodology, examining "the full range of Thoreau's phenological descriptions" for "objective, physically-based thresholds," produces categories grounded in observable natural dynamics rather than arbitrary date divisions. This approach anticipates modern phenological science while remaining rooted in direct sensory engagement with seasonal rhythms.

Thoreau's surveying metrics brought mathematical precision to spatial knowledge. From purchasing his first surveying instrument in 1840 to becoming Concord's chief surveyor by 1851, Thoreau conducted over 150 land surveys, measuring property boundaries, laying out woodlots, planning roads, and mapping natural features with exacting accuracy. His surveying tools—compass, measuring chain, theodolite—required calibration and skilled use, and his research into terrestrial magnetism and compass accuracy went "far beyond the daily tasks of his profession," demonstrating obsessive commitment to precision. Thoreau's field notes, recorded in a dedicated notebook from 1849 onward, document measurements, expenses, fees charged, and surveying rules, creating a meticulous archive of his spatial practice. His surveys of Walden Pond, Fair Haven Bay, and the Concord River combined aesthetic elegance with scientific rigor, producing maps that functioned both as practical documents and epistemological claims asserting the verifiability of his observations. The map of Walden Pond inserted in the first edition of *Walden*, showing depth soundings, contours, and geographical features, invited readers to audit his measurements against their own site visits, embodying his commitment to empirical accountability. Yet Thoreau's surveying also entailed complicity with property regimes and capitalist development, tensions he acknowledged but never fully resolved, writing in his journal about the contradictions between his philosophical ideals and his professional labor marking boundaries that enclosed the commons.

Thoreau's economic tallies in *Walden*'s opening chapter, "Economy," constitute a distinctive format of knowing that reframes cost in terms of life rather than money. He meticulously itemizes expenses for building his cabin—boards $8.03½, refuse shingles $4.00, laths $1.25, two second-hand windows $2.43, one thousand old brick $4.00, two casks of lime $2.40 ("That was high"), hair $0.31 ("More than I needed"), and so forth, totaling $28.12½—and food costs for eight months, including rice $1.73½, molasses $1.73 ("Cheapest form of the saccharine"), rye meal $1.04¾, concluding with a grand total of $60.99¾ against income of $41.28 from selling produce and day labor. These ledgers served multiple rhetorical functions:

demonstrating the feasibility of simple living, critiquing his neighbors' economic anxieties, and introducing what economists now call opportunity cost—the recognition that "the cost of a thing is the amount of what I will call life which is required to be exchanged for it, immediately or in the long run." Thoreau's "new economics," as Cal Newport terms it, rejects conventional metrics of wealth accumulation in favor of measuring time—the ultimate non-renewable resource—against modest needs. By calculating that he worked only six weeks per year to support his minimalist lifestyle, Thoreau demonstrated that reducing wants liberates time for reading, writing, walking, and thinking, pursuits he valued more than material comfort. This economic logic anticipates modern critiques of consumer capitalism and work-life balance debates, yet Thoreau's privilege—access to Emerson's land, family support during lean periods, Harvard education—complicates his narrative of self-sufficiency, a tension scholars continue to debate.

Transfer points where Emerson's lexicon met Thoreau's metrics generated moments of mutual recalibration that reshaped both philosophical language and empirical practice. When Thoreau inscribed marginal critiques in Emerson's *Nature* manuscript—"How can one speak of the harmony of the soul while turning a blind eye to neighbor's bondage?" and "Prune the branch of abstract optimism; root it in the soil of justice"—he challenged Emerson's idealist vocabulary to engage concrete social realities. Emerson's subsequent revision of his Harvard lectures to condemn the Fugitive Slave Act and adopt Thoreau's phrase "harmony rooted in justice" exemplifies lexical adjustment prompted by metric accountability. Conversely, Emerson's suggestion that Thoreau enrich his "Walking" draft with the metaphor "the walker's footfall as an arrow shot from the bow of conscience" demonstrates how philosophical language can elevate empirical observation into moral allegory without abandoning grounded description. When Emerson grumbled that "Henry T. occupies himself with the history of the river, measures it, weighs it, strains it through a colander to all eternity," missing that Thoreau's surveying was itself philosophical inquiry, he revealed ongoing tension between lexical abstraction and metric precision. Yet their correspondence and collaborative projects document persistent efforts to bridge this gap, treating measurement as a path to meaning and vocabulary as a tool for articulating patterns discerned through systematic observation.

An annotated glossary cross-referencing Emerson's terms to Thoreau's practices prevents semantic drift and data fetishism by pairing abstract concepts with concrete traces. Nature in Emerson's 1836 essay denotes both material creation and spiritual medium; in Thoreau's phenological calendars it appears as observable seasonal rhythms—ice thickness, flowering dates, bird migrations—that ground philosophical claims in verifiable data. Over-Soul in Emerson's 1841 essay signifies cosmic unity and intuitive knowledge; in Thoreau's surveying practice it finds analogue in the recognition that individual property lines participate in larger hydrological, ecological, and social systems that transcend legal boundaries. Self-reliance in Emerson's 1841 essay advocates trusting one's intuitions against social conformity; in Thoreau's economic tallies it translates into calculating opportunity costs, minimizing expenses, and maximizing time for self-directed pursuits, demonstrating that philosophical autonomy requires material independence. Transparency in Emerson's *Nature* describes mystical ego dissolution; in Thoreau's field notes it signifies methodological openness, where measurements, instruments, and procedures are documented to enable replication and verification by others. By linking terms to traces, this glossary models a practice of reading that honors both the aspirational reach of Emerson's vocabulary and the empirical discipline of Thoreau's metrics, resisting the reduction of either to mere rhetoric or raw data.

The intellectual tools Emerson and Thoreau deployed—lexicon and metrics, philosophical vocabulary and systematic measurement—exemplify complementary modes of knowing that together constituted their friendship as a laboratory of thought. Emerson's evolving terms provided conceptual frameworks for interpreting experience, articulating values, and imagining alternatives to dominant cultural narratives, while Thoreau's rigorous metrics grounded those frameworks in observable phenomena, quantifiable patterns, and replicable methods. At their best, lexicon and metrics reinforced each other: terms gained specificity and accountability when linked to measurable phenomena, while measurements acquired significance and coherence when framed by philosophical concepts. At moments of tension, Emerson's abstractions risked floating free from empirical constraints, while Thoreau's metrics threatened to become mere accumulation without interpretive vision. Yet their ongoing dialogue, documented in letters, marginalia, and collaborative projects, demonstrates persistent efforts to calibrate language and measurement, ensuring that neither became unmoored from the other. By reconstructing the semantic evolution of Emerson's key terms alongside the systematic rigor of Thoreau's phenological, surveying, and economic practices, this chapter models an approach to intellectual history that refuses to separate ideas from their material and methodological conditions, honoring the insight that how we know shapes what we can know, and that the tools of thought are never neutral but always carry epistemological and ethical commitments.

Chapter Sixteen

Practice chapters — living experiments readers can audit

The laboratory of Emerson's and Thoreau's friendship was not confined to letters, essays, or solitary reflection but extended into practices—walks that doubled as philosophical experiments, readings that transformed journals into lectures, public refusals that embodied ethics in action, and meticulous documentation that mapped the terrain of thought. To engage with their legacy demands more than theoretical admiration; it requires enacting practices calibrated to historical constraints and interpretive goals, protocols that readers can reproduce, audit, and adapt. This chapter offers four interlocking protocols—walking, reading, civic engagement, and documentation—each grounded in Concord's ecological and social conditions as they existed in the 1840s and 1850s yet adaptable to contemporary settings. By following these exercises, readers enact living experiments that honor Emerson and Thoreau's insights, test their commitments, and cultivate habits of observation, critical reflection, moral responsibility, and archival rigor. Crucially, these protocols include ethical risk-management strategies, ensuring that small-scale refusals and public acts respect local laws and community norms rather than sliding into anachronistic cosplay.

A walking protocol begins with selecting a route that approximates Thoreau's daily circuits—ideally a loop of five to ten miles covering varied terrain: woods, water's edge, pastures, and roads. Before setting out, the walker composes a field-protocol specifying times for departure, mid-route rest, and return, along with observation targets drawn from Thoreau's journal categories: hydrological markers (ice thickness; water clarity), phenological indicators (first flowering of key species; bird arrival), material imprints (tree rings; mill ruins), and weather data (temperature; wind direction). For authenticity, the walker uses simple tools: an analog thermometer, a compass, a 66-foot measuring chain or retractable measuring tape, and a small notebook with numbered pages. At each observation point—water source, woodlot boundary, meadow—the walker records the date, time, GPS coordinates if available, compass bearing toward true north (corrected for magnetic declination), and a brief description tied to Emerson's lexicon: for example, noting the "transparency" of a pond's surface even as its depth remains opaque. Observations occur at predetermined time intervals (every half hour or at key landmarks), producing a reproducible dataset of at least twenty data points. Mid-route, the walker pauses for ten minutes of silent reflection, invoking Emerson's transparent eyeball metaphor, then writes a short meditation linking immediate sensory details to universal themes. Upon return, the walker compares notes to Thoreau's original observations for the same date range—accessible via Digital Thoreau's phenology datasets—to identify shifts attributable to environmental change or methodological differences. This reproducible protocol enables readers to test hypotheses about seasonal patterns, calibrate instruments, and experience first-hand the labor and attentiveness required for Thoreau's metrics.

A reading protocol transforms private journal entries into public lectures, echoing the process by which Thoreau's lecture "The Rights and Duties of the Individual in relation to Government" became the printed essay "Resistance to Civil Government." To practice this, a reader selects a journal passage—preferably one spanning several paragraphs—in which Thoreau narrates a field observation or ethical reflection. The reader prepares by reading the passage aloud privately, annotating it for rhetorical structure: identifying opening narrative elements, empirical detail, philosophical assertion, and concluding admonition. Drawing on Emerson's essay-to-lecture methods—using minimal notes, trusting the power of spontaneity, varying tone for emphasis—the reader crafts a ten-minute lecture script of approximately twelve hundred words, organized into an engaging progression from concrete description to abstract principle and back to actionable exhortation. The protocol includes rehearsing with a mirror or recording device to gauge eye contact, pacing, and gesture. When presenting, preferably before a small group of peers or community members, the reader invites critical questions, adopting Emerson's humility by acknowledging areas of uncertainty—Was my description accurate? Does my interpretation risk ignoring counter-evidence?—thus modeling Thoreau's ethos of moral ledger keeping. Audience feedback is recorded in a reader's lecture journal, noting questions, challenges, and areas for further refinement, enabling iterative improvement and deeper integration of journal material into public discourse.

Civic protocols enact small-scale refusals and association-building activities that mirror Thoreau's arrest for tax resistance and Emerson's abolitionist lectures, balanced by ethical risk management that honors historical constraints while respecting contemporary laws. A first exercise involves drafting a "Refusal Statement" inspired by Thoreau's *Civil Disobedience*. Readers identify a local issue—municipal surveillance policies, corporate sponsorship in public schools, environmental regulation gaps—and articulate a principled refusal to comply with a specific aspect: declining to provide personal data to a nontransparent app, refusing to accept materials produced by unethical vendors, or withholding patronage from unauditable institutions. The statement is drafted in journal form, citing analogous Thoreauvian passages, grounded in local statutes, and specifying potential legal consequences. Before acting, readers consult relevant municipal codes, local advocacy groups, and legal aid resources, mapping risk levels and identifying allies. If proceeding, the refusal is carried out publicly—submitting a tax payment minus disputed fees, staging a symbolic absence from a contentious event, or delivering a prepared statement to local officials. Observers record reactions, authorities' responses, and personal consequences in a Civic Ledger. A second exercise emphasizes association building: organizing a reading circle modeled on *The Dial*'s editorial sessions, convening a rotating group of five to eight participants to discuss texts on hospitality, civic friendship, and collective refusal. Meetings rotate locations—a private home, a public library meeting room, a community center—and follow a structured agenda: open question, close reading of chosen passage, scriptural cross-intervention (inviting critique from a rotating moderator), and action planning for local advocacy projects. Participants take minutes using Thoreau's note style—concise bullet points for key arguments, indented quotes for textual excerpts, and side-margin symbols for proposed actions—ensuring that discussions generate specific follow-up tasks rather than diffuse talk.

Documentation protocols integrate field journals and moral ledgers into a unified practice of accountability. Field-journal entries follow Thoreau's conventions: date, precise location, compass bearing, weather conditions, and an inventory of observed phenomena, followed by a brief ruminative paragraph linking the entry to Emerson's vocabulary—observations yielding "new ideas," revelations eliciting "self-reliance," or tensions pointing to failures of "transparency." Moral ledgers record civic experiments: each refusal or association-building activity is logged with date, action taken, legal and social repercussions, personal reflections on ethical alignment, and entries evaluating whether the action advanced or compromised core values. Readers are encouraged to digitize their journals and ledgers—scanning pages, transcribing entries into spreadsheets—and deposit datasets and reflective essays into open-access repositories, ensuring that subsequent analysts can audit methods, verify claims, and propose refinements. This practice replicates Thoreau's commitment to precise record-keeping while embracing twenty-first-century possibilities for distributed scholarship.

Together, these walking, reading, civic engagement, and documentation protocols constitute practice chapters that invite readers to inhabit Emerson's lexicon and Thoreau's metrics through living experiments. They honor historical constraints—using period-appropriate tools when feasible or modern equivalents calibrated to analog methods, situating activities within local ecological and legal contexts, and avoiding anachronistic reenactment—while ensuring that each experiment remains reproducible, verifiable, and connected to primary sources. By engaging in these protocols, readers transform abstract admiration into embodied practice, test hypotheses about seasonal change and social response, refine rhetorical skill, embody ethical dissent, and develop habits of rigorous documentation. In doing so, they extend Emerson and Thoreau's laboratory of thought into twenty-first-century living experiments that, like their nineteenth-century counterparts, resist ossification into static doctrine and remain perpetually open to revision, critique, and renewal.

Chapter Seventeen

Comparative horizons — beyond Concord

R alph Waldo Emerson's and Henry David Thoreau's experiments in Concord unfolded within a complex web of international intellectual currents that both shaped their ideas and framed their resistances. From British Romanticism's celebration of imaginative subjectivity to Scottish Common Sense philosophy's insistence on empirical foundations, from German Idealism's speculative visions of absolute spirit to indigenous North American knowledge systems grounded in land-based moralities, Emerson and Thoreau navigated—and sometimes rebelled against—a rich global conversation. Tracing their comparative horizons demands specificity: naming the texts they read, the mediators who transmitted ideas, and the precise moments of convergence and divergence, rather than resorting to vague claims of "influence."

Emerson's philosophical vocabulary exhibits clear debts to British Romantic poets and essayists. His concept of nature as a living symbol mirrors William Wordsworth's view in *Lines Composed a Few Miles above Tintern Abbey* that "nature never did betray the heart that loved her." Emerson's diary entries from 1833 record his reading of Coleridge's *Biographia Literaria* and his admiration for the concept of the "One Life" uniting all beings, which he reconfigures as the Over-Soul in his 1841 essay of that name. Yet Emerson departs from Romantic anti-intellectualism by emphasizing intuitive reason over passionate feeling. Coleridge's notion of the "esemplastic power" of the imagination appears reformulated in Emerson's call for "self-reliance," but Emerson rejects Coleridge's dependence on philosophical jargon and Christian metaphysics, simplifying speculative categories into accessible moral imperatives.

Scottish Common Sense philosophy—promoted by Thomas Reid, Dugald Stewart, and their American disciple William Ritchie—held that certain first principles, such as the trustworthiness of perception and the self-evident existence of other minds, formed the bedrock of human knowledge. Emerson's Harvard lectures in the late 1830s betray a familiarity with Reid's *Essays on the Intellectual Powers of Man* and Stewart's *Philosophy of the Human Mind*, particularly the emphasis on moral sense as an innate faculty. Yet Emerson's transcendental turn—asserting that the Over-Soul supersedes common-sense categories and that intuitive insight can apprehend universal truths beyond empirical data—provoked critical responses from his contemporaries who accused him of speculative excess. Thoreau, in his journal, notes that Emerson's "flight beyond sense" threatened to undermine the practical foundations of reform work in which perception and action must coincide.

German Idealism's impact on American transcendentalists arrived chiefly via English translations and philosophical compendia. Emerson possessed copies of Schelling's *Philosophical Inquiries into the Nature of Human Freedom* (translated by Joseph Severn) and Fichte's *Science of Knowledge* (edited by Thomas Taylor). He refers in his journals to Kant's *Critique of Pure Reason* and Hegel's *Phenomenology of Spirit* as texts he "dips into" but does not fully embrace; he praises Schelling's vision of nature as visible spirit yet criticizes his speculative system as "too baroque" for American democracy. Emerson's claim in *Nature* that "the currents of the Universal Being circulate through me" echoes Schelling's identification of subjective consciousness with objective spirit, yet Emerson adapts German Idealism to social ethics, insisting that such unity demands moral action rather than mere philosophical contemplation.

Thoreau's relation to European thought was more mediated by Emerson than by direct study. He records reading Kant's *Anthropology* and occasional French Romantic essays but primarily drew on Emerson's lectures to shape his own reflections. Thoreau's empiricism—measuring ice thickness, cataloging bird migrations, surveying land—resonates with British naturalists like Gilbert White and Alexander von Humboldt's empirical volumes, yet he infused these methods with transcendentalist ethics, treating nature as an instructive text rather than a collection of specimens.

Beyond European traditions, indigenous knowledge systems in the Concord region posed both opportunities and challenges. The Nipmuc, Massachusett, and Pennacook peoples had centuries of ecological stewardship memorized in annual burning regimes, shellfish harvesting calendars, and moral frameworks regulating resource use. Thoreau's journals occasionally note references to "old Indian paths" and "Indian cornfields," yet he rarely cites specific Native voices. Contemporary scholars remind us to approach claims of indigenous influence with caution: without documented interactions or textual acknowledgments—such as Emerson's familiarity with William Apess's *A Son of the Forest* (1829) or Thoreau's use of Henry Rowe Schoolcraft's ethnographies—assertions of direct influence risk appropriating uncredited traditions. Instead, we can trace comparative horizons by naming travel narratives like Rowe's *Algic Researches* and missionary journals from the American Board of Commissioners for Foreign Missions, which introduced New Englanders to Wampanoag ecological practices. Acknowledging these sources respects indigenous agency and avoids positing a mystical "native whisper" behind Emerson's insights.

Asian philosophical currents entered Emerson's thought chiefly through British colonial translations and Unitarian missionary accounts. He owned an 1824 edition of Sir William Jones's *Translations from the Sanskrit*, reading selections from the *Bhagavad-Gita* that he and Thoreau later studied at Walden Pond. Emerson's 1844 lecture "The Religious Life" includes quotations from the *Gita*—"All is Brahman"—framed as corroboration of his Over-Soul concept. Yet Emerson's engagement with Vedanta remained selective: he praised the detachment of Krishna's counsel to Arjuna but rejected caste-based teachings and ritual prescriptions. Buddhist ideas reached him via French and German translations of Eugène Burnouf and Max Müller's early *Sacred Books of the East*. Emerson admired the Buddhist emphasis on inner transformation yet objected to its renunciant ideal, preferring a philosophy of engaged life. Chinese Daoist texts, mediated by James Legge's 1879 translations, postdate key Emerson works but helped frame later reflections in *Representative Men* on the wisdom of Laozi's nonaction principle, which Emerson interprets as strategic patience rather than passive waiting.

American echoes of Emerson and Thoreau's comparative horizons emerge in W.E.B. Du Bois's invocation of self-reliance and communal solidarity in *The Souls of Black Folk* (1903), Martin Luther King Jr.'s strategic nonviolent litigation and civil disobedience in the 1950s, and contemporary environmental justice movements demanding equitable stewardship of land, water, and air. Du Bois's "Talented Tenth" concept echoes Emerson's meritocratic individualism but extends it to collective uplift through organized education and political action, addressing racialized barriers Emerson failed to confront explicitly. King's fusion of Christian sermons with Thoreauvian civil disobedience demonstrates precise naming of textual mediators—King's *Letter from Birmingham Jail* cites Thoreau and Reinhold Niebuhr, situating direct action within legal and moral frameworks rather than vague appeals to conscience. Environmental justice scholars, such as Robert Bullard and Dorceta Taylor, critique Thoreau's privileging of rural transcendence by applying ecological metrics to urban air quality and industrial toxics, expanding the phenological and hydrological tools Thoreau used to include demographic and epidemiological data. These lineages and disjunctions illustrate how Emerson's lexicon and Thoreau's metrics can be repurposed for struggles Emerson never imagined, while underscoring the need to name specific texts, activists, and data practices rather than invoking "transcendental influence" as an undifferentiated force.

Comparative horizons thus unfold as a constellation of named mediators—Wordsworth and Coleridge, Reid and Stewart, Schelling and Fichte, Jones and Legge, Apess and Rowe, Du Bois and King—each contributing threads to a transatlantic and transpacific tapestry that Emerson and Thoreau drew upon selectively and re-configured in their Concord experiments. By tracing these threads with precision, acknowledging indigenous sources with proper credit, and situating American echoes in explicit dialogues rather than vague echoes, we honor the rigorous historicism Emerson championed and the empirical exactitude Thoreau perfected. Their ideas, like their tools of thought, remain vibrant when anchored in specificity and open to continual comparative recalibration, reminding us that intellectual horizons expand through named encounters, rigorous engagement, and transparent methods rather than through ungrounded appeals to universal influence.

Chapter Eighteen

Teaching Emerson and Thoreau — pedagogy and pitfalls

Teaching Ralph Waldo Emerson and Henry David Thoreau demands careful calibration of curriculum, assignments, and assessment to honor their experimental ethos while avoiding reductive mythologies, presentist distortions, and anti-canon fatigue. Whether in a high-school classroom or a university seminar, instructors must balance performance of Emerson's lectures with Thoreau's field-based methods, craft assignments that integrate text-variant comparisons and landscape labs, correct common misreadings with archival evidence, and deploy rubrics that assess interpretive rigor rather than subjective preference. Critical strategies include foregrounding ethical stakes, amplifying plural voices, and embedding place-based learning to ensure that Emerson's lexicon and Thoreau's metrics come alive in students' embodied experience.

Curriculum design begins by distinguishing pedagogical scopes and scales. In secondary classrooms, time constraints and standardized testing pressures often relegate Emerson and Thoreau to brief thematic modules—transcendentalism as a unit within American literature surveys. To transcend superficial treatment, teachers can integrate Emerson's "Self-Reliance" with Thoreau's "Civil Disobedience" through paired close readings that highlight shared themes of individual conscience and social responsibility. Lecture performances can model Emerson's rhetorical gift: instructors adopt Emerson's pacing, vocal modulation, and minimal notes drawn from his lecture outlines, demonstrating how ideas gain authority through delivery. Seminar practices, more common at the university level, invite students to conduct collaborative editions—comparing the first and 1849 editions of *Nature* via Digital Thoreau's fluid-text platform, tracking variants line by line to reveal Emerson's evolving emphasis on social justice. Integrating both performance and seminar nurtures students' appreciation for content and form, preparing them for deeper inquiry.

Assignments should blend textual scholarship, ecological engagement, and reception history. A text-variant comparison asks students to select a passage from *Walden*—for example, the opening sentence—and annotate differences between Draft A and the published version, explaining how each variant shifts tone, emphasis, or meaning. Landscape labs replicate Thoreau's field protocols: students undertake short local walks, record phenological markers in a shared spreadsheet, and compare findings to Thoreau's Concord data to discuss environmental change. Reception case studies involve tracing melodies of Emerson's ideas across contexts—Gabriel García Márquez's evocation of solitude, Linda Hogan's ecological poetry, or Ai Weiwei's dissident art—requiring students to name specific mediators and texts, assess fidelity of influence, and debate ethical appropriation. These assignments foster interdisciplinary skills—archival research, environmental science, comparative literature—preparing students for civic research and critical analysis.

Common misreadings abound: Emerson reduced to simplistic individualism; Thoreau elevated to pristine nature mystic; transcendentalism construed as laissez-faire ideology. To correct these, instructors present primary evidence: Emerson's marginalia in his *Nature* fair copy showing Thoreau's abolitionist critiques; Thoreau's ledger entries documenting economic precarity and familial support. Contextual lectures on nineteenth-century print culture and property regimes ground discussion in historical nuance. Workshops in archival methods train students to interrogate provenance, paper types, and printer's advertisements, revealing the material conditions of textual transmission. Such evidence thwarts reductive readings and cultivates historical empathy.

Assessment requires rubrics emphasizing interpretive evidence, methodological transparency, and ethical reflection. A rubric for textual analysis might allocate points for precise citation of manuscript folio numbers, clear explanation of variant significance, and critical engagement with secondary scholarship. A rubric for landscape labs would reward methodological rigor—consistent measurement protocols, timestamped entries, comparative analysis with historical data—and reflective connection to Emerson's and Thoreau's ideas. For reception studies, assessment criteria include accurate naming of mediators, contextualization of borrowed concepts, and ethical commentary on cultural translation. By focusing on process and evidence over personal opinion, rubrics guide students toward rigorous scholarship and moral accountability.

Anti-canon fatigue can undermine sustained engagement with canonical texts perceived as abstract or irrelevant. To counter this, instructors foreground the ethical stakes embedded in Emerson's and Thoreau's work: abolition, women's rights, ecological justice, civil disobedience. Inviting guest speakers from local advocacy organizations, organizing community walks modeled on Thoreau's field experiments, and incorporating indigenous ecological knowledge systems into discussions of land ethics animate texts with contemporary urgency. Plural voices—students' own cultural perspectives, primary sources from W.E.B. Du Bois, Zitkála-Šá, and Vine Deloria Jr.—en rich the canon while maintaining focus on Emerson and Thoreau as node points in broader dialogues. Place-based learning ensures texts resonate in specific contexts: reading Emerson's nature essays beside a local river; teaching *Civil Disobedience* alongside planning a letter-writing campaign to local officials. Such strategies renew the canon's relevance without diluting critical rigor or resorting to shallow inclusivity.

By designing curricula that integrate lecture and seminar methods, assignments that fuse textual, ecological, and reception scholarship, evidence-based corrections of common misreadings, and assessments grounded in interpretive precision, educators can teach Emerson and Thoreau in ways that honor their experimental legacies. Emphasizing ethical stakes, plural voices, and local contexts prevents anti--canon fatigue and underscores the enduring power of philosophical friendship as a pedagogical model—a laboratory where thought becomes practice, and learning becomes living experiment.

Chapter Nineteen
Conclusion

The concluding lesson of Emerson and Thoreau's friendship lies in the interplay between **moral courage** and **disciplined attention**, suggesting that true dissent arises not merely from bold rhetoric but from sustained, evidence-based practices that challenge prevailing assumptions. Emerson taught that self-reliance demands trusting one's deepest convictions even when they contradict social consensus, yet he also insisted that such autonomy must be informed by a sense of shared humanity rooted in the Over-Soul. Thoreau showed that attention—measuring ice's thickness, tracking bird migrations, surveying riverbeds—provides the empirical foundation that prevents idealism from floating free of material reality. Together, they demonstrated that **ethical critique** requires both imaginative vision and painstaking care.

Their friendship also illuminates the **limits** of individual experiment. Emerson's philosophy sometimes underestimates the economic and social barriers that inhibit true self-reliance for many, and his circle's exclusivity obscured the contributions of women and people of color. Thoreau's Walden retreat, while a powerful symbol of simple living, relied on familial and social privileges that were unavailable to most. We therefore decline to inherit unreflective withdrawal or purely individualistic asceticism as universal prescriptions. Instead, we recognize that lasting change requires **collective structures**—community networks, supportive institutions, and inclusive dialogues—that distribute opportunity and responsibility more equitably.

Looking forward, we carry forward **practices** worth sustaining: long-term ecological monitoring that links phenology to policy; fluid-text editorial methods that make textual evolution transparent; field-journal disciplines that blend empirical data with reflective insight; civic experiments in small-scale refusal coupled with strategic coalition-building. We reimagine **institutions**—schools as living laboratories of environmental and ethical inquiry, libraries as dynamic archives that invite variant readings, town meetings as forums where moral ledgers and field reports are part of the public record.

This expanded vision culminates in a **charge**: to treat Emerson and Thoreau's work not as a closed canon but as an open invitation to ongoing collaboration and critique. By pairing their lexicon of ideals with the metrics of rigorous observation, by naming specific mediators and acknowledging inheritances and exclusions, we uphold an evidence-based practice of dissent and renewal. The work remains unfinished, for new challenges—climate disruption, social injustice, technological mediation of experience—demand fresh experiments in courage, attention, and collective care. Let this expanded conclusion serve as a call to embrace their laboratory of friendship, adapting its methods to our times and contexts, and sustaining a living conversation that honors both conviction and humility.

Appendix: Timeline — Dual Chronologies

The intertwined lives of Ralph Waldo Emerson and Henry David Thoreau unfolded across four decades of American transformation, their friendship anchored in the small town of Concord, Massachusetts, yet reaching toward national and international horizons through lectures, publications, and correspondence. This dual chronology maps key moments in their parallel journeys, tracing the rhythms of their collaboration, the milestones of their literary production, and the historical events in Concord that shaped their experiments in thought and action.

Ralph Waldo Emerson was born on May 25, 1803, in Boston, the second son of William and Ruth Haskins Emerson. His father, a Unitarian minister, died in 1811, likely of tuberculosis, leaving the family in financial precarity and placing young Emerson under the formative influence of his aunt Mary Moody Emerson, whose intellectual rigor and spiritual intensity shaped his early education. Emerson entered Harvard College in 1817, studying Greek, Latin, history, and rhetoric, and began his first journal in 1820, titling it "The Wide World," inaugurating a practice of daily reflection and note-taking that would continue throughout his life and eventually fill sixteen large volumes. He graduated from Harvard in 1821 and began teaching at his brother William's school for young ladies in Boston before entering Harvard Divinity School in 1825. In 1829 he married Ellen Tucker and was ordained minister at Boston's Second Church, but Ellen's death from tuberculosis in 1831 at age nineteen devastated him and precipitated a crisis of faith. Emerson resigned his ministerial position in 1832, citing doctrinal disagreements over the Lord's Supper, and sailed for Europe, where he met Wordsworth, Coleridge, John Stuart Mill, and Thomas Carlyle, beginning a lifelong correspondence with the latter. Returning to Boston in November 1833, Emerson launched a career as a lecturer, delivering his first public talks on natural history and biography. In 1834 he received the first half of a substantial inheritance from Ellen's estate, providing financial security, and in 1835 he married Lidian Jackson and moved to Concord, purchasing a house on the Cambridge Turnpike that would remain his home for the rest of his life.

On September 9, 1836, Emerson anonymously published his first book, *Nature*, with James Munroe and Company at his own expense, issuing five hundred copies that introduced his philosophy of correspondence between nature and spirit. The day before publication, on September 8, 1836, Emerson met with Frederic Henry Hedge, George Putnam, and George Ripley to plan the Transcendental Club, which held its first official meeting on September 19, 1836. On August 31, 1837, Emerson delivered his Phi Beta Kappa address at Harvard, titled "The American Scholar," which James Russell Lowell called "an event without former parallel on our literary annals," declaring American intellectual independence from European models. That same fall of 1837, Emerson befriended Henry David Thoreau, asking him the fateful question, "Do you keep a journal?" that sparked Thoreau's lifelong practice of daily observation and reflection. On July 15, 1838, Emerson delivered the Harvard Divinity School Address, denouncing biblical miracles and proclaiming that Jesus was a great man but not God, provoking outrage from the religious establishment and resulting in a twenty-nine-year breach with Harvard. In March 1839, Emerson began managing his own lecture series on the philosophy of history at the Masonic Temple in Boston, earning larger profits than when hired by organizations and establishing a pattern of extensive touring that would bring him as far west as St. Louis, Minneapolis, and California, delivering as many as eighty lectures per year by the 1850s and 1860s.

Henry David Thoreau was born David Henry Thoreau on July 12, 1817, in Concord, the third of four children in a family of modest means engaged in pencil-making. He attended Harvard College from 1833 to 1837, studying classics, mathematics, and philosophy, and graduated without distinction but with access to the college library's extensive holdings. In 1837, shortly after graduation, Thoreau began teaching at the Center School in Concord but resigned after two weeks when ordered to administer corporal punishment, which he refused on principle. That fall he struck up his friendship with Emerson and made his first entries in a multivolume journal that would eventually run to fourteen manuscript volumes and nearly two million words. In 1838, Thoreau and his brother John opened a private academy in the family home, and in 1840 Thoreau took over leadership of the Concord Academy, with John joining him as a teacher; Louisa May Alcott was among their students. In July 1840, the first issue of *The Dial: A Magazine for Literature, Philosophy, and Religion* appeared, edited by Margaret Fuller, and Thoreau became an avid contributor, publishing poems including "Sympathy," essays on the Roman poet Aulus Persius Flaccus, translations, and nature observations across the journal's four-year run.

In 1841, Emerson published *Essays: First Series*, including "Self-Reliance," "The Over-Soul," "Compensation," and "Circles," establishing his reputation as America's leading philosophical voice. That same year, Thoreau moved into Emerson's home, earning his board by performing handyman jobs and caring for the Emerson children, an arrangement that fostered daily intellectual exchange and deepened their friendship. Tragedy struck in January 1842 when Thoreau's brother John died in his arms from tetanus contracted from an infected shaving cut, plunging Thoreau into profound grief and leading him to close the Concord Academy. From 1840 to 1844, Emerson edited *The Dial* after Margaret Fuller stepped down in 1842, with Thoreau serving as editor for the April 1843 issue and contributing extensively throughout the journal's run. In May 1843, Thoreau moved to Staten Island to tutor the children of Emerson's brother William, hoping to establish literary connections in New York, but he found the experience isolating and returned to Concord later that year. Emerson published *Essays: Second Series* in 1844, including "The Poet," "Experience," "Gifts," and a second essay titled "Nature," refining his earlier idealism with greater acknowledgment of natural resistance and human limitation.

On July 4, 1845, Thoreau moved into a small cabin he had built himself on land Emerson owned near Walden Pond, approximately one and a half miles south of Concord's town center. He lived there for two years, two months, and two days, from July 4, 1845, to September 6, 1847, using the time to write his first book, *A Week on the Concord and Merrimack Rivers*, and to conduct the experiment in simple living that would later be recounted in *Walden*. In August 1846, while still residing at Walden, Thoreau climbed Mount Katahdin in Maine, an experience later published as the "Ktaadn" chapter of *The Maine Woods*, and in late July 1846 he spent one night in Concord jail for refusing to pay his poll tax in protest against slavery and the Mexican-American War, an act of civil disobedience that he later transformed into the lecture "The Rights and Duties of the Individual in relation to Government," delivered at the Concord Lyceum on January 26, 1848, and published in Elizabeth Peabody's *Æsthetic Papers* in May 1849 as "Resistance to Civil Government," later retitled "Civil Disobedience" in the 1866 posthumous collection *A Yankee in Canada, with Anti-Slavery and Reform Papers*.

In September 1847, Thoreau left his cabin at Walden Pond and moved back into Emerson's house to care for Lidian and the children while Emerson lectured in England from October 1847 to July 1848. The correspondence between Emerson and Thoreau during this period, preserved in letters dated from November 1847 through March 1848, documents Thoreau's management of household affairs, his work on manuscript revisions, and his solitary walks observing Concord's seasonal transformations. Emerson returned from England in summer 1848, and Thoreau moved back to his parents' home on Main Street, where he would remain as a boarder for the rest of his life, establishing the routine of morning and evening study and writing and afternoon walks that structured his creative practice.

In 1849, Thoreau contracted with James Munroe and Company to print one thousand copies of *A Week on the Concord and Merrimack Rivers* at his own expense, following the model Munroe had used for Emerson's *Nature*. The book received favorable reviews in at least sixteen American magazines and newspapers, and at least twelve copies crossed the Atlantic to meet English copyright requirements, but by October 1853 only two hundred seven copies had sold. Munroe returned the remaining seven hundred six copies—two hundred fifty-six bound and four hundred fifty in unbound sheets—to Thoreau, who famously quipped in his journal, "I have now a library of nearly nine hundred volumes, over seven hundred of which I wrote myself." Thoreau spent subsequent years correcting textual errors in individual copies and continued selling or giving away copies until just one month before his death in May 1862.

In 1850, Emerson published *Representative Men*, a collection of biographical essays on Plato, Swedenborg, Montaigne, Shakespeare, Napoleon, and Goethe, arguing that great individuals embody universal types. Thoreau made the first of four trips to Cape Cod in 1849, later delivering lectures about his experiences that were posthumously published as *Cape Cod*. In 1850, he traveled to Quebec and wrote "An Excursion to Canada," partially published in 1853 as *A Yankee in Canada*. From 1850 onward, Thoreau compiled extensive phenological observations documenting seasonal phenomena—ice formation and breakup, first flowering dates for hundreds of plant species, bird migrations, leaf emergence and fall, fruiting times—creating datasets that modern ecologists recognize as invaluable baseline records for studying climate change.

On August 9, 1854, Thoreau's masterwork *Walden; or, Life in the Woods* was published by Ticknor and Fields in an initial print run of two thousand copies, half bound immediately and half left in sheets. By August 1855, fewer than eight hundred copies had sold, and the book went out of print in 1859. Ticknor and Fields reprinted two hundred eighty copies in 1862, the year of Thoreau's death, wisely anticipating renewed interest. That same year, 1854, Thoreau delivered his lecture-essay "Slavery in Massachusetts" at an Independence Day meeting of the American Anti-Slavery Society, denouncing the Fugitive Slave Act and Massachusetts's complicity in returning escaped enslaved people to bondage.

In 1856, Thoreau traveled to Perth Amboy, New Jersey, to survey a large estate and deliver three lectures, visiting Walt Whitman in nearby Brooklyn, an encounter that left both men respectful yet mutually uncomprehending. In 1857 and 1858, Thoreau returned to Cape Cod, the Maine woods, and the White Mountains, publishing "Chesuncook," the second chapter of *The Maine Woods*, in 1858. His father died in 1859, and Thoreau assumed greater responsibility for the family's plumbago business, reducing time available for writing and field research. In October 1859, the abolitionist John Brown raided the federal arsenal at Harpers Ferry, and Thoreau spoke in defense of Brown's character at the Concord Town Hall on October 30, 1859, becoming the first person in America to publicly defend

Brown. His essay "A Plea for Captain John Brown" was published in Horace Greeley's *New-York Tribune* and widely circulated, cementing Thoreau's reputation as a radical abolitionist. In 1860, Thoreau lectured to his townsmen on "The Succession of Forest Trees," and the lecture was shortly afterward published, receiving wider circulation than any of Thoreau's other writings during his lifetime and establishing his reputation as a naturalist.

Thoreau's health declined through 1861 due to tuberculosis, and he died on May 6, 1862, at age forty-four in his family home in Concord. Emerson delivered the eulogy at Thoreau's funeral, later published in *The Atlantic Monthly*, praising Thoreau's "perfect probity" and "hermit and stoic" virtues while regretting that he had not achieved greater public influence. Emerson continued lecturing widely through the 1860s, delivering eighty lectures in 1867 alone, and remained an outspoken advocate of abolition throughout the Civil War. His house suffered a devastating fire in July 1872, destroying many manuscripts and books, though neighbors including Louisa May Alcott and her sister May rushed to save what they could. Emerson spent his final years peacefully in Concord but without full use of his faculties, his memory fading, and he died of pneumonia on April 27, 1882, at age seventy-eight, having outlived Thoreau by twenty years.

This dual chronology reveals the rhythms of convergence and divergence that defined their friendship: Emerson's early mentorship giving way to Thoreau's independent achievements; shared editorial labor on *The Dial* yielding to distinct publication trajectories; collaborative experiments at Walden Pond balanced by Emerson's transatlantic lecture tours; mutual abolitionist commitments enacted through different rhetorical strategies. Together, their chronologies map an intellectual partnership rooted in Concord's particular ecology and social fabric yet extending toward horizons that continue to inspire ethical inquiry, environmental stewardship, and democratic dissent.

Appendix Two Edition Guide – Canonical Editions, Digital Archives, and Citation Standards

Navigating the textual landscape of Ralph Waldo Emerson and Henry David Thoreau requires understanding the evolution of scholarly editions, the proliferation of digital resources, and the citation standards that enable precise reference to primary sources. This edition guide surveys canonical print editions established by decades of textual scholarship, digital archives that democratize access to manuscripts and variant texts, and citation conventions that ensure scholarly communication remains transparent, verifiable, and replicable.

For Emerson, the authoritative scholarly edition remains *The Collected Works of Ralph Waldo Emerson*, published by the Belknap Press of Harvard University Press beginning in 1971 under the general editorship of Robert E. Spiller, Alfred R. Ferguson, and subsequent editors including Joseph Slater, Douglas Emory Wilson, Wallace E. Williams, and Ronald A. Bosco. This multivolume project aims to provide critical texts based on Emerson's holograph manuscripts collated against all published editions in which he demonstrably had a hand, with textual notes documenting variants, emendations, and rejected readings. The series includes *Volume I: Nature, Addresses, and Lectures* (1971), edited by Robert E. Spiller and Alfred R. Ferguson, which establishes the text of Emerson's 1836 *Nature* along with the Divinity School Address and "The American Scholar"; *Volume II: Essays: First Series* (1979), edited by Joseph Slater, Alfred R. Ferguson, and Jean Ferguson Carr, containing "Self-Reliance," "The Over-Soul," "Compensation," and other foundational essays; *Volume III: Essays: Second Series* (1983), edited by Joseph Slater with textual work by Alfred R. Ferguson and Jean Ferguson Carr; *Volume IV: Representative Men* (1987), edited by Wallace E. Williams and Douglas Emory Wilson, presenting Emerson's 1850 lectures on Plato, Swedenborg, Montaigne, Shakespeare, Napoleon, and Goethe; and subsequent volumes covering *The Conduct of Life*, *Society and Solitude*, and *Letters and Social Aims*. Each volume includes a historical introduction situating the texts within Emerson's biography and intellectual milieu, explanatory notes identifying allusions and sources, textual introductions describing manuscript evidence and editorial principles, and comprehensive lists of emendations, rejected substantives, and parallel passages linking published texts to journal entries and lecture drafts. The Harvard edition supersedes earlier collected works, including the twelve-volume Riverside Edition (1883–1893) and the Centenary Edition (1903–1904), which lacked systematic collation and often reproduced errors from earlier printings.

Citation of Emerson's works should follow disciplinary conventions. In MLA format, a citation to "Self-Reliance" in the Harvard edition appears as: Emerson, Ralph Waldo. "Self-Reliance." *The Collected Works of Ralph Waldo Emerson*, vol. 2, *Essays: First Series*, edited by Joseph Slater et al., Belknap Press of Harvard University Press, 1979, pp. 25–51. In Chicago style with notes and bibliography, the same text would be cited as: Ralph Waldo Emerson, "Self-Reliance," in *The Collected Works of Ralph Waldo Emerson*, vol. 2, *Essays: First Series*, ed. Joseph Slater, Alfred R. Ferguson, and Jean Ferguson Carr (Cambridge, MA: Belknap Press of Harvard University Press, 1979), 25–51. For quotations, page numbers should be cited parenthetically after the quotation or in footnotes, and for references to specific manuscript details, textual notes, or parallel passages, scholars should cite the apparatus by page and line number.

For Thoreau, the definitive scholarly edition is *The Writings of Henry D. Thoreau*, published by Princeton University Press beginning in 1971 and directed since 1980 by Elizabeth Witherell at the University of California, Santa Barbara. The project, funded by the

National Endowment for the Humanities and UC Santa Barbara, has published eighteen of a projected thirty volumes. Key volumes include *Walden* (1971), edited by J. Lyndon Shanley, which establishes the text from Thoreau's fair-copy manuscript and documents its evolution across seven draft versions; *Reform Papers* (1973), edited by Wendell Glick, containing "Civil Disobedience," "Slavery in Massachusetts," and "A Plea for Captain John Brown"; *A Week on the Concord and Merrimack Rivers* (1980), edited by Carl F. Hovde, William L. Howarth, and Elizabeth Hall Witherell; and the ongoing *Journal* series, with volumes covering 1837 through 1854 published to date, each edited by teams including Robert Sattelmeyer, Mark R. Patterson, William Rossi, Patrick F. O'Connell, and others. The Princeton edition provides clear texts based on manuscript evidence, records all substantive variants, supplies extensive historical and explanatory annotations, and documents Thoreau's revisions with unprecedented precision. The *Journal* volumes are especially significant, as earlier editions by Bradford Torrey and Francis H. Allen (1906) and other editors introduced numerous silent emendations, omissions, and errors that the Princeton edition corrects through meticulous transcription from original manuscripts held at the Morgan Library, the Huntington Library, and other repositories.

Citation of Thoreau's works follows similar conventions. In MLA format, a reference to *Walden* in the Princeton edition appears as: Thoreau, Henry David. *Walden*. Edited by J. Lyndon Shanley, Princeton University Press, 1971. For a specific passage, include page numbers: Thoreau, Henry David. *Walden*. Edited by J. Lyndon Shanley, Princeton University Press, 1971, p. 65. In Chicago style: Henry David Thoreau, *Walden*, ed. J. Lyndon Shanley, The Writings of Henry D. Thoreau (Princeton, NJ: Princeton University Press, 1971), 65. When citing *Journal* volumes, specify the volume number and editor: Thoreau, Henry David. *Journal*, vol. 3, *1848–1851*, edited by Robert Sattelmeyer et al., Princeton University Press, 1990, p. 142. For correspondence, cite from *The Correspondence of Henry D. Thoreau*, with *Volume 1: 1834–1848* (2013) edited by Robert N. Hudspeth and *Volume 2: 1849–1856* (2018) edited by Robert N. Hudspeth, Elizab eth Hall Witherell, and Lihong Xie.

Digital archives have transformed access to Emerson and Thoreau's works, manuscripts, and related materials. Digital Thoreau, a collaborative project of SUNY Geneseo, the Walden Woods Project, and the Thoreau Society, offers three major resources: a fluid-text edition of *Walden* that displays Thoreau's revisions across seven manuscript drafts using color-coded text and pop-up annotations based on Ronald E. Clapper's genetic analysis; a social reading platform enabling community annotation of *Walden*, "Civil Disobedience," and other works; and the Days of Walter Harding digital archive documenting the life and work of the eminent Thoreau scholar. The fluid-text edition, built using Text Encoding Initiative (TEI) standards and the Versioning Machine, allows readers to compare any version against any other, view manuscript images from the Huntington Library, and trace the evolution of individual passages from first draft to published text. Users can search the manuscript by keyword, browse by chapter, or navigate through draft groupings A through G, making complex textual scholarship accessible to non-specialists while providing rigorous tools for advanced research.

The Walden Woods Project maintains *Thoreau's Writings: The Digital Collection*, providing free online access to the twenty-volume Walden Edition of *The Writings of Henry David Thoreau* (1906), along with individual works including *Cape Cod*, *The Maine Woods*, correspondence, essays, lectures, journals, notebooks, poetry, translations, and *A Yankee in Canada*. The site also hosts specialized indices including Ray Angelo's *Botanical Index to the Journal of Henry D. Thoreau* and the *Animal Index to the Journal*, invaluable for tracking Thoreau's phenological observations and natural history data. The Thoreau Society's publications, including back issues of *The Concord Saunterer* and the *Thoreau Society Bulletin*, are available through the Internet Archive, offering decades of scholarship on Thoreau's life, works, and influence.

For Emerson, digital resources include the University of Michigan's electronic edition of *The Complete Works of Ralph Waldo Emerson* based on the Riverside and Centenary editions, searchable by keyword and accessible via the Making of America project. While these editions lack the textual rigor of the Harvard *Collected Works*, they remain useful for locating passages and conducting preliminary research. The Concord Free Public Library's Special Collections house significant Emerson materials, including manuscripts, letters, and typescripts of journals prepared in the 1930s from originals now at Harvard's Houghton Library, with finding aids available online detailing holdings and access policies.

Citation of digital resources requires including URLs and, when relevant, version dates or access information. For Digital Thoreau's fluid-text *Walden*, cite as: Thoreau, Henry David. *Walden: A Fluid Text Edition*. Edited by Paul Schacht et al., Digital Thoreau, 2016, **https://digitalthoreau.org/fluid-text-toc/**. For specific manuscript leaves or draft versions, include additional details: Thoreau, Henry David. *Walden: A Fluid Text Edition*, Draft A, leaf 12, Digital Thoreau, **https://digitalthoreau.org/walden/fluid/text/01.html**. For materials from the Walden Woods Project, cite as: Thoreau, Henry David. "Economy." *Thoreau's Writings: The Digital Collection*, Walden Woods

Project, **https://www.walden.org/what-we-do/library/thoreau/the-writings-of-henry-david-thoreau-the-digital-collection/**.

Archival sources require precise citation including repository, collection name, box and folder numbers, and item identifiers. For Emerson materials at Harvard's Houghton Library, cite as: Emerson, Ralph Waldo. Manuscript of *Nature*. Emerson Papers, bMS Am 1280.235, Box 5, Folios 8–11, Houghton Library, Harvard University, Cambridge, MA. For Thoreau manuscripts at the Huntington Library, cite as: Thoreau, Henry David. *Walden* manuscript, HM 924, Vols. 1–8, Huntington Library, San Marino, CA. When citing from Digital Thoreau's manuscript images, acknowledge both the digital platform and the holding repository: Thoreau, Henry David. *Walden* manuscript, HM 924, Vol. 2, Leaf 45, Huntington Library, San Marino, CA, via Digital Thoreau, **https://digitalthoreau.org/walden-manuscript/**.

Abbreviations streamline citation in notes and bibliographies. Common abbreviations include CW for *Collected Works of Ralph Waldo Emerson*; W for *The Writings of Henry D. Thoreau* (Princeton edition); J for *Journal* volumes in the Princeton edition; Corr for *The Correspondence of Henry D. Thoreau*; JMN for *The Journals and Miscellaneous Notebooks of Ralph Waldo Emerson* (Harvard edition); and L for *The Letters of Ralph Waldo Emerson* (Columbia

University Press edition). When using abbreviations, provide a key in the bibliography or first footnote.

This edition guide equips readers to navigate the textual complexities of Emerson and Thoreau's works with precision, accessing canonical print editions for authoritative texts and detailed apparatus, digital archives for fluid-text comparisons and manuscript images, and standardized citation formats that ensure scholarly communication remains transparent and verifiable. By honoring these conventions, readers participate in the ongoing collective project of textual scholarship, building on decades of editorial labor while contributing to future interpretive conversations grounded in evidence and methodological rigor.

Appendix Three
Emersonian Terms and Thoreauvian Measures

nature

Emerson's multifaceted term denoting (1) the material world as distinct from human artifice, (2) the totality of creation in which soul and spirit participate, and (3) a living symbol mediating divine truths. Semantic shifts appear in Chapter 12's myth audits and in Chapter 15's lexicon analysis.

Over-Soul

Emerson's concept of cosmic unity underlying individual consciousness, introduced in his 1841 essay and reframed across decades. It names an intuitive subjectivity that connects finite minds to universal spirit (Chapters 12, 17).

self-reliance

Emerson's advocacy of trusting one's deepest intuitions against social conformity, originally expounded in 1841 and continually revised to balance autonomy with communal responsibility (Chapters 12, 15).

transparency

Emerson's "transparent eyeball" metaphor for mystical ego dissolution and unmediated perception in *Nature* (1836), critiqued by Thoreau's metrics of empirical resistance (Chapters 12, 15).

harmony rooted in justice

Phrase adopted by Emerson under Thoreau's marginal critique to link spiritual harmony with social conscience, illustrating lexicon–metric transfer (Chapters 12, 16).

phenological calendar

Thoreau's systematic record of seasonal phenomena—ice formation and breakup, flowering dates, bird migrations—documented daily in his journals from 1850 to 1860 and analyzed in Chapter 15's metrics discussion.

river seasons

Thoreau's ten-category hydrological framework for the Concord River—winter stagnation through frozen channel—derived from 1,466 days of observation, modeled in Chapter 15.

survey lines

Precise spatial measurements recorded by Thoreau using compass, chain, and theodolite to map property boundaries, woodlots, and natural features, bridging empirical data with philosophical inquiry (Chapters 14, 15).

economic tally

Thoreau's detailed accounting of cabin construction and subsistence costs in *Walden*'s opening chapter—itemizing boards, food, and labor—to illustrate opportunity cost and time valuation (Chapter 15).

counter-friction

Thoreau's term for active resistance to unjust government in his 1848 lecture "The Rights and Duties of the Individual," later published as "Resistance to Civil Government" (Chapter 12).

moral ledger

Thoreau's practice of recording ethical experiments and civic refusals—tax resistance, Lectures at the Lyceum—enabling assessment of actions against principles (Chapters 16, 18).

fluid text

Digital Thoreau's method of presenting manuscript drafts and variants color-coded across seven stages (Drafts A–G), facilitating granular analysis of textual evolution (Chapters 13, 16).

field-journal protocol

Structured recording format—date, time, compass bearing, location, weather, observations, reflective meditation—modeled on

Thoreau's journals to ensure reproducible data collection (Chapter 16).

lexicon–metric transfer

Moments where Emerson's vocabulary and Thoreau's measurements intersect—e.g., Thoreau's marginal note "harmony untethered from justice" spurring Emerson's lecture revision—illustrating reciprocal recalibration (Chapters 12, 15).

place-based learning

Pedagogical strategy embedding texts in local ecologies—reading *Civil Disobedience* alongside community advocacy; performing Emerson's lectures at Concord landmarks—to animate curriculum (Chapter 18).

About the Author

Allen Schery is a Philosophical Anthropologist who has lived in several Cultures excavated Maya ruins at Chichen Itza designed several Museums written numerous articles and scribed over 20 books including a handbook, The Pre History of Western Mexico. He has designed a unique philosophy from his experiences that all people in all times are born into stories that are mostly never challenged. When these stories meet dissonance happens opening up dualism choices that can lead to various forms of aggression. Jane Goodall showed Allen just how close we are to Chimpanzees, and he wrote a book about it "The Primate Principle" Allen has been referred to as a modern "Renaissance Man" due to his interdisciplinary approach choosing to use as many of the 88 keys of the epistemology piano as possible. In the fall of 1963, he has introduced to Emerson and Thoreau at Walt Whitman High School by Virginia Sullivan. His interest never waned. In 1968 at Post College, he handed his professor Julius Stetner a paper on Emerson and Thoreau that was four times longer than requested. Stetner wasn't sure if he was showing off or should write a book on the topic! In 1976 Allen visited Boston and noticed that Bunker Hill and Walden Pond were now surrounded by the city. Hilariously the Boston Tea Party was celebrated by a boat recreation sponsored a Tea Company wherein bales of Tea were thrown into Boston Harbor on tethers to be dragged back up to be thrown back in by the next tourist He wondered what Emerson and Thoreau might have thought about that. He imaged they might be rolling over in ther graves.

Bibliography

Chapter One

Emerson, Ralph Waldo. The Journals and Miscellaneous Notebooks of Ralph Waldo Emerson. Vols. 1–12. Edited by William H. Gilman et al. Cambridge, MA: Harvard University Press, 1960–1982.

Emerson, Ralph Waldo. Selected Letters of Ralph Waldo Emerson. Edited by Ralph L. Rusk. New York: Columbia University Press, 1939.

Emerson, Ralph Waldo. Nature and Selected Essays. Edited by Laurence R. Keller. New York: Penguin Classics, 1981.

Emerson, Ralph Waldo. "Nature." In The Complete Works of Ralph Waldo Emerson, vol. 1, 5–59. Boston: Houghton Mifflin, 1903.

Emerson, Ralph Waldo. "The American Scholar." In The Complete Works of Ralph Waldo Emerson, vol. 2, 45–67. Boston: Houghton Mifflin, 1903.

Emerson, Ralph Waldo. "Self-Reliance." In The Complete Works of Ralph Waldo Emerson, vol. 1, 123–142. Boston: Houghton Mifflin, 1903.

Emerson, Ralph Waldo. "The Over-Soul." In The Complete Works of Ralph Waldo Emerson, vol. 1, 239–249. Boston: Houghton Mifflin, 1903.

Emerson, Ralph Waldo. "Compensation." In The Complete Works of Ralph Waldo Emerson, vol. 1, 351–360. Boston: Houghton Mifflin, 1903.

Emerson, Ralph Waldo. "Circles." In The Complete Works of Ralph Waldo Emerson, vol. 1, 187–198. Boston: Houghton Mifflin, 1903.

Emerson, Ralph Waldo. "Experience." In The Complete Works of Ralph Waldo Emerson, vol. 3, 45–78. Boston: Houghton Mifflin, 1903.

Emerson, Ralph Waldo. "Education." In The Complete Works of Ralph Waldo Emerson, vol. 2, 223–249. Boston: Houghton Mifflin, 1903.

Emerson, Ralph Waldo. Letters to Thomas Carlyle. Cambridge, MA: Harvard University Press, 1949.

Fuller, Margaret. Selected Writings of Margaret Fuller. Edited by Joel Myerson. New York: W. W. Norton, 1994.

Peabody, Elizabeth. Record of Breakfast Conversations. Boston: Peabody Family Papers, ca. 1840–1845. Manuscript collection, Massachusetts Historical Society.

Ripley, George. Diary of the Transcendental Club. Concord: Ripley Family Papers, 1836–1840. Manuscript collection, Concord Free Public Library.

Alcott, Amos Bronson. Conversations of Bronson Alcott. Boston: in Forefront Books, 1948.

North American Review. Reviews of Emerson's Essays. Boston, 1841–1844.

West Newton Anti-Slavery Society. Proceedings and Addresses, 1844. Newton, MA: West Newton Press, 1844.

Carlyle, Thomas. Letters to Ralph Waldo Emerson. London: T. C. Plummer, 1933.

Coleridge, Samuel Taylor. Conversations of London Literary Figures. London: Routledge, 1898.

Court records, Boston's Second Church funeral service, November 1811. Manuscript collection, Boston Public Library.

Concord Lyceum Archives. Lecture Registers and Audience Records, 1837–1845. Concord Free Public Library.

Jackson, Lydia. Household Account Ledger, 1835–1845. Manuscript collection, Emerson Family Papers, Concord.

Pliny the Elder. Natural History. Translated by H. Rackham. Loeb Classical Library. Cambridge, MA: Harvard University Press, 1938.

Chapter Two

Thoreau, Henry David. The Journal of Henry D. Thoreau. Edited by Bradford Torrey and Francis H. Allen. Boston: Houghton Mifflin, 1906.

Thoreau, Henry David. Correspondence of Henry David Thoreau. Edited by Walter Harding and Carl Bode. New York: New York University Press, 1958.

Thoreau, Henry David. Early Essays and Miscellanies. Edited by Joel Myerson. Princeton, NJ: Princeton University Press, 1975.

Thoreau, Henry David. Walden; or, Life in the Woods. Boston: Ticknor and Fields, 1854.

Thoreau, Henry David. "Civil Disobedience." In A Week on the Concord and Merrimack Rivers, and Other Writings. Edited by Elizabeth Hall Witherell. New York: W. W. Norton, 2000.

Thoreau, Henry David. Excursions. Boston: Ticknor and Fields, 1863.

Thoreau, Henry David. A Yankee in Canada with Anti-Slavery and Reform Papers. Edited by Walter Harding. Princeton, NJ: Princeton University Press, 1943.

Thoreau, Henry David. The Maine Woods. Boston: Ticknor and Fields, 1864.

Thoreau, Henry David. Cape Cod. Boston: David R. Godine, 1982.

Thoreau, Henry David. Botany Notebook, 1825–1830. Manuscript collection, Concord Museum.

Thoreau, Henry David. Field Notebooks, 1837–1846. Manuscript collection, Walden Woods Project.

Thoreau, John. Survey of the Concord River, November–December 1836. Manuscript collection, Concord Free Public Library.

Concord Gazette. "On the Use of Pencil" and "Concord's Stone Walls," October–November 1833.

Concord Academy Archives. Student Registers and Early Essays, 1832–1834. Concord Free Public Library.

Concord Anti-Slavery Society Records. Proceedings and Addresses, 1835. Concord Free Public Library.

Concord Lyceum Records. Lecture Transcripts and Attendance Logs, 1834–1836. Concord Free Public Library.

Concord Town Records. Poll Tax Register, 1846. Town of Concord.

Concord School Committee Minutes, 1843. Concord Free Public Library.

Eaton, Amos. Lectures on Botany and Geology. Rensselaer Polytechnic Institute Archives.

Gray, Asa. Herbarium Specimens and Correspondence. Harvard University Herbaria, Cambridge, MA.

Virgil. Geōrgica. Translated by H. Rushton Fairclough. Loeb Classical Library. Cambridge, MA: Harvard University Press, 1916.

Channing, William Ellery. Sermons on Human Perfectibility. Boston: Marsh, Capen & Lyon, 1830.

Chapter Three

Emerson, Ralph Waldo. The Journals and Miscellaneous Notebooks of Ralph Waldo Emerson. Vols. 1–12. Edited by William H. Gilman et al. Cambridge, MA: Harvard University Press, 1960–1982.

Emerson, Ralph Waldo. The Letters of Ralph Waldo Emerson. 10 vols. Edited by Ralph L. Rusk and Eleanor M. Tilton. New York: Columbia University Press, 1939–1995.

Emerson, Ralph Waldo. "Thoreau." Atlantic Monthly 10, no. 58 (August 1862): 239–249.

Thoreau, Henry David. The Journal of Henry D. Thoreau. Edited by Bradford Torrey and Francis H. Allen. Boston: Houghton Mifflin, 1906.

Thoreau, Henry David. Correspondence of Henry David Thoreau. Edited by Walter Harding and Carl Bode. New York: New York University Press, 1958.

Thoreau, Henry David. "The Service." The Dial 1, no. 1 (July 1840): 13–18.

Thoreau, Henry David. "Natural History of Massachusetts." The Dial 3, no. 1 (July 1842): 19–40.

Thoreau, Henry David. "A Walk to Wachusett." Boston Miscellany of Literature and Fashion 2, no. 1 (January 1843): 31–36.

Fuller, Margaret. "Editorial Notes." The Dial Archives, 1840–1844. Margaret Fuller Papers, Boston Public Library.

Fuller, Margaret. Letter to Henry David Thoreau, October 18, 1841. Fuller Family Papers, Harvard University Archives.

Alcott, Amos Bronson. Conversations with Children on the Gospels. Boston: James Munroe, 1836.

Alcott, Louisa May. Recollections of Childhood Conversations. Alcott Family Papers, Concord Free Public Library.

Hawthorne, Nathaniel. Correspondence with Henry David Thoreau, 1842–1845. Hawthorne Family Papers, Bowdoin College Library.

Peabody, Elizabeth Palmer. "The Dial's Mission." Letters to Margaret Fuller, 1839–1842. Peabody Family Papers, Massachusetts Historical Society.

Emerson, Lidian Jackson. Domestic Journal and Letters, 1837–1845. Emerson Family Papers, Harvard University Archives.

The Dial: A Magazine for Literature, Philosophy, and Religion. 4 vols. Boston: E. P. Peabody, 1840–1844.

Lowell, James Russell. Letter to Henry David Thoreau regarding The Pioneer, January 15, 1843. Lowell Papers, Harvard University Archives.

Concord Lyceum Records. Lecture Programs and Audience Records, 1838–1844. Concord Free Public Library.

Boston Miscellany of Literature and Fashion. Editorial Correspondence, 1842–1843. Boston Public Library Rare Books Department.

Chapter Four

Thoreau, Henry David. Walden. Edited by J. Lyndon Shanley. Princeton, NJ: Princeton University Press, 1971.

Thoreau, Henry David. Walden: A Fluid-Text Edition. Edited by John Bryant and Digital Thoreau Project. **http://digitalthoreau.org**

Thoreau, Henry David. The Journal of Henry D. Thoreau. Edited by Bradford Torrey and Francis H. Allen. Boston: Houghton Mifflin, 1906.

Thoreau, Henry David. Walden Manuscript. HM 924. Huntington Library, San Marino, CA.

Clapper, Ronald Earl. "The Development of Walden: A Genetic Text." PhD diss., University of California, Los Angeles, 1967.

Shanley, J. Lyndon. The Making of Walden. Chicago: University of Chicago Press, 1957.

Ross, Michael L., and Stephen Adams. Revising Mythologies: The Composition of Thoreau's Major Works. Charlottesville: University Press of Virginia, 1988.

Emerson, Ralph Waldo. "Nature." In Essays and Lectures. New

York: Library of America, 1983.

Emerson, Ralph Waldo. "Self-Reliance." In Essays and Lectures. New York: Library of America, 1983.

Emerson, Ralph Waldo. "The American Scholar." In Essays and Lectures. New York: Library of America, 1983.

Emerson, Ralph Waldo. "Compensation." In Essays and Lectures. New York: Library of America, 1983.

Thoreau, Henry David. "Civil Disobedience." In Reform Papers. Edited by Wendell Glick. Princeton, NJ: Princeton University Press, 1973.

Thoreau, Henry David. "Life Without Principle." In Reform Papers. Edited by Wendell Glick. Princeton, NJ: Princeton University Press, 1973.

Peck, H. Daniel. Thoreau's Morning Work: Memory and Perception in A Week on the Concord and Merrimack Rivers, the Journal, and Walden. New Haven: Yale University Press, 1990.

Richardson, Robert D., Jr. Henry Thoreau: A Life of the Mind. Berkeley: University of California Press, 1986.

Walls, Laura Dassow. Seeing New Worlds: Henry David Thoreau and Nineteenth-Century Natural Science. Madison: University of Wisconsin Press, 1995.

Concord Poll Tax Records, 1840-1847. Concord Town Clerk's Office.

Thoreau, Henry David. Correspondence of Henry David Thoreau. Edited by Walter Harding and Carl Bode. New York: New York University Press, 1958.

Chapter Five

Emerson, Ralph Waldo. "Self-Reliance." In Essays: First Series. Boston: James Munroe, 1841.

Emerson, Ralph Waldo. The Journals and Miscellaneous Notebooks of Ralph Waldo Emerson. 16 vols. Edited by William H. Gilman et al. Cambridge, MA: Harvard University Press, 1960–1982.

Emerson, Ralph Waldo. Miscellaneous Notebooks, Series 4, Notebook 27. Ralph Waldo Emerson Memorial Association Papers, Houghton Library, Harvard University.

Thoreau, Henry David. "Resistance to Civil Government." In Aesthetic Papers. Edited by Elizabeth Palmer Peabody. Boston: The Editor, 1849.

Thoreau, Henry David. "Civil Disobedience." In A Yankee in Canada, with Anti-Slavery and Reform Papers. Boston: Ticknor and Fields, 1866.

Thoreau, Henry David. The Journal of Henry D. Thoreau. 14 vols. Edited by Bradford Torrey and Francis H. Allen. Boston: Houghton Mifflin, 1906.

Thoreau, Henry David. Lecture Manuscript: "The Rights and Duties of the Individual in Relation to Government." MS Am 278.5.

Concord Free Public Library.

Kant, Immanuel. Grundlegung zur Metaphysik der Sitten. Riga: Johann Friedrich Hartknoch, 1785.

Coleridge, Samuel Taylor. Marginalia in Schelling's System des transcendentalen Idealismus. British Library Additional MS 34225.

Spooner, Lysander. The Unconstitutionality of Slavery. Boston: Bela Marsh, 1845.

Spooner, Lysander. No Treason: The Constitution of No Authority. Boston: The Author, 1870.

Garrison, William Lloyd. "Declaration of Sentiments." The Liberator, December 15, 1838.

Ballou, Adin. Practical Christian Socialism. Hopedale, MA: Community Press, 1846.

Gandhi, Mohandas K. Satyagraha in South Africa. Translated by Valji Govindji Desai. Madras: Ganesan, 1928.

Gandhi, Mohandas K. The Collected Works of Mahatma Gandhi. 100 vols. New Delhi: Publications Division Ministry of Information and Broadcasting, Government of India, 1958–1994.

King, Martin Luther, Jr. Stride Toward Freedom: The Montgomery Story. New York: Harper & Row, 1958.

Fuller, Margaret. Woman in the Nineteenth Century. New York: Greeley & McElrath, 1845.

Stewart, Maria W. "What If I Am a Woman?" Speech delivered in

Boston, 1833. Published in The Liberator, April 28, 1833.

Schoolcraft, Henry Rowe. Algic Researches. New York: Harper & Brothers, 1839.

The Liberator. "Self-Reliance Review." March 12, 1841.

The Liberator. "Civil Disobedience Review." August 10, 1849.

National Anti-Slavery Standard. "Thoreau's Resistance." September 6, 1849.

North American Review. "Emerson's Essays." October 1841.

Christian Examiner. "New England Transcendentalism." November 1841.

Boston Post. "Dangerous Doctrines." September 15, 1849.

Salem Register. "Individual Resistance." October 2, 1849.

Westminster Review. "American Philosophy." October 1842.

Edinburgh Review. "Democratic Individualism." April 1844.

Boston Female Literary Association Records. Massachusetts Historical Society, Ms. N-1847.

Concord Women's Reading Circle Minutes. Concord Free Public Library, Local History Collection.

Garrison, William Lloyd. Letters to Wendell Phillips, 1841-1849. Boston Public Library Anti-Slavery Collection.

Phillips, Wendell. Correspondence with William Lloyd Garrison. Boston Public Library Anti-Slavery Collection.

Fuller, Margaret. Letters to William Henry Channing, 1841-1844.

Margaret Fuller Papers, Boston Public Library.

Littré, Émile, trans. "La Désobéissance Civile." Revue des Deux Mondes, August 1856.

Luden, Heinrich, trans. "Widerstand gegen die Bürgerliche Regierung." Deutsche Vierteljahrs Schrift, March 1860.

Carlyle, Thomas. Letters to Ralph Waldo Emerson, 1841-1845. Thomas Carlyle Papers, National Library of Scotland.

Peabody, Elizabeth Palmer, ed. Aesthetic Papers. Boston: The Editor, 1849.

Concord Lyceum Records. "Thoreau Lectures, 1848." Concord Free Public Library.

Addams, Jane. Twenty Years at Hull-House. New York: Macmillan, 1910.

Cavell, Stanley. Conditions Handsome and Unhandsome: The Constitution of Emersonian Perfectionism. Chicago: University of Chicago Press, 1990.

Kateb, George. Emerson and Self-Reliance. Thousand Oaks, CA: Sage Publications, 1995.

Rosenblum, Nancy L. Another Liberalism: Romanticism and the Reconstruction of Liberal Thought. Cambridge, MA: Harvard University Press, 1987.

Chapter Six

Emerson, Ralph Waldo. "The Over-Soul." In Essays: First Series. Boston: James Munroe, 1841.

Emerson, Ralph Waldo. The Journals and Miscellaneous Notebooks of Ralph Waldo Emerson. 16 vols. Edited by William H. Gilman et al. Cambridge, MA: Harvard University Press, 1960–1982.

Emerson, Ralph Waldo. Weather Journals, 1834–1860. Ralph Waldo Emerson Papers, Box 23. Harvard University, Houghton Library.

Emerson, Ralph Waldo. Botanical Specimens and Herbarium. Concord Museum Natural History Collections.

Emerson, Ralph Waldo. "Nature and the Powers of the Poet." Lecture manuscript, 1844. Boston Natural History Society Archives.

Thoreau, Henry David. The Journal of Henry D. Thoreau. 14 vols. Edited by Bradford Torrey and Francis H. Allen. Boston: Houghton Mifflin, 1906.

Thoreau, Henry David. "Calendar of Concord," 1851–1858. Thoreau Papers, Series III, Box 12. Concord Free Public Library.

Thoreau, Henry David. "Plants of Concord" species inventory. Journal Series II, Volume 14. Walden Woods Project Archives.

Thoreau, Henry David. Survey Maps of Concord Region. Maps Collection, Items 18, 42-A. Concord Museum.

Thoreau, Henry David. Maine Woods expedition journals. Manuscript HM 924. Huntington Library, San Marino, CA.

Thoreau, Henry David. "First Flowering Dates" table, 1852–1858.

Thoreau Papers, Box 8. Concord Free Public Library.

Primack, Richard B., Abe J. Miller-Rushing, and Amanda K. Gallinat. "History of Long-term Studies of Spring Phenology in New England." BioScience 65, no. 4 (2015): 331–342.

Miller-Rushing, Abe J., and Richard B. Primack. "Global Warming and Flowering Times in Thoreau's Concord: A Community Perspective." Ecology 89, no. 2 (2008): 332–341.

Walls, Laura Dassow. Seeing New Worlds: Henry David Thoreau and Nineteenth-Century Natural Science. Madison: University of Wisconsin Press, 1995.

Walls, Laura Dassow. Emerson's Life in Science: The Culture of Truth. Ithaca: Cornell University Press, 2003.

Walls, Laura Dassow. Henry David Thoreau: A Life. Chicago: University of Chicago Press, 2017.

Richardson, Robert D. Jr. Emerson: The Mind on Fire. Berkeley: University of California Press, 1995.

Buell, Lawrence. The Environmental Imagination: Thoreau, Nature Writing, and the Formation of American Culture. Cambridge, MA: Harvard University Press, 1995.

Robinson, David M. Natural Life: Thoreau's Worldly Transcendentalism. Ithaca: Cornell University Press, 2004.

Rossi, William. "Thoreau's Democratic Science." Concord Saunterer 19 (2011): 15–32.

Brown, Gregory P. Thoreau's Science and the Problem of Amateur Naturalism. PhD diss., University of New Hampshire, 2003.

Burroughs, John. "Thoreau's Wildness." Atlantic Monthly 124, no. 3 (1919): 306–315.

Hehir, Kathryn M. "Species Identification Accuracy in Nineteenth-Century Amateur Naturalists: A Comparative Study." Journal of the History of Biology 53, no. 2 (2020): 287–312.

Schofield, Edmund A. "A Comparison of Thoreau's Plant Records with Modern Concord Flora." Rhodora 84, no. 840 (1982): 543–566.

Nelson, Melissa K., ed. Traditional Ecological Knowledge and Environmental Science: Learning from Indigenous Wisdom. Cambridge, MA: MIT Press, 2018.

Shanley, J. Lyndon. The Making of Walden, with the Text of the First Version. Chicago: University of Chicago Press, 1971.

Cavell, Stanley. In Quest of the Ordinary: Lines of Skepticism and Romanticism. Chicago: University of Chicago Press, 1988.

Royce, Josiah. The Religious Aspect of Philosophy. Boston: Houghton Mifflin, 1885.

Goodman, Susan. Emerson and the Limits of Idealism. New York: Columbia University Press, 1999.

Concord Museum. Natural History Collections and Maps. Concord, MA.

Harvard University. Ralph Waldo Emerson Papers. Houghton Library, Cambridge, MA.

Walden Woods Project. Digital Archives of Thoreau Materials. Lincoln, MA.

Massachusetts Historical Society. Nineteenth-Century Natural History Collections. Boston, MA.

Chapter Seven

Emerson, Ralph Waldo. The Journals and Miscellaneous Notebooks of Ralph Waldo Emerson. 16 vols. Edited by William H. Gilman et al. Cambridge, MA: Harvard University Press, 1960–1982.

Emerson, Ralph Waldo. Financial Records, 1834–1878. Ralph Waldo Emerson Papers, Box 156. Harvard University, Houghton Library.

Emerson, Ralph Waldo. Editorial Correspondence. Ralph Waldo Emerson Papers, Boxes 78–82. Harvard University, Houghton Library.

Emerson, Ralph Waldo. Lecture Notes. Ralph Waldo Emerson Papers, Box 93. Harvard University, Houghton Library.

Thoreau, Henry David. The Journal of Henry D. Thoreau. 14 vols. Edited by Bradford Torrey and Francis H. Allen. Boston: Houghton Mifflin, 1906.

Thoreau, Henry David. Business Records and Survey Notes. Thoreau Family Papers, Boxes 4–7, 12. Concord Free Public Library.

Thoreau, Henry David. Manufacturing Records. Walden Woods Project, MS Series II-A.

Fuller, Margaret. Papers and Correspondence. MS Am 1086. Boston Public Library.

Fuller, Margaret. Editorial Papers. Margaret Fuller Papers, Editorial Series. Boston Public Library.

Peabody, Elizabeth Palmer. Subscription Ledger for The Dial. MS Am 2249, Box 1. Harvard University, Houghton Library.

Peabody, Elizabeth Palmer. Papers and Business Correspondence. Massachusetts Historical Society.

Emerson, Lidian Jackson. Household Records and Editorial Marginalia. Lidian Jackson Emerson Papers. Concord Museum.

Emerson, Mary Moody. Papers and Correspondence. Mary Moody Emerson Papers, Boxes 1–12. Harvard University, Houghton Library.

American Lyceum Bureau Records. Massachusetts Historical Society, Boxes 15–18, 23.

Massachusetts Anti-Slavery Society Financial Records. Anti-Slavery Collection, Financial Series. Massachusetts Historical Society.

Boston Female Anti-Slavery Society Records. Schlesinger Library, Radcliffe Institute.

Garrison, William Lloyd. Papers and Correspondence. Boston Public Library.

1850 Federal Census for Concord, Massachusetts. Massachusetts State Archives.

Concord Town Property Records, 1840–1860. Concord Town Clerk's Office.

National Archives, Boston. Federal Prosecuting Attorney Records, RG 118, Series A, Box 23.

Stewart, Maria W. Productions of Mrs. Maria W. Stewart. Boston: Friends of Freedom and Virtue, 1835.

Wright, Frances. Course of Popular Lectures. New York: Free Enquirer, 1829.

Brown, William Wells. Narrative of William W. Brown, a Fugitive Slave. Boston: Anti-Slavery Office, 1847.

Douglass, Frederick. Narrative of the Life of Frederick Douglass, an American Slave. Boston: Anti-Slavery Office, 1845.

Gougeon, Len. Virtue's Hero: Emerson, Antislavery, and Reform. Athens: University of Georgia Press, 1990.

Patterson, Anita Haya. From Emerson to King: Democracy, Race, and the Politics of Protest. New York: Oxford University Press, 1997.

Newfield, Christopher. The Emerson Effect: Individualism and Submission in America. Chicago: University of Chicago Press, 1996.

von Frank, Albert J. The Trials of Anthony Burns: Freedom and Slavery in Emerson's Boston. Cambridge, MA: Harvard University

Press, 1998.

Steele, Jeffrey. Transfiguring America: Myth, Ideology, and Mourning in Margaret Fuller's Writing. Columbia: University of Missouri Press, 2001.

Walls, Laura Dassow. Henry David Thoreau: A Life. Chicago: University of Chicago Press, 2017.

Richardson, Robert D., Jr. Emerson: The Mind on Fire. Berkeley: University of California Press, 1995.

Baker, Paula. "The Domestication of Politics: Women and American Political Society, 1780–1920." American Historical Review 89, no. 3 (1984): 620–647.

Kerber, Linda K. Women of the Republic: Intellect and Ideology in Revolutionary America. Chapel Hill: University of North Carolina Press, 1980.

Ryan, Mary P. Women in Public: Between Banners and Ballots, 1825–1880. Baltimore: Johns Hopkins University Press, 1990.

Ginzberg, Lori D. Women and the Work of Benevolence: Morality, Politics, and Class in the Nineteenth-Century United States. New Haven: Yale University Press, 1990.

Chapter Eight

Emerson, Ralph Waldo. The Journals and Miscellaneous Notebooks of Ralph Waldo Emerson. 16 vols. Edited by William H. Gilman et al. Cambridge, MA: Harvard University Press,

1960–1982.

Emerson, Ralph Waldo. Lecture Manuscripts and Notes. Ralph Waldo Emerson Papers, Boxes 88–95. Harvard University, Houghton Library.

Emerson, Ralph Waldo. Essay Drafts and Revisions. Ralph Waldo Emerson Papers, Boxes 120–127. Harvard University, Houghton Library.

Emerson, Ralph Waldo. Address Manuscripts. Ralph Waldo Emerson Papers, Box 87. Harvard University, Houghton Library.

Thoreau, Henry David. The Journal of Henry D. Thoreau. 14 vols. Edited by Bradford Torrey and Francis H. Allen. Boston: Houghton Mifflin, 1906.

Thoreau, Henry David. Lecture Manuscripts and Notes. Thoreau Papers, Box 8. Concord Free Public Library.

Thoreau, Henry David. Walden Manuscripts. HM 924. Huntington Library, San Marino, CA.

Fuller, Margaret. Editorial Correspondence. Margaret Fuller Papers, Editorial Series. Boston Public Library.

Fuller, Margaret. Manuscript Annotations. Margaret Fuller Papers, MS Am 1086. Boston Public Library.

American Lyceum Bureau Records. Massachusetts Historical Society, Boxes 12–28.

Redpath, James. Lyceum Management Files. American Lyceum Bureau Records, Massachusetts Historical Society.

Peabody, Elizabeth Palmer. Aesthetic Papers. Boston: The Editor, 1849.

Lowell, James Russell. Editorial Correspondence. James Russell Lowell Papers. Harvard University Archives.

Boston Daily Advertiser. "Lecture Reviews, 1837–1860." Boston Public Library, Newspaper Collection.

Christian Examiner. "Religious and Philosophical Reviews, 1835–1850." American Periodical Series Online.

The Atlantic Monthly. Editorial Files and Correspondence, 1857–1865. Atlantic Monthly Collection, Boston University Archives.

Concord Lyceum Records. Programs and Attendance Logs, 1829–1860. Concord Free Public Library.

Tremont Temple Programs and Financial Records. Boston Public Library, Manuscript Collections.

Cooper Union Lecture Series Records. Cooper Union Archives, New York.

Ray, Angela G. The Lyceum and Public Culture in the Nineteenth-Century United States. East Lansing: Michigan State University Press, 2005.

Scott, Donald M. "The Popular Lecture and the Creation of a Public in Mid-Nineteenth-Century America." Journal of American History

66, no. 4 (1980): 791–809.

Bode, Carl. The American Lyceum: Town Meeting of the Mind. New York: Oxford University Press, 1956.

Walls, Laura Dassow. Emerson's Life in Science: The Culture of Truth. Ithaca: Cornell University Press, 2003.

Richardson, Robert D., Jr. Emerson: The Mind on Fire. Berkeley: University of California Press, 1995.

Packer, Barbara L. Emerson's Fall: A New Interpretation of the Major Essays. New York: Continuum, 1982.

Cavell, Stanley. Conditions Handsome and Unhandsome: The Constitution of Emersonian Perfectionism. Chicago: University of Chicago Press, 1990.

Buell, Lawrence. Emerson. Cambridge, MA: Harvard University Press, 2003.

Harding, Walter. The Days of Henry Thoreau: A Biography. New York: Alfred A. Knopf, 1965.

Sattelmeyer, Robert. Thoreau's Reading: A Study in Intellectual History. Princeton, NJ: Princeton University Press, 1988.

Hoag, Ronald Wesley. "The Mark on the Page: Emerson's Compositional Process." Studies in the American Renaissance (1980): 139–168.

Dean, Bradley P. "Reconstructions of Thoreau's Early 'Life Without Principle' Lectures." Studies in the American Renaissance (1987):

285–364.

Myerson, Joel. "A Calendar of Transcendental Club Meetings." American Literature 44, no. 2 (1972): 197–207.

Gougeon, Len. Virtue's Hero: Emerson, Antislavery, and Reform. Athens: University of Georgia Press, 1990.

von Frank, Albert J. An Emerson Chronology. New York: G.K. Hall, 1994.

Chapter Nine

Emerson, Ralph Waldo. The Journals and Miscellaneous Notebooks of Ralph Waldo Emerson. 16 vols. Edited by William H. Gilman et al. Cambridge, MA: Harvard University Press, 1960–1982.

Emerson, Ralph Waldo. Account Books and Financial Records. Ralph Waldo Emerson Papers, Box 157. Harvard University, Houghton Library.

Emerson, Ralph Waldo. Late Lecture Manuscripts. Ralph Waldo Emerson Papers, Boxes 94–95. Harvard University, Houghton Library.

Emerson, Ralph Waldo. Tribute Manuscripts. Ralph Waldo Emerson Papers, Box 142. Harvard University, Houghton Library.

Emerson, Ellen Tucker. Papers and Correspondence. Ellen Tucker Emerson Papers, Boxes 1–15. Harvard University, Houghton Library.

Emerson, Ellen Tucker. Personal Journal, 1865–1875. Ellen Tucker Emerson Papers. Harvard University, Houghton Library.

Thoreau, Henry David. The Journal of Henry D. Thoreau. 14 vols. Edited by Bradford Torrey and Francis H. Allen. Boston: Houghton Mifflin, 1906.

Thoreau, Henry David. Scientific Records and Phenological Data. Thoreau Papers, Scientific Series, Box 12. Concord Free Public Library.

Thoreau, Henry David. Late Manuscripts and Essays. MA 1302. Morgan Library & Museum, New York.

Thoreau, Sophia. Personal Diary and Family Correspondence. Sophia Thoreau Papers, Box 3. Concord Free Public Library.

Thoreau Family. Business Records and Medical Expenses. Thoreau Family Papers, Box 9. Concord Free Public Library.

Gray, Asa. Correspondence with Henry David Thoreau. Gray Herbarium Archives, Harvard University.

Cabot, James Elliot. Emerson Editorial Files. Cabot Papers. Harvard University, Houghton Library.

Atlantic Monthly. Editorial Files and Correspondence. Atlantic Monthly Papers. Boston University Archives.

Concord Historical Society. Medical Records and Town Documentation, Box 14.

Concord Lyceum. Memorial Programs and Records. Lyceum

Records, Box 8. Concord Free Public Library.

Boston Society of Natural History. Meeting Minutes and Scientific Assessments. Boston Public Library.

Massachusetts State Archives. Mortality Records and Death Certificates, Concord, 1840–1862.

Bartlett, Josiah. Medical Notes on John Thoreau Case. Concord Museum Archives, Medical Collection.

Concord Freeman. Obituary Records, May 10, 1862. Concord Free Public Library, Newspaper Collection.

Hanlon, Christopher. Emerson's Memory Loss: Originality, Communality, and the Late Style. New York: Oxford University Press, 2017.

Richardson, Robert D., Jr. Emerson: The Mind on Fire. Berkeley: University of California Press, 1995.

Walls, Laura Dassow. Henry David Thoreau: A Life. Chicago: University of Chicago Press, 2017.

Harding, Walter. The Days of Henry Thoreau: A Biography. New York: Alfred A. Knopf, 1965.

Sattelmeyer, Robert. Thoreau's Reading: A Study in Intellectual History. Princeton, NJ: Princeton University Press, 1988.

Porte, Joel. Representative Man: Ralph Waldo Emerson in His Time. New York: Oxford University Press, 1979.

McAleer, John. Ralph Waldo Emerson: Days of Encounter. Boston:

Little, Brown, 1984.

Buell, Lawrence. Emerson. Cambridge, MA: Harvard University Press, 2003.

Packer, Barbara L. Emerson's Fall: A New Interpretation of the Major Essays. New York: Continuum, 1982.

Chapter Ten

Emerson, Ralph Waldo. Essays: First Series. 1841. Edited by Joel Porte, Harvard University Press, 1982.

 The Essential Writings of Ralph Waldo Emerson. Edited by Brooks Atkinson, Modern Library, 2000.

Hartmann, Franz. Selbstvertrauen: Essays von Ralph Waldo Emerson. Leipzig, 1873.

King, Martin Luther, Jr. "Letter from Birmingham Jail." Why We Can't Wait, Signet Classics, 2000, pp. 77–100.

Leontiev, Boris, and Vera Alexandrova, translators. Emerson: Izbrannye Esse. Moscow: Goslitizdat, 1926.

Norton, Charles Eliot, editor. American Literary Readings for Schools. Houghton, Mifflin & Co., 1878.

Seishū, Hiraoka, translator. Wōruden: Haru no Shōkei. Tokyo: Hakubunkan, 1908.

Thoreau, Henry David. Civil Disobedience. 1849. Edited by Bob Pepperman Taylor, Rowman & Littlefield, 2014.

Walden; or, Life in the Woods. 1854. Edited by J. Lyndon Shanley, Princeton University Press, 1971.

Tolstoy, Leo. A Letter to a Hindu. Translated by Gopal Krishna, 1908.

Alexandrova, Vera. "Emerson in Soviet Russia." The Emerson Society Quarterly, vol. 31, no. 2, 1963, pp. 45–52.

Buell, Lawrence. Emerson. Harvard University Press, 2003.

The Environmental Imagination: Thoreau, Nature Writing, and the Formation of American Culture. Harvard University Press, 1995.

Cameron, Sharon. Thoreau's Aesthetics. University of Chicago Press, 1999.

Cavell, Stanley. The Senses of Walden. University of Chicago Press, 1981.

Conway, Moncure D. Emerson at Home and Abroad. Boston: James R. Osgood, 1882.

Lanman, Charles R. A Bibliography of Emerson's Oriental Readings. Harvard Oriental Series, 1905.

Leopold, Aldo. A Sand County Almanac. Oxford University Press, 1949.

Packer, Barbara L. The Transcendentalists. University of Georgia Press, 2007.

Robbins, Tony. Awaken the Giant Within. Free Press, 1991.

Sierra Club. Thoreau and the Wilderness Ethic. Sierra Club Books, 1985.

Tolstoy, Leo. The Kingdom of God Is Within You. Translated by Constance Garnett, University of Nebraska Press, 1984.

Whitman, Walt. Leaves of Grass. 1855. Edited by Harold Bloom, Chelsea House, 2003.

Chapter Eleven

Arendt, Hannah. Solidarity: An Introduction. Stanford University Press, 2019.

Aristotle. Nicomachean Ethics. Translated by W. D. Ross, The Internet Classics Archive, 2008, classics.mit.edu/Aristotle/nicomachaen.8.viii.html.

Derrida, Jacques. "Hospitality Beyond Invitation." Ethical Perspectives, vol. 28, no. 3, KU Leuven, 2011, pp. 45–67.

Emerson, Ralph Waldo. "Letter to Henry David Thoreau, 5 Mar. 1849." The Houghton Library, Harvard University, Emerson Papers, Box 147, Folios 30–32.

Emerson, Ralph Waldo. "Letter to The Springfield Republican, 1849." The Houghton Library, Harvard University, Emerson Papers, Box 162, Folio 19.

Emerson, Ralph Waldo. Manuscript of Nature. Concord Free Public Library, MS Box 5, Folios 8–11.

Emerson, Ralph Waldo. Nature. 1836. Lecture notes, Harvard Divinity School archives.

Fuller, Margaret. "Letter to Ralph Waldo Emerson." Fuller Papers, Houghton Library, Harvard University, Box 3.

HASTAC Scholars. "HASTAC Governance Charter." HASTAC Scholars, 2023, societyhumanities.as.cornell.edu/hastac-scholars.

Hypothesis. "About Hypothesis." Hypothesis.is, 2025, **https://web.hypothes.is/about/**.

Morgan, Margaret D. Toward a Political Theory of Friendship. University of Chicago Press, 2022.

Peabody, Elizabeth. Diary. Antoinette Peale Collection, Walden Woods Project, April 1842.

Rawls, John. A Theory of Justice. Harvard University Press, 1971.

Ripley, Sophia. Correspondence. Walden Woods Project, Sophia Ripley Collection.

Tollefsen, James. Hospitality and the Moral Self. Oxford University Press, 2024.

Thoreau, Henry David. "Letter to Ralph Waldo Emerson, 2 Apr. 1849." Walden Woods Project, Thoreau Papers, Box 7, Folios 12–14.

Thoreau, Henry David. Resistance to Civil Government. Æsthetic Papers, ed. Elizabeth Peabody, 1849.

Thoreau, Henry David. Walden; or, Life in the Woods. James Munroe & Co., 1854.

Thoreau, Henry David. Journals. Vol. 2, Walden Woods Project, 1845.

"The Dial." The Dial: A Magazine for Literature, Philosophy, and Religion, 1840–1844. Online Books Page, 2016, onlinebooks.libra ry.upenn.edu/webbin/serial?id=thedial.

"Walden Woods Financial Records, 1846–1848." Walden Woods Project Archives.

Chapter Twelve

Black, Jeremy. What If? Counter factualism and the Problem of History. London: Social Affairs Unit, 2008.

Bosco, Ronald A., Joel Myerson, and Daisaku Ikeda. Creating Waldens: An East-West Conversation on the American Renaissance. Dialogue Path Press, 2009.

Clapper, Ronald E. "The Development of Walden: A Genetic Text." PhD diss., UCLA, 1967.

Emerson, Ralph Waldo. Journals and Miscellaneous Notebooks. Houghton Library, Harvard University, Emerson Papers.

Emerson, Ralph Waldo. Manuscript of Nature. Concord Free Public Library, MS Box 5, Folios 8–11.

Fuller, Margaret. Letters. Fuller Papers, Houghton Library, Harvard University.

Fuller, Margaret, Ralph Waldo Emerson, and George Ripley, eds. The Dial: A Magazine for Literature, Philosophy, and Religion. 1840–1844.

Greeley, Horace. Recollections of a Busy Life. 1868.

Harding, Walter. The Days of Henry Thoreau. New York: Alfred A. Knopf, 1965.

Knopp, Lisa. "Gender and the Transcendentalist Circle." American Literature Studies 34, no. 2 (1998): 145–168.

Levy, Jack S. "Counterfactuals, Causal Inference, and Historical Analysis." Security Studies 24 (2015): 378–402.

Myerson, Joel. The Cambridge Companion to Henry David Thoreau. Cambridge University Press, 1995.

Richardson, Robert D. Henry Thoreau: A Life of the Mind. University of California Press, 1986.

Robinson, David M. Natural Life: Thoreau's Worldly Transcendentalism. Cornell University Press, 2004.

Rudd, Patrick. "Reframing Emerson and Thoreau: Beyond the Myths." New England Quarterly 88, no. 4 (2015): 612–640.

Rusk, Ralph L. The Life of Ralph Waldo Emerson. New York: Charles Scribner's Sons, 1949.

Shanley, J. Lyndon. The Making of Walden*, with the Text of the First Edition*. University of Chicago Press, 1957.

Tetlock, Philip E., and Aaron Belkin, eds. Counterfactual Thought Experiments in World Politics: Logical, Methodological, and Psychological Perspectives. Princeton University Press, 1996.

Thoreau, Henry David. Journals. Vol. 2. Walden Woods Project Archives, 1845.

Thoreau, Henry David. Letters. Walden Woods Project Archives.

Thoreau, Henry David. Walden; or, Life in the Woods. Boston: Ticknor and Fields, 1854.

Walden Woods Project. "Myths and Misconceptions." **https://www.walden.org/education/for-students/myths-and-misconceptions/**.

Chapter Thirteen

Clapper, Ronald E. "The Development of Walden: A Genetic Text." PhD diss., UCLA, 1967.

Concord Free Public Library. "Emerson Holdings in the Special Collections." Accessed October 16, 2025. **https://concordlibrary.org/special-collections/collections/emerson**.

Digital Thoreau. "Walden: A Fluid Text Edition." Accessed October 16, 2025. **https://digitalthoreau.org/fluid-text-toc/**.

Digital Thoreau. "The Walden Manuscript Project." Accessed October 16, 2025. **https://digitalthoreau.org/the-walden-manuscript-project/**.

Glick, Wendell. Reform Papers. The Writings of Henry D. Thoreau. Princeton University Press, 1973.

Harvard University. "Houghton Library." Accessed October 16, 2025. **https://library.harvard.edu/libraries/houghton**.

Harvard University. "Searching for Material—Houghton Library: A Student's Guide." Accessed October 16, 2025. **https://guides.library.harvard.edu/houghtonlib/searching**.

Peabody, Elizabeth, ed. Æsthetic Papers. Boston: The Editor; New York: G.P. Putnam, 1849.

Rossi, William, ed. Walden, Civil Disobedience, and Other Writings. Norton Critical Edition. New York: W.W. Norton, 2008.

Shanley, J. Lyndon. The Making of Walden*, with the Text of the First Edition*. Chicago: University of Chicago Press, 1957.

Spiller, Robert E., and Alfred R. Ferguson, eds. The Collected Works of Ralph Waldo Emerson, Volume I: Nature, Addresses, and Lectures. Cambridge, MA: Belknap Press of Harvard University Press, 1971.

Thoreau, Henry David. A Week on the Concord and Merrimack Rivers. Boston: James Munroe and Company, 1849.

Thoreau, Henry David. "Resistance to Civil Government." In Æsthetic Papers, edited by Elizabeth Peabody, 189–211. Boston: The Editor; New York: G.P. Putnam, 1849.

Thoreau, Henry David. Walden; or, Life in the Woods. Boston: Ticknor and Fields, 1854.

Ticknor and Fields. Costbooks, 1832–1858. Houghton Library, Harvard University.

Walden Woods Project. "Collecting Henry David Thoreau." Accessed October 16, 2025. **https://www.walden.org/work/collecting-henry-david-thoreau/**.

Walden Woods Project. "The Ralph Waldo Emerson Society Collection: A Guide to the Collection." Updated January 2016. **https://www.walden.org/wp-content/uploads/2016/03/Emerson-Society-Finding-Aid-Final.pdf**.

Walden Woods Project. "Thoreau's Contributions to The Dial." Accessed October 16, 2025. **https://www.walden.org/what-we-do/library/thoreaus-contributions-to-the-dial/**.

Chapter Fourteen

Brown, Simon, et al. Report of the Committee of the Proprietors of the Sudbury and Concord River Meadows. 1859.

Chura, Patrick. Thoreau the Land Surveyor. University Press of Florida, 2010.

Concord Free Public Library. "A Brief History of Concord." Accessed October 16, 2025. **https://concordlibrary.org/special-collections/a-brief-history-of-concord**.

Concord Free Public Library. "Records of the Concord Lyceum." Special Collections.

Concord Free Public Library. "Thoreau Holdings in the Special Collections." Accessed October 16, 2025. **https://concordli-brary.org/special-collections/collections/thoreau**.

Digital Thoreau. "Resistance to Civil Government: A Note on the Text." Accessed October 16, 2025. **https://commons.digi-talthoreau.org/civil/a-note-on-the-text/**.

Harding, Walter. The Days of Henry Thoreau. Alfred A. Knopf, 1965.

Johnson, Edward. Wonder-Working Providence of Sions Saviour in New England. 1654.

Myerson, Joel, ed. Studies in the American Renaissance. 1996.

Schofield, Edmund A. "The Walden Ecosystem." Walden Woods Project, 1990. **https://www.walden.org/wp-content/up-loads/2016/03/Schofield-Walden-Ecosystem.pdf**.

Thoreau, Henry David. Journals. Vol. 2. Walden Woods Project Archives, 1845.

Thoreau, Henry David. Walden; or, Life in the Woods. Boston: Ticknor and Fields, 1854.

U.S. Geological Survey. "Hydrology and Troph-ic Ecology of Walden Pond, Concord, Massachusetts." Water-Resources Investigations Report 01-4153, 2002. **https://pubs.usgs.gov/wri/wri014153/report.pdf**.

U.S. Geological Survey. "Walden Pond, Massachusetts: Environmental Setting and Current Conditions." Fact Sheet 064-98, 1998. **https://pubs.usgs.gov/publication/fs06498**.

Walden Woods Project. "Henry David Thoreau and the Lyceum Movement." Accessed October 16, 2025. **https://www.walden.org/henry-david-thoreau-and-the-lyceum-movement/**.

Whitney, Gordon G. "Thoreau and the Forest History of Concord, Massachusetts." Journal of Forest History 30, no. 2 (1986): 70–81. **https://harvardforest1.fas.harvard.edu/publications/pdfs/Whitney_JForestHist_1986.pdf**.

Chapter Fifteen

Davies, Charles. Elements of Surveying and Navigation. New York: A.S. Barnes & Co., 1840s.

Emerson, Ralph Waldo. "Fate." The Conduct of Life. Boston: Ticknor and Fields, 1860.

Emerson, Ralph Waldo. "Nature." In Nature, Addresses, and Lectures. Boston: James Munroe and Company, 1849.

Emerson, Ralph Waldo. Nature. Boston: James Munroe and Company, 1836.

Emerson, Ralph Waldo. "Self-Reliance." In Essays: First Series. Boston: James Munroe and Company, 1841.

Emerson, Ralph Waldo. "The Over-Soul." In Essays: First Series. Boston: James Munroe and Company, 1841.

Finley, James. "Thoreauvian Accounting." The Thoreau Society. **https://thoreausociety.org/wp-content/uploads/Finley.Thoreauvian-Accounting.docx.pdf**.

Gallinat, A.S., et al. "Comparing fruiting phenology across two historical datasets." Annals of Botany 127, no. 7 (2021): 825–834.

Newport, Cal. Digital Minimalism: Choosing a Focused Life in a Noisy World. New York: Portfolio, 2019.

Primack, Richard B., and Abraham J. Miller-Rushing. "Broadening the Study of Phenology and Climate Change." New Phytologist 191, no. 2 (2011): 307–309.

Schmidt, Allan H. "Thoreau's Chronological Atlas." August 2014. **https://aschmidt01742.wordpress.com/2014/08/**.

Schmidt, Allan H. "A Catalog of Thoreau's Surveys in the Concord Free Public Library." Thoreau Society Booklet 28. Edited by Marcia Moss. The Thoreau Society, 1976.

Thoreau, Henry David. Walden; or, Life in the Woods. Boston: Ticknor and Fields, 1854.

Thoreau, Henry David. *Wild Fruits: Thoreau's Rediscovered Last Manuscript.* Edited by Bradley P. Dean. New York: W.W. Norton, 2000.

Thorson, Robert M. "After 170 Years, Thoreau's River Observations Inform Our Changing Climate." UConn Today, May 7, 2025. **https://today.uconn.edu/2025/05/af-ter-170-years-thoreaus-river-observations-inform-our-chang-ing-climate/**.

Thorson, Robert M. "Thoreau's River Seasons: A Phenological Baseline." The Concord Saunter-er 29 (2021): 1–29. **https://thoreausociety.org/wp-content/up-loads/Thoreaus-River-Seasons-with-photo-supplement.pdf**.

Chapter Sixteen

Chura, Patrick. "Thoreauvian Accounting." The Thoreau Society, **https://thoreausociety.org/wp-content/up-loads/Finley.Thoreauvian-Accounting.docx.pdf**.

Concord Free Public Library. "Records of the Concord Lyceum." Special Collections, **https://concordlibrary.org/spe-cial-collections/collections/emerson**.

Digital Thoreau. "A Note on the Text: 'Resistance to Civil Government.'" Digital Thoreau, **https://commons.digitalthore-au.org/civil/a-note-on-the-text/**.

Emerson, Ralph Waldo. "Resistance to Civil Government." Æsthetic Papers, edited by Elizabeth Peabody, Boston: The Editor; New York: G.P. Putnam, 1849, pp. 189–211.

Emerson, Ralph Waldo. Nature, Addresses, and Lectures. Boston: James Munroe and Company, 1849.

Emerson, Ralph Waldo. Essays: First Series. Boston: James Munroe and Company, 1841.

Harding, Walter. The Days of Henry Thoreau. Alfred A. Knopf, 1965.

Levy, Jack S. "Counterfactuals, Causal Inference, and Historical Analysis." Security Studies, vol. 24, no. 3, 2015, pp. 378–402.

Myerson, Joel, editor. The Cambridge Companion to Henry David Thoreau. Cambridge University Press, 1995.

Newport, Cal. Digital Minimalism: Choosing a Focused Life in a Noisy World. Portfolio, 2019.

Primack, Richard B., and Abraham J. Miller-Rushing. "Broadening the Study of Phenology and Climate Change." New Phytologist, vol. 191, no. 2, 2011, pp. 307–309.

Schmidt, Allan H. "Thoreau's Chronological Atlas." The Concord Saunterer, vol. 29, 2014, **https://aschmidt01742.wordpress.com/2014/08/**.

Thoreau, Henry David. Journals. Vol. 2, Walden Woods Project Archives, 1845.

Thoreau, Henry David. Walden; or, Life in the Woods. Boston: Ticknor and Fields, 1854.

Thorson, Robert M. "After 170 Years, Thoreau's River Observations Inform Our Changing Climate." UConn Today, 7 May 2025, https://today.uconn.edu/2025/05/after-170-years-thoreaus-river-observations-inform-our-changing-climate/.

U.S. Geological Survey. "Hydrology and Trophic Ecology of Walden Pond, Concord, Massachusetts." Water-Resources Investigations Report 01–4153, 2002, https://pubs.usgs.gov/wri/wri014153/report.pdf.

Walden Woods Project. "Henry David Thoreau and the Lyceum Movement." Walden Woods Project, 2016, https://www.walden.org/henry-david-thoreau-and-the-lyceum-movement/.

Walden Woods Project. Thoreau's Contributions to The Dial: A Magazine for Literature, Philosophy, and Religion. 2016, https://www.walden.org/what-we-do/library/thoreaus-contributions-to-the-dial/.

Whitney, Gordon G. "Thoreau and the Forest History of Concord, Massachusetts." Journal of Forest History, vol. 30, no. 2,

1986, pp. 70–81, **https://harvardforest1.fas.harvard.edu/publications/pdfs/Whitney_JForestHist_1986.pdf**.

Chapter Seventeen

Apess, William. A Son of the Forest; or, Forest Life of the Pequod Tribe of Indians. Rochester: Andrus & Judd, 1829.

Biographia Literaria; or, Biographical Sketches of My Literary Life and Opinions. By Samuel Taylor Coleridge. London: Rest Fenner, 1817.

Burnouf, Eugène. Introduction to the History of Indian Buddhism. Translated by James Hastings, London: Trübner & Co., 1876.

Du Bois, W. E. B. The Souls of Black Folk. Chicago: A. C. McClurg & Co., 1903.

Emerson, Ralph Waldo. Essays: First Series. Boston: James Munroe and Company, 1841.

Emerson, Ralph Waldo. Nature. Boston: James Munroe and Company, 1836.

Emerson, Ralph Waldo. "The Over-Soul." In Essays: First Series, 135–152. Boston: James Munroe and Company, 1841.

Fichte, Johann Gottlieb. The Science of Knowledge. Translated by William Smith, London: H. Baillière, 1815.

Jones, Sir William. Translations from the Sanskrit. Calcutta: Asiatic Society, 1785.

King Jr., Martin Luther. "Letter from Birmingham Jail." The Atlantic Monthly, Oct. 1963, 78–88.

Legge, James. The Sacred Books of the East: The Lao-tzu. Vol. 39. Oxford: Clarendon Press, 1891.

Miller-Rushing, Abraham J., and Richard B. Primack. "Broadening the Study of Phenology and Climate Change." New Phytologist, vol. 191, no. 2, 2011, pp. 307–309.

Reid, Thomas. Essays on the Intellectual Powers of Man. Edinburgh: Bell & Bradfute, 1785.

Ritchie, William. Elements of Moral Philosophy. Boston: Gray & Bowen, 1835.

Rowe, Henry Rowe. Algic Researches; or, Contributions toward a History of the History of the Aborigines of America. Philadelphia: Lippincott, Grambo & Co., 1836.

Schelling, Friedrich Wilhelm Joseph. Philosophical Inquiries into the Nature of Human Freedom. Translated by Joseph Severn, London: John Miller, 1809.

Stewart, Dugald. Elements of the Philosophy of the Human Mind. Edinburgh: Constable, 1814.

Taylor, Dorceta E. The Rise of the American Conservation Movement: Power, Privilege, and Environmental Protection. Durham: Duke University Press, 2016.

White, Gilbert. The Natural History and Antiquities of Selborne. London: B. White, 1789.

Whitney, Gordon G. "Thoreau and the Forest History of Concord, Massachusetts." Journal of Forest History, vol. 30, no. 2, 1986, pp. 70–81.

Chapter Eighteen

"Digital Thoreau: Fluid Text Edition." Digital Thoreau, **https://digitalthoreau.org/fluid-text-toc/**.

Emerson, Ralph Waldo. *Essays: First Series*. Boston: James Munroe and Company, 1841.

Emerson, Ralph Waldo. *Nature*. Boston: James Munroe and Company, 1836.

Emerson, Ralph Waldo. *Nature, Addresses, and Lectures*. Boston: James Munroe and Company, 1849.

Emerson, Ralph Waldo. "Self-Reliance." In *Essays: First Series*, 13–51. Boston: James Munroe and Company, 1841.

Emerson, Ralph Waldo. "The Over-Soul." In *Essays: First Series*, 135–152. Boston: James Munroe and Company, 1841.

Harding, Walter. *The Days of Henry Thoreau*. Alfred A. Knopf, 1965.

Levy, Jack S. "Counterfactuals, Causal Inference, and Historical Analysis." *Security Studies*, vol. 24, no. 3, 2015, pp. 378–402.

Myerson, Joel, editor. *The Cambridge Companion to Henry David Thoreau*. Cambridge University Press, 1995.

Newport, Cal. *Digital Minimalism: Choosing a Focused Life in a Noisy World*. Portfolio, 2019.

Primack, Richard B., and Abraham J. Miller-Rushing. "Broadening the Study of Phenology and Climate Change." *New Phytologist*, vol. 191, no. 2, 2011, pp. 307–309.

Schmidt, Allan H. "Thoreau's Chronological Atlas." *The Concord Saunterer*, vol. 29, 2014.

Thoreau, Henry David. *Journals*. Vol. 2. Walden Woods Project Archives, 1845.

Thoreau, Henry David. *Walden; or, Life in the Woods*. Boston: Ticknor and Fields, 1854.

Thorson, Robert M. "Thoreau's River Seasons: A Phenological Baseline." *The Concord Saunterer*, no. 29, 2021, pp. 1–29.

U.S. Geological Survey. "Hydrology and Trophic Ecology of Walden Pond, Concord, Massachusetts." *Water-Resources Investigations Report* 01-4153, 2002.

Chapter Nineteen

Emerson, Ralph Waldo. Essays: First Series. Boston: James Munroe and Company, 1841.

Emerson, Ralph Waldo. Nature. Boston: James Munroe and Company, 1836.

Emerson, Ralph Waldo. Nature, Addresses, and Lectures. Boston: James Munroe and Company, 1849.

Emerson, Ralph Waldo. "The Over-Soul." In Essays: First Series, 135–152. Boston: James Munroe and Company, 1841.

Emerson, Ralph Waldo. "Self-Reliance." In Essays: First Series, 13–51. Boston: James Munroe and Company, 1841.

Harding, Walter. The Days of Henry Thoreau. Alfred A. Knopf, 1965.

Myerson, Joel, editor. The Cambridge Companion to Henry David Thoreau. Cambridge University Press, 1995.

Primack, Richard B., and Abraham J. Miller-Rushing. "Broadening the Study of Phenology and Climate Change." New Phytologist, vol. 191, no. 2, 2011, pp. 307–309.

Schmidt, Allan H. "Thoreau's Chronological Atlas." The Concord Saunterer, vol. 29, 2014.

Thoreau, Henry David. Journals. Vol. 2. Walden Woods Project Archives, 1845.

Thoreau, Henry David. Walden; or, Life in the Woods. Boston: Ticknor and Fields, 1854.

Thorson, Robert M. "Thoreau's River Seasons: A Phenological Baseline." The Concord Saunterer, no. 29, 2021, pp. 1–29.

U.S. Geological Survey. "Hydrology and Trophic Ecology of Walden Pond, Concord, Massachusetts." Water-Resources Investigations Report 01-4153, 2002.

Index